PHIL SMITH was born in milltown Lancashire where he has lived for most of his life. 30 years working as a freelance reporter on all things Northern for BBC Radio gave him the opportunity to trek around the region and develop a knowledge and love of the North's history and landscape. Amongst his published books are 'Tales from the Straggling Town', 'The Century Speaks', 'Real Lancashire' and, published by Yoricks Press, 'Demdike, A Lancashire Witches Tale'.

Above: the author and his wife, the book's photographer, outside the stables at Snape Castle.
Front cover: Ribblehead, where viaduct, track and mountain take you irresistibly northwards.

NORTH

Phil Smith

A journey through the landscape and history of the North of England

YORICKS PRESS

Lines from 'Cathedral Builders' by John Ormond appear by
permission of the publishers of 'John Ormond: Selected Poems',
Seren Books, 1987.
Lines from 'Four Quartets' by T.S Eliot are by kind permission of
Faber & Faber.

Published by Yoricks Press.
The Stables, The Old Coach House, Holme-in-Cliviger, Burnley,
BB10 4SY.
www.philsmithwrites.co.uk
info@philsmithwrites.co.uk

Printed by Tyson Press, UK

ISBN 978-0-9927115-0-4

To Elliot, for his invaluable help.

CONTENTS

INTRODUCTION

This book is the record of a journey of exploration which leaves behind the well-worn image of the North of England as the graveyard of the Industrial Revolution and celebrates the inspirational and poetical appeal of its rural landscape and more distant history. The North of its title is the pre-Anglo Saxon region beyond the Humber, drawing a line westwards to north of the Ribble Estuary to dispose of the Lancashire and Yorkshire conurbations and leaving us with the North's soul, the place where the mind switches to when it leaves the towns and cities behind; where sensible people put on their walking boots and escape to at the weekend.

Geology has so much to do with defining the North. Our hills and mountains give us a unique sense of perspective, especially of time. So the Carboniferous limestone of 300 million years ago is where we begin, the stained and weathered cliff face of Malham Cove with its glaciated pavements above, the bare bones of the Northern Pennines. And the human history of the North begins here too, in the glacial lake of Malham Tarn where the prehistoric arrivals hunted and fished before settling, leaving their bone harpoons and flints in Victoria Cave above Settle and Dowkerbottom in Littondale, or their own huddled remains in potholes like Elbolton Cave in Wharfedale. Further east they left the three megaliths of the Devil's Arrows at Boroughbridge, the mysterious giant henges further north at Thornborough and the megalith at Rudston in the old East Riding, more imposing than any of the sarsens at Stonehenge.

Then there are the Iron Age remains of the Yorkshire Dales, the field strips and stock enclosures visible among the scoured limestone pavements of the last ice age. Or the hillfort remains of the belligerent Brigantes who built their camp high on the top of Ingleborough where they could beat their naked chests at the terrified

Romans. You can, incidentally, observe a similar practice today from their ancestors in many of our northern towns on a Saturday night where youths and even maidens bare their torsos in sub-zero temperatures to the astonishment and dismay of elderly passers-by like myself.

But despite our native uncouthness the Romans left their civilising mark all over the North. As well as statements of their military might and singleness of purpose like the camps across Stainmore, the spectacularly located fort on Hardknott Pass in the Lake District and the road which climbs to 2,700 feet across High Street, they left us the bathhouse at Ravenglass, still standing after almost two millennia, the countless sculptures and other artefacts to be seen in our museums and the miraculously preserved details of everyday life in the age of Hadrian in the Vindolanda letters. But it is that enduring symbol of conquest, Hadrian's Wall, which steals all the superlatives, defining the North as a frontier war zone for over a thousand years after the Romans left, a region of successive invasions and foreign settlement, Angles, Saxons, Vikings, Normans and marauding Scots all leaving their indelible print upon the landscape.

Mutilated skeletons uncovered in the burnt out Roman signal station on the North Yorkshire coast at Goldsborough near Whitby are a reminder of the violent transition from Roman rule to Anglo-Saxon settlement. Even the figure of King Arthur hovers in the Dark Age shadows of our region at this time, at Birdoswald on the Wall by the River Irthing where it's been suggested one of his battles against the Anglo-Saxon invaders may have taken place. This area, around Bewcastle, is the haunt of the old Celtic war god, Cocidius. Even today it's not difficult to sense the taint of violence and fear which hangs about these bleak wastes and forests beyond the pale of the Wall and civilisation, fear that haunted the Anglo-Saxon imagination, finding expression in the monsters of 'Beowulf' and bringing the amazing seventh century Christian cross to Bewcastle to exorcise its demons. But perhaps unsuccessfully. For in the sixteenth century the Scottish reivers cut a trail of larcenous destruction across this landscape and only as little as fifty years ago the forest of

Spadeadam was the site of a secret laboratory where the Blue Streak missile, a terrifying modern weapon of mass destruction, was developed.

Violence, it seems, is in the blood here in the North. Tests have revealed a significant proportion of Viking DNA in our population. The material legacy of our Viking forebears is to be found in the crosses and tombstones scattered throughout the Lune valley and western Cumbria, an enigmatic fusion of both Christian and violent pagan imagery. In the Jorvic Centre the daily life of the tenth century Viking settlers of York is displayed. So too is death, in the remains of bodies ravaged by disease and battle.

But the story of the North isn't all of Dark Age brutality. A journey in search of the remains of Cuthbert and Bede to Lindisfarne and Jarrow will reveal the North of the seventh and eighth centuries as an age of enlightenment, art and scholarship inferior to none in Western Europe at the time. Many monasteries from Lindisfarne to Whitby were built, like the abbey church at Hexham which contains the finest Anglo-Saxon crypt in England, and Lastingham on the edge of the North Yorkshire Moors where the church has been in continuous use since founded by St Cedd in 654. To me, a devout sceptic, this must be the holiest place in England, where the stonework whispers of 1,400 years of Christian faith. And at Escomb in Durham the church of St John survives from before the Synod of Whitby, astonishing historical resonances if you ignore the setting on the edge of a modern housing estate. But this travelogue rather than merely historical approach will allow for such observations and impressions to be recorded and maybe throw up some insights into the present as well as the past.

But, as I say, this is not just history, though I hope the historical approach will give the narrative some shape. What it is is an evocation, an effort to unearth not only the ghosts of the region's past but to resurrect the spirits of its places, those shy local gods which give a place its unique magic and as a whole give the North its fascination, its depth, its cultural richness, which engages the imagination and helps to define the region in terms of its real roots and spiritual ancestry, which in an age when regional identity is threatened by cultural conformity allows us to celebrate, nay, exult in, our distinctiveness.

The Norman invasion brought both power and piety to the North, the might of castles and the spiritual splendour of the monasteries, starkly beautiful statements in ruined stones which still speak to us today in castles like Richmond and Helmsley and the great abbeys of Rievaulx and Fountains. And while during the post-Conquest years the North dips in and out of political obscurity, a high point was reached in the late Middle Ages with the emergence of the great dynasties of warrior knights like the Percies, whose wealth won in France and against the Scots contributed to the decorative splendour of churches like the Abbey at Selby and the Minster at Beverley. Much of the wealth of East Yorkshire came from what some might rightly regard as the symbol of the rural North, the ubiquitous sheep, but for the humble peasant it was his downfall in those deserted villages like Wharram Percy where to make more money the landlords evicted their tenants and turned their land over to grazing. With the miseries of the Black Death it is of little surprise that one of the most popular poems of the early fifteenth century was about the end of the world and is depicted in the stark images of the stained glass of the Pricke of Conscience window in the church of All Saints in York.

Wharram Percy is set within the Yorkshire Wolds which, to me, a Pennine man, is a strangely secretive landscape of bare chalk escarpments and empty dry valleys. Yet it is astonishingly rich in history, not least in Neolithic burial mounds like Duggleby Howe, all rifled and their contents recorded by tireless Victorian amateur archaeologists. The Yorkshire Wolds add to a remarkable diversity of landscapes to be discovered in the relatively small area I've chosen to explore. There couldn't be a greater contrast than that between the gently undulating chalk Wolds - the remains of marine animals laid down during the Cretaceous period 80 million or so years ago - and the rugged volcanic mountains of the Lake District, older, at 500 million years, than the Himalayas. Yet they are separated by little over 100 miles, a comfortable afternoon's drive. And through what further variety of landscape and history! There are the rich plains of the Vale of York, scenes of so many historical battles, the limestone hills of the Dales where the Vikings settled the dale heads, the lush Lune valley beyond with its string of mediaeval defensive castles and finally the high mountains of Cumbria themselves where the Lake District poets discovered a new kind of Nature.

During these journeys I have endeavoured to evoke a feel for the landscape as well as for its history. For me, the two combine to form a heady emotional appeal, something close to that essence which I began by describing as the 'soul' of the North. My observations are, indeed, often deeply personal, and when it comes to how our Northern ancestors in their turn responded to their surroundings they are often speculative, too. Were the prehistoric henges around the River Ure a reflection of the endless circular dance of procreative life they found around them? Can once-sacred groves or theatres of violent conflict retain a lasting imprint, a psychical stain that creeps into the present and can still be felt today? In fact, does this whole psychogeographical approach to landscape and history make any sense at all in an age of reason? And how, in these modern scientific times do we respond to nature (or should that be Nature?) especially in its more dramatic manifestations like in the mountains of the Lake District? Do we react still with some of the shock and horror of those earlier visitors to Gordale Scar, or do we feel along with Wordsworth the reverence in the presence of some great moral Entity? The answer may be neither, we're just out for a good walk. But if by drawing attention to some of these historic reactions I've helped to enrich your response to the Northern landscape, I'll consider the months of foot-slogging worthwhile.

Finally, this doesn't claim to be in any way an exhaustive survey of the North's inspirational places. Nor do I claim to possess the expert knowledge of the region's history, archaeology etc of others. Look upon it as the work of an enthusiastic layman and Northerner eager to share his passion and in the process to move a little closer to understanding those feelings inspired by the word 'North'.

1. THE LANGUAGE OF STONES

You come in winter to Malham Cove and the fields lie yellow and sullied, untidily strewn with molehills and withered sticks of dead thistles. You walk along the river from the village and here's the limestone at your feet, boulders blotched with lichen, some black, some creamy white like birdlime. Only the river seems to show any animation, like all children - for this is a tributary of the infant Aire - scrambling over the hidden stones, dancing in its joy to be free of the darkness beneath the Cove. On the way from the car park in the village you have been primed with notices telling you what you are about to see. The Cove was probably formed 50,000 years ago when it was once a giant waterfall, with meltwater from the ice age glaciers tumbling down the line of the Craven Fault, exposing the petrified remains of billions of sea creatures which lived in the warm seas of the Carboniferous era 300 million years ago. But nothing can quite prepare you for the visual impact if you clamber over the wet stones to the very foot of the cliff and look up at the towering curve of the rock. It's a Cyclops, rising to 250 feet, bellying out threateningly. It engulfs you, absorbs you into its massive lithic embrace. To look up is to feel the terrible cold strength of the rock. In the book 'Climbers' by M. John Harrison, the author describes a small child stepping out of a car to look up at a rock wall for the first time and screaming. That's what Malham Cove does to the over-protected modern mind: it drags to the surface the primordial instincts, the awe, the fear. I've visited it in the past to find climbers straddled out across the overhanging rock, dressed in Day-Glo silkskin dance-tights like gaudy spiders, young men pitting themselves against the rock's alien, primal power. Today, I for one wouldn't touch the stone. It has the appearance of dirty tallow, sweating and dribbling before your eyes, streaked with ugly stains of black, tar-like stuff which I can only assume is some kind of lichen. Amazingly, vegetation clings to it. There are bare ash trees and a colony of ivy hanging from a ledge. The rock needs water again from the ice age waterfalls to cleanse it and restore its limestone purity. Only when the sunlight appears, bathing the rock in light until it glows like warm skin, does the fear and chill of the Cove recede.

'I wonder what it must have looked like 50 million years ago?' says a visitor standing nearby. I think he must have meant 50 thousand years ago, but in this landscape thousands can easily blur into millions as we fail to grasp the immensity of geological time. It reinforces a conviction that here in the North, where landscape can so often brutally assert itself, elbowing its way into our lives every now and then, our perspectives are altered. We are awed, afraid and humbled by turn. So it is with Malham Cove. Pushy executives and self-regarding media personalities should be made to visit here regularly to be cut down to size.

If you chose not to climb the Cove by your fingertips with a rope belayed to one of the many pitons that glint in the sun, there's always the steps. The limestone has grown polished and treacherous with all the feet that make the pilgrimage. The steps wind up the western side of the cliff and will deposit you, puffing and panting, on top where the ice age glaciers have scoured bare the limestone pavements. Another helpful notice will tell you that the cracks in the pavement are known as grykes - which sounds to me like the name for a bad-tempered Yorkshireman. The grykes are small fissures, open sutures in the rock dissolved by the effects of acid rainwater on the limestone. They provide a secretive haven for rare plants like the hart's tongue fern whose ribbed tongues rise out of the mossy darkness to lick at the daylight. We watched a Labrador dog stranded in the middle of the pavement, fearful perhaps of falling down one of the grykes. Or maybe she was afraid that something might reach up out of the dark and grab her? Who knows in a landscape of primal fear? Eventually her owner had to come along and pick her up and carry her away to safety.

The poet W.H. Auden liked limestone for its lack of durability, because, like humans, it is inconstant. Walk the limestone pavements above Malham Cove with their surface hollows filled with rainwater and you are treading in the weathered footprints of time itself. It heightens your awareness of mutability, of change. After all, what is limestone but a transformation itself? Living, moving creatures turned to rock. And now, the rock itself is no longer permanent. I wonder if anyone has measured the rate at which the limestone is dissolving in all the acid rain of our polluted atmosphere? I've stood on the roof of York Minster and seen mediaeval gargoyles turned to featureless lumps. If rock is no longer permanent what is to be the next stage in this landscape's history? See, I'm already in the grip of this limestone, asking questions to which we can never hope to be around long enough to know the answers.

Malham affords a perspective on human history as well as geological time. The plateau that stretches northwards from the top of the Cove has been under human occupation since after the last ice age around 10,000 BC. The first visitors were hunters foraging the area around Malham Tarn. They left behind their bone harpoons and flint arrowheads which are still to be found today by the diligent scavenger of molehills. The area must have suited them because the lower land would have been difficult and swampy from the glacial meltwater and the trees would have been thinner on the high lands making movement easier for them to hunt and fish. The first true settlers came later, making use of the many caves for shelter where rudimentary pottery has been found along with animal bones of deer, wolf and wild boar as well as cattle. Polished axes that have been discovered seem to suggest that they began clearing the trees to allow their cattle to graze. They were the first farmers.

Three rather grisly occupants of one of the local caves can be inspected today in the Craven Museum in the High Street in Skipton. The museum can be a welcome refuge from the excesses of the weather on the Malham moor tops and the displays provide an excellent and sometimes dramatic picture of prehistoric life thereabouts. Three human skulls discovered in Elbolton Cave are on display. The yellowish bones rest incongruously upon the neat modern Styrofoam upholstery of the display cabinet. Two of the skulls are complete, with cavernous and dusty eye sockets and ragged empty nose holes. The third is only half a head, chopped off from the top like a boiled egg. His colleagues seem to be looking on, still wincing. They have been numbered in a rather undignified manner with white paint: 150 and 152, on their foreheads, 151, on the shattered surface of his lower face. As an aid to the imagination there's an artist's impression of what the remains looked like when they were found. It shows two skeletons in a crouching position and looking all too disturbingly animated, as if they were waiting for the artists to go home before they began a rattling sort of dance around the cave, something they'd been doing since Neolithic times around 5,000 years ago. The implication of these discoveries is that the local caves were used for burials rather than dwellings, though the account of the excavations of Elbolton Cave in 1888 perhaps suggests a rather grim accommodation of the two. According to the excavation leader, the Reverend E Jones, 'semi-circular fenders of large stones were placed between the bodies and the rest of the cave'. Of course, I had to go and have a look where this Elbolton Cave was.

Elbolton Hill is an uncommonly round hill rising to 1150 feet close to the hamlet of Thorpe a couple of miles southeast of Grassington, seven miles from Malham cove as the crow flies. The hill is actually a reef knoll, the remains of a coral reef when the area was flooded by the warm Carboniferous seas of 300 million years ago. The cave is more like a pothole, with a small shaft going vertically into the earth. I knew this before setting out because I'd seen a picture on the computer in the Craven Museum taken during the original excavation in Victorian times. They must have been pretty keen not to have their work interfered with because they sealed off the shaft with a couple of trapdoors like those you sometimes see draymen opening in the pavement outside pubs in order to deliver barrels of beer into the cellars. But the precise location of the cave was a mystery to me, so after making a few enquiries I went to see the landowner, a cheerful farmer called Robin Hall. Farming in Thorpe, a Danish place name, made me wonder if he could trace his ancestry back to those invaders who gave such trouble back in the ninth century, their boats nosing their way menacingly up the Humber intent upon grabbing so much of the land of Saxon England. He seemed far from troublesome and gave me instructions on how to find the cave: up a v-shaped valley and on the eastern side of Elbolton Hill. The hill is very steep and is covered in stone-filled hollows which could all be shafts until you arrive there and find nothing but broken rock and stones.

I reached the top without any luck. There's a wonderful sense of openness and freedom on the summit of Elbolton Hill, with 360 degree panoramas of Nidderdale, Wharfedale and, far to the west, Ribblesdale. There's a real feeling of peace, of being separated from the modern world, with only the distant mumble of traffic on the road past Cracoe quarry to distract you. It's a good preparation for letting the mind slip back into prehistoric times, to imagine those first farmers standing here on this hill and looking out towards the northwest above the wooded Wharfedale valley over Mastiles and watching the smoke rise from the neighbouring settlements on Malham Moor. Were they a threat to one another or did they exist peaceably side-by-side? Did their shared intimacy with the natural environment lead them to live in harmony or did the realities of survival mean their lives were lived in savage and intense hostility? Questions to which the gaping Elbolton skulls provide no answers.

There's a pothole right on the top of Elbolton Hill but it's not the entrance to the cave. Again I remembered the picture on the computer in the museum. There'd been a short escarpment above the shaft into the cave where the Victorian excavators stood. So I went back over the top of the hill and down several yards to below the scar. And there it was, a narrow hole in the ground no more than a metre wide with a metal bar across the top where you could hitch a rope to climb down. Well, I wasn't doing that. Instead, I sat on the grass at the edge and peered gingerly in. A vertical shaft about 30 feet deep disappeared into the gloom. The cold of the earth rose to meet me. I began to scribble down my impressions of the place when suddenly, a man and woman appeared, hurrying anxiously round the side of the hill towards me. Hanging there over the edge of the hole, pencil and paper in hand, a distracted expression on my face, I think they must have thought I was a suicide case writing a farewell note before throwing myself in. They were dashing towards me in a bid to persuade me not to do it, that after all, life was sweet and tomorrow I might even win the Lottery. We laughed a lot when I explained my mission, and the man, a former member of the Upper Wharfedale Cave Rescue team, told me that he'd been down and that after the shaft it opened out into a roomy cave and a network of potholes. So did these Neolithic people live down here or just die here? Found amongst the skeletons were also pottery, animal bones and charcoal. Articles of subsistence or offerings to their gods?

For the Celts, the later inhabitants of these hills, holes like this would be seen as entrances to the Otherworld. They were scenes of magic and rituals performed to propitiate their volatile and unpredictable gods. They were the gateway to where those arbiters of their fate, of everything that was good or bad that could happen to them, lived; where votive offerings of sacred possessions and even human life itself were sacrificed. As I sat there, on my own again, peering into the shadows of time and feeling that chill breath of the earth on my face, I suddenly became aware of a noise coming from below. It was a dull, irregular thud. I strained to listen, waiting a minute, maybe two, before it was repeated, a hollow knocking sound coming from deep within the cave. What was it? A potholer about to emerge? Or something else? I didn't hang around to find out. I think I probably hold the world record for the rapid descent of a reef knoll.

But I still had to overcome my troglophobia - if such a word exists. I suppose I could try Victoria Cave on Langcliffe Scar above Settle which is both famous and easily accessible. From the tools and ornaments found there, Victoria Cave has a history of human occupation of around 10,000 years, right up to Roman times. It's worth a stroll up from Langcliffe village just for the fine expansive views up Ribblesdale. But the cave is a victim of its own fame and you are unlikely to be alone. The Health and Safety people have been there too, and on my last visit there was a notice warning you not to step inside without a hard hat in case of falling rock. Now a hard hat is not the sort of thing most people take with them on a country walk, unless they happen to be a construction worker who can't wait for Monday morning. This is namby-pambyism gone mad and there's not much sense of adventure to be had standing on the slopes outside the cave and just staring into the shadows of its cavernous mouth. So I'll give Victoria Cave a miss for now and opt for the more remote and less-frequented cave of Dowkerbottom, or Douky Bottom, as the OS map has it, rather more quaintly.

Now this is a place of atmosphere. High up on the empty moors west of Littondale, you approach it by climbing up Sleet's Gill. Some potholers lounge about planning a descent into Sleet's Gill pot and they direct me towards Douky Bottom. The talk is of shallow valleys and rocky outcrops, vague and primal landmarks. With only the sheep tracks to follow, it's easy to imagine yourself tramping in the footsteps of those early settlers. The landscape is prehistoric too, bare outcrops, strewn stones and an empty, featureless moortop squeezed between a vast expanse of bare sky. To the north a disconcerting feature is a group of scattered stones on the skyline which look rather menacing, like cowled figures looking out, the guardians of this place. You can't seem to lose them but they're always there, creeping into the tail of your eye even when your back is turned. There is a consistency about this landscape, as if nature had taken its cue from the rocks themselves, producing nothing but bare and weathered things. I pass a gnarled thorn tree whose twisted branches scratch at the sky. Another grows out of the very rock until, sucked dry, all that remains is the contorted grain of the trunk projecting like some grotesque gargoyle. Everywhere underfoot are rabbit bones, bleached and inarticulated. Rock, wood, bone, all of a kind. The basic elements of this place scattered under the wide sky. The history of the earth's long and painful evolution laid out.

It's not the first time I've been here and felt the same chilling sense of an alien and inhospitable landscape. I'm reminded of the poem by Robert Browning, 'Childe Rowland to the Dark Tower Came', where

21

the landscape takes on the ominous despair of the knight's fateful mission. Maybe it's because I know I shall have to enter the darkness and danger of underground soon and I'm projecting my apprehension onto the landscape. I'd done some potholing as a teenager, goaded on against my natural instincts by peer pressure. I'd hated crawling around in those, narrow, black, claustrophobic passages, away from everything we naturally revel in: light and air and colour and open spaces. I grow breathless just thinking about it.

And then, suddenly, I was there at the cave. The potholers had told me to look for a wall corner and from there it was just 200 metres away to the right. And they were spot on. Out of nothing, a sudden fissure in the flat surface of the ground about 12 metres across, a gaping hole at either end. Maximum apprehension now as I stood irresolutely. I could see the scuff marks on the rocks where others must have climbed down. But do I dare follow? Not so young anymore and on my own. What if I fell? Broke my ankle? Had a heart attack? I'd borrowed a mobile phone, yes, but it told me there was no signal available here. You wouldn't expect modern technology to work in such a raw, primal place. But I'd brought a torch and I was determined to go down and have a look. People had lived down here. They were beckoning.

But which hole of the two to go down? The one to the right with hart's tongue ferns waving (a warning?) or to the left where a briar bent over the entrance, its thorns bristling with hostility? I try the right. There's an unnatural green glow issuing from the hole from all the moss-strewn boulders at the entrance, nature's last-ditch effort to cling onto the light before blind white fish and stuff like that take over. And then I spot a hook driven into the rock. Potholers again with their ropes and ladders. Not for me. So it's to the left I go, under the arching briar. And it's easy. A scramble down some rocks before lowering myself down another and I'm in the chamber of the cave. It's black, cold and silent, and I think it must be like being dead. At the far end of the chamber a passage leads out and further down. The potholers had told me it went on for a thousand metres. I followed it for a few steps, but the roof is getting lower and lower and all daylight from the entrance has now disappeared. I hate it. The silence, the mass of rock above me, the darkness, are squeezing the life out of me, the spirit, like a candle flame slowly being snuffed. I start to panic. I turn round and hurry back, convinced that something is stumbling out of the passage behind me. Something from the Otherworld. All thoughts of the past and the people who lived in here is put to flight. The only thought I have is that to live down here you must have something much worse to fear on the surface.

As I clamber out the daylight returns like an enormous friendly smile. The air smells sweet and warm. And suddenly a curlew calls, great bubbling cadences of sound that swell to fill the whole sky before melting away into a melancholy loneliness. I stride away back down into Littondale, elated at my own bravery.

Another day and I'm back at Malham. I'm already drawn to the place, like thousands of others who come here throughout the year. I don't quite know what it is yet that I find so magnetic but for the time being I'm content to call it my Malham mania. This time I've come to the Tarn, about a mile or so north of the Cove. It's a beast of an afternoon in late January and the place is deserted. Again it is beginning to feel like I've slipped back into a prehistoric age, somewhere basic and elemental, belonging to the bare aeons of geology which have fashioned this lake, marooned at 1200 feet by a ring of empty moorland hills. Grey bones of limestone scars peep through the leafless branches of the trees behind the Field Centre, the only sign of human habitation. The weather is atavistic, a brutal wind and cold, stinging rain. It has swept the shorelines bare as tundra. The heavy rain has left small lakes that mirror the bruised sky. The limestone walls hint at ownership, at husbandry, though it's hard to tell they're limestone in places for the black stains of lichen and the vivid green coatings of moss. There are squads of sheep that when disturbed swirl in tight formation as if trained. They're ragged warriors, their wool stained with blood-like dye, with low-slung horns like headdresses, black-faced with grey muzzles as if dipped in ash, a hint of amber in the eyes which gaze out steadily from those shadowy faces. These sheep are the true heirs of this country. They look like how I imagine our Mesolithic ancestors to have been, the hunters who first came here after the ice to lose their tiny flint arrowheads around the Tarn and on the Lings. I wondered what became of those first Northerners, the nomad hunters who grazed the land like sheep before moving on. And at what point in their long, slow history did they stop simply being food-gatherers and settle to become farmers, stockading the beasts they fed upon and clearing the land of trees to grow their crops? When did they submit to that most civilising of human instincts and lay down roots, growing to know and love the landscape intimately enough to call it home and ultimately to be buried in the earth that sustained them?

The earliest evidence of settlement comes from burials like that at Elbolton. A more curious and seemingly improvised method of burial was discovered in 1936 nine miles west of Malham Tarn near Selside in Ribblesdale. The skeleton of a woman aged between 35 and 40 was found in one of the limestone fissures or grykes. It had been partially covered by limestone blocks. Nearby was a polished stone axe, probably from the Langdale axe factory on Stickle Pike. You can speculate about the axe. Was it hers, as seems likely? So was there an even distribution of labour 4,000 years ago, women as well as men clearing the forest? Equal opportunities and none of that, 'You stick to the smoky fire and cooking pot and looking after the black-faced kids, my dear'. The remains of the skeleton were apparently well enough preserved for the discoverers to first report their find to the police. Sir Arthur Keith, who examined the remains, wrote of a 'very feminine' woman who 'had kept many of her girlish features into her maturity'. Quite what he meant by that, I don't know, though I'm told it might be something to do with the development of the skull bone. The remains were dated to the later Neolithic period around the late third millennium BC. Knowledge of this discovery soon had me peering into the grykes on the pavements above Malham Cove. But the only human remains I came across were the crisp packets and plastic pop bottles discarded by some of the visitors and carefully concealed between the stones. What will the archaeologists of the future make of these? Votive offerings to the giant food and drink corporations that sustain us today?

With the arrival of the Bronze Age there seems to have been a dramatic change of location for burial sites around the Malham area. No longer were the bodies stuffed into narrow grykes or left crouching with their knees to their chests in dark caves. Now it was a barrow on the most prominent hilltop with the bones often burnt and placed inside an urn surrounded by a stone cist or chamber piled with stones. Well, this is how it was for the most important people in the tribe. To judge from the relative rarity of barrows and crematory urns in the area, the rest must have disappeared like birds seem to do when they die, their remains scattered and absorbed into the great cycle of nature: 'Rolled round in earth's diurnal course, With rocks and stones and trees', in Wordsworth's immortal lines.

Near the crossroads just southeast of the Tarn on Malham Moor is Seaty Hill. On the top is a shallow ditch with a small bank enclosing a low mound around 60 feet in diameter. A seated skeleton was found here in a hole in the centre of the mound, thought to date from around 1800 years BC or the early Bronze Age. You can't fail to be impressed by the view from the hilltop. If the dead had eyes they would count themselves kings of their surroundings, which, as I say, they probably were, though, presumably, the prominence of the burial site was more for the benefit of the living than the dead, a reminder, akin to the follies that rich Victorian men built on hilltops, to carry their prestige or that of their tribe beyond the grave. The clamour for this immortal ostentation seems to be illustrated by the fact that, according to Arthur Raistrick, the eminent recorder of all things to do with the history of Malham, there were at least 13 other burials made in the mound dating from the later Iron Age or the first century BC. Amongst the bones, beads and iron knives dug up there was a rather more extraordinary object. It isn't clear from which grave it was removed but a bone whistle with three finger holes, fashioned out of the leg of a sheep, was also discovered. Back in the Craven Museum is a cast of the instrument, the original having disappeared to a museum in Leeds. By pressing a button on the display cabinet you can listen to a recording of someone playing the whistle. Now you may have heard the recording of someone blowing a ceremonial trumpet found in the tomb of Tutankhamen. It is an uncanny experience. Knowing that the instrument was last pressed to the lips of someone over 3,000 years ago, raises the hairs on the back of your neck. It is the same when you hear this whistle being blown, only more so if you just happen to have read the story of the antiquarian and scholar M.R. James, 'Oh, Whistle and I'll Come to You!' It's the tale of a curious investigator who discovers an ancient whistle at an archaeological site and foolishly elects to blow it. The sound resurrects a terrifying apparition which then proceeds to pursue him, driving him to the edge of madness. For a long time I refused to touch the button on the display cabinet. But then my curiosity got the better of me and I tentatively pressed it. Rising out of the background crackle of the recording came the thinnest, most whispery and forlorn sound I've heard. At the risk of sounding melodramatic, if the dead could whistle, this would be the sound they would make. It immediately took me back to Malham Tarn on that late winter afternoon when I first visited the barrow on Seaty Hill. The waters of the Tarn grey as zinc, trembling in a bitter north wind. The surrounding hills beginning to darken and crouch at the onset of night. Ragged ribbons of unmelted snow etching the outline of the dry-stone walls. A small flock of returning curlews circling aimlessly, piping plaintively. But then another, stranger scene takes shape. Ragged figures circle the barrow at the top of the hill, among them a cowled priesthood of druids muttering and chanting, calling on the spirits which so manifestly inhabit this place to welcome the dead man to their Otherworld, along with his precious whistle. Of course, for others the sound of the Malham whistle may evoke a less fanciful response. They may be cheered by the thought that however brutish and short their lives may have been, our early ancestor still found time and possessed the sensitivity to make music.

Closer to the Tarn, above the track to the Field Centre, lie the remains of another even more prominent barrow. It's on Great Close Scar, over 1400 feet above sea level and, according to Arthur

Raistrick, is an Iron Age tumulus which contained multiple burials. You'll find a ring of stones about six metres in diameter which from a distance looks like a cairn but on closer inspection is a hollow crater full of broken stones and moss. There was such a freezing wind blowing on the day I climbed there that the only respite I could get was to lie down in the circle below the shallow wall of stones. With no other option but to stare up at the sky, I began to think about those Iron Age people who lived here for about six centuries between 250BC and around the fifth century AD, the Celtic tribe of the Brigantes. What was their relationship with the sky? We know they believed in an Otherworld, the access to which was through caves and wells and votive shafts. And yet here they are burying their dead in high places as if their gods were more sky-bound. Or perhaps their relationship with the sky wasn't spiritual at all but physical. They lived and died upon these high hills because they were their defensive stronghold. Look at their hillfort, which some think of as their city, high on the top of Ingleborough. This was their fortress against the Romans, come the beginning of the first millennium and the arrival of the Roman armies. I recalled a phrase I'd seen in the museum in Skipton which said that the word Brigantes meant 'the High Ones' and was a direct reference to the way they lived high in the hills. But Anne Ross in her book 'Everyday Life of the Pagan Celts' insists that the Brigantes took their name from the powerful goddess Brigit or Brigantia, the 'High One', and because the tribe was a confederation occupying a wide area of Northern England, not just sites as outlandish as the tops of mountains, I'm more inclined to believe this to be the true derivation of the name. Nevertheless, because the true essence of the North seems to me to belong in the high places like the Pennine Hills and the exhilarating sense of physical and spiritual expansiveness which we enjoy in being in such places, I am inclined to adopt the Brigantes as a symbol of Northernness and feel a need to know more about these rugged and independent people. So I shall be returning to them.

But while we are still in this fairly uncharted territory of the numinous effects of our landscape, I must mention an incident that took place on my visit to Great Close Scar. On the way up to the tumulus I'd noticed a figure at the foot of the scar near the eastern edge of the Tarn. He stood quite motionless, staring upwards at the bare limestone rock. When I returned half an hour later I was amazed to see that he was still there and didn't appear to have moved. What was he up to? At first I thought he might have been a climber planning an ascent. Or perhaps a geologist from the nearby Field Centre reading the mysterious calligraphy of rocks and strata as only geologists can do. But then I remembered my own feelings at the foot of the Cove and how I'd felt the ominous power of the rock and I could only think that the poor man was himself locked in the spell of the rock, chained Prometheus-like by some primal instinct of mingled awe and terror. I'd liked to have hailed him to discover what he was thinking. But you don't shake someone out of a trance or disturb a person at prayer.

Outnumbering the burial sites on and around Malham Moor by many times are the remains of prehistoric houses. Only, for this explorer, they were the very Devil to find. The problem is that the landscape, when not covered with limestone pavements, is scattered with stones and boulders and moss-encrusted bumps. The art is to identify some man-made pattern, some geometrical shape of either a rectilinear enclosure or roundhouse amongst all this surface pandemonium. Easier said than done. I have spent hours wandering the plateau between the two Craven faults and clambering to the top of the shallow scars to try and get a bird's eye view of the land to make out the remains of the many ancient settlements. Many years ago I was taken to some Iron Age huts and enclosures by the admirable field historian of these hills, Alan King, somewhere off the dry valley at the top of the Cove. But could I find them again? Even with a good OS map and the word settlement printed in that special antique-looking font, there's no guarantee you won't end up wandering about fruitlessly. But then Dr Raistrick came to the rescue. His precise description, with grid reference, of not an Iron Age but a Bronze Age house, had me scurrying off to Combe Scar, a shallow escarpment to the east of the dry valley, at the head of a small valley of its own just deep enough to afford shelter from the cold east winds I'd become familiar with. It was a well-preserved stone circle with walls about two feet high enclosing an area of about 20 feet in diameter. The wall would have been the base for branches to be laid up to a central post which supported the roof. There was a stone in the centre of the circle and another nearby which may perhaps have been a hearth stone. A gap in the circle of stones looked like an entrance. We squatted down inside the stones and imagined enjoying some Bronze Age hospitality. A jackdaw came to join us, balancing precariously on a boulder in the wind, feathers ruffled untidily. I felt a sense of privilege to sit there, knowing it was a place where people lived, ate, slept, made love and died almost 4,000 years ago. What sort of life was it? Stressful because of the harsh pressures of trying to stay alive? Or measured and peaceful, paced only by the cycles of the sun and the seasons? The land below that caught all the light was perhaps where they grew their grain and housed their breeding stock of sheep and goats. And the pavement above was a place to stand and look out over the land, 30 miles, from Pendle Hill in the west to Simon's Seat in the east. Perhaps they went no further than this moor all their lives and today lie deep in the grykes which channel the rocks. One gryke has collapsed, leaving a dark cave of splintered rock, but it's too narrow to explore.

To feel the same warm sun on your face as these people did, the same cold wind on your back, to share the same curiosity and sense of wonder, of awe and bafflement at why we are here and what will become of us in the end, is to feel an affinity with these people whose age was defined by the material they used, despite the thousands of years which separate us from them in today's age of plastic. Because for all our technological sophistication, we share the same joys and fears, the same vulnerable humanity. I wonder if this is what makes Malham so popular, that brings people here at all times of the year and in all weathers to wander the moor tops? For there is nothing here to buy or sell or make an irritating noise, nothing to allow us to flaunt our status or wealth, none of the things that normally draw the modern crowds. There is just a quiet sense of continuity in the knowledge that we are treading the paths of our ancient ancestors.

Over the scar from the Bronze Age house, a few hundred yards eastwards towards the road which leads to the Tarn lies another ancient settlement. It's marked on the map and I visited it on another winter's day, walking up from the village. It was a day of sun and broken cloud, the sun chasing the shadows across Ewe Moor to the west of the river valley that leads from the Cove. As you climb the hill on the Tarn road the limestone walls are granite-grey, lit by clusters of powdery lichen, some lime-white, others bright orange. Over the wall to the left are the terraced strips of land known as lynchets. It was a way of cultivating sloping ground, terracing one side of the strip with stone banks so that the soil wouldn't be washed away and the strips were flat enough to plough. They're visible on both sides of the valley between the village and the Cove and are evidently the work of the first farmers to settle in the village, the Anglians, who came over the North Sea from Germany in the seventh century to live here. We naturally think of our history as a rectilinear thing, events and people following one another in neat progression. But get into the field and the evidence left behind is a puzzling unsequential jumble, waiting for the eye of the expert who can date it from recognising a pattern or discovering a precious artefact, someone who can read the language of the stones that litter the landscape for the benefit of the naïve enthusiast like me, bent only upon encountering the shadowy spirits of our ancestors. It's all a muddle, an exhilarating and fascinating muddle.

Once at the top of the winding lane to the Tarn there's a stile that takes you onto the footpath to Prior Rakes. This leads you past the settlement I was searching for. I have to take it on trust that a settlement was once here. It's like walking down a village street that has long disappeared and returned to rough, stony heathland. The sheep, stained with an emerald green dye, gaze disinterestedly at me as I stroll by. One drinks at a rain-filled hollow in a rock. Others lounge on the bare pavements, trying to extract whatever heat they can from the sun-splashed stones. A rook waddles amongst the molehills, closely patrolled by his own black shadow. He jabs at the black soil, having found something tasty to rooks. The only hint you get that you might be approaching a settlement is when the path crosses the foundations of a long wall, too straight and purposeful not to be man-made. This, I guess, must be the remains of the settlement's perimeter wall. Defensive or merely to prevent their stock from wandering? To the west side of the path is a shallow scar, strewn with a jumble of broken rocks. Is there a pattern there? Small, square enclosures, set out next to one another like a row of houses. I stand inside one of them and notice that some of the stones have been placed one upon the other. Today they're mortared together by moss, but there's deliberation here, selection, a sense of purpose. Am I in someone's living room? A recollection of travelling in one of those trains through the Viking village in the Yorvik Centre at York trundles into my mind. And then, at the other side of the 'street', two long houses. I measure them, tread them out. 16 metres in length by 6 metres wide. Viking longhouses? The Vikings were sheep farmers who settled these lonely, hilly area in the tenth century and gave their names to many of the places. So here's another web in the complex fabric of settlement that is spread over Malham Moor.

Arthur Raistrick writes of a rectangular house on the edge of Great Close, north of here, known as the Priest's House. Excavations there unearthed a bronze brooch with gold inlay as well as bronze book edgings and straps, all dating from the seventh century and similar to material found in the Anglian monastery at Whitby. He concludes that the house probably belonged to a hermit priest looking after the spiritual welfare of the scattered native population. Despite a grid reference I had no luck in locating the remains of this house, although, with the blessing of the farmer and the National Trust, I have trawled the area. I was ostensibly searching for Iron Age hutments, a village of 19 huts of the tribe of the Brigantes who cultivated small fields of corn and barley and kept herds of sheep and cattle. Round huts like these dating from the third century BC are by far the commonest ancient settlements to be found on Malham Moor according to Dr Raistrick. For some reason I found the ones in Great Close Pasture impossible to locate. Identification was made difficult by the fact that there'd been a heavy fall of snow the week before and the ground was scattered with frozen patches of drifts. But I did come across the remains of two more rectangular buildings, side-by-side and about 30 feet long with a definite entrance on the Pasture side. Perhaps another Viking farm? Or there again, the remains of mediaeval dwellings? Sometimes the past seems so comprehensively obscured. The landscape is like a mediaeval parchment or palimpsest, where the old writing is scratched out to make way for the new and can only be discerned by the faintest of outlines. Maybe you have to start to rely on other senses than sight on a raw day like today with a skin-peeling northerly wind blowing. You start to notice the difference in temperature in the more sheltered places and think, 'Yes, this would be a good place for a house'. It's something the sheep know about when they lie down for the night, sensing the places that are a degree or two warmer. They are old, buried instincts that modern man has lost, that have atrophied in an age of loft insulation and double-glazing.

As I say, sometimes the imprint of the past on Malham moor survives in the place names. The Viking suffix -gil was the name given to places in the deep upland valleys settled by the Norsemen. So, Thorgill House and Tennant Gill House off Darnbrook Fell north of the Tarn. As Arthur Raistrick points out, over the door of one of the houses at Water Houses are the initials MT MT on either side of the date 1635. He tells us that these are the initials of Matthew Towler and his wife, descendants of Matthew and Thomas Toller who held the land under Fountains Abbey a hundred years earlier. You see, after the Norman Conquest, the lands around Malham fell into the hands of Norman barons who later transferred them to the monks of Fountains Abbey and Bolton Priory who held them for the next 300 years. Now wasn't it a Towler, Stephen Towler, I'd rung up to ask permission to walk on Great Close Pasture to look for the Iron Age hutments? Towlers, it seems, are still rearing their sheep here as they have done since the Dissolution of the Monasteries almost 500 years ago. And for how long before that? It's not improbable that the farmer digging out that drainage channel with his JCB or delivering that fodder to his sheep on a quad bike could trace his DNA to the Vikings and even beyond. It completes the link in the 7,000 year occupation of Malham Moor, bringing it right up to date to the people who live and work here today.

I think this is the unique appeal of Malham Moor. I know of no other place where you can trace its human occupation uninterruptedly through so many years of history by means of material remains available to the casual observer: from the sightless skulls of the Neolithic occupants of Elbolton Cave, through the Bronze Age tumuli and round houses, the Iron Age hutments, the Anglian terraced fields and Viking longhouses, to the modern farmers whose ancestors grazed their sheep at the behest of one of the great Cistercian monasteries. It is as if the crowds who come here, ambling their way along the river path to the Cove on a Sunday afternoon before climbing the steps onto the limestone pavements above and fanning out to explore the plateau beyond, felt it with something akin to the instinct of the salmon that finds its way back to the source of the river where it was born, or the sixth sense of the aboriginal who gets in touch with the spirits of his ancestors, and were returning to the happy hunting grounds of their forebears.

The old access road to Malham and the farms around the Tarn is from the east along Mastiles Lane from Kilnsey over in Wharfedale. The route is scattered with prehistoric settlements, one of them at Bordley to the south. It's worth travelling along there to get an idea of what Malham Moor is today, in a working sense, away from the visitors and tourists who can sometimes seem to overrun the place. You don't need to go down into Bordley but can stand on the hill above Mastiles Lane and look down onto it, tucked into a hollow. You soon see that it's not a village or even a hamlet but a farm or maybe two, I never was sure. I think I counted two houses amongst all the barns and outbuildings set into a clutter of yards and muddy paddocks with tractors, muck heaps and black plastic silage bales glinting in the watery sunlight. There are the cries of children playing in the garden of one of the houses, of rooks grumbling in a small wood on the slopes of a gill which runs back up the hill where I'm standing. A cock crows and a dog barks. But it is not these sounds that you really notice. It is the cacophony of bleeting sheep that seems to fill the valley to bursting point. Sheep are the real business of this place. Bordley is a sheep factory. The sheep are bleeting because they're hungry and they'll soon be ready to lamb. In the field where I'm standing they've been muck-spreading. And that is what it's all about: spreading muck, growing grass, feeding and breeding sheep and harvesting their meat. We can think that with the loss of cotton, steel, shipbuilding and all the other urban industries, the North is no longer a place for manufacturing. Not it. We are the great manufacturers of meat here in the Pennine Hills and have been since the Vikings and before. The thread which links the modern dalesman to his ancient ancestors is a woollen one. It is the enduring constant which defines these Northern hills. Mutton, lamb, dress it as you will, it's sheep meat. It used to be wool as well but the demand for that no longer seems to keep the coat on the farmer's back. How long before the meat of these sheep goes the same way and succumbs to market forces, changing trends, climate change? Who knows? Meanwhile, what could be more suited to survive in this environment, this upland fastness of tough bents and moor grass, hostile winds and months of rain? What could look the part more than these ragged warriors of the fells that stare with blank indifference to the long, slow passage of time?

Back up Mastiles Lane to the north of Bordley is what's left of a stone circle. Three standing stones are all that remain. The stones are pale grey, smooth and greasy with the rubbing of sheep. They're known locally as the Druids' Circle. The setting is awe-inspiring, surrounded by high and ranging moorland, lonely and empty, the barest elements of landscape. The land is pale yellow in the late winter sunlight, flecked with the chasing shadows of clouds. What were the stones for? What happened here? The mind lurches back into the shadows of pre-history again, to a time of dark magic and

34

obscure ritual, of minds preoccupied with strange gods. We must leave Malham Moor behind to explore some of the monoliths and henges of the North to attempt to answer some of the questions posed by stones like these.

2. SACRED CIRCLES

It is a short step from natural monoliths like Malham Cove to the man-made ones. They share the same capacity to awe, a power over the mind which is ancient and terrifying. The Devil's Arrows at Boroughbridge, 300 yards to the east of the A1, rise from the fields like giant molars, yellow with age, their cusps ribbed and fluted with weathering. There are three of them, almost in a straight line parallel with the North Road, the old Roman Dere Street. The tallest is around 22 feet high, the widest eight and a half feet thick and probably 25 feet in circumference. I couldn't even begin to guess at their weight. A vast undertaking to drag them here and root them in the earth; a huge and inscrutable undertaking.

Like all ancient mysteries, the Devil's Arrows are largely ignored by the self-absorbed modern world. The stones are set incongruously between the busy road and a modern housing estate. The traffic swishes past, drivers foot down, eye on the needle, hurrying home for the match on the box, the next episode of a soap. The houses so neat with their terracotta pantiles, homes for well-ordered suburban minds too busy for mysteries, for questions without answers. In Druid's Meadow and Arrows Drive they sleep untroubled by any echoes of the past still lurking in the avenue of oak trees that shadows the stones. Even the farmer, who lives by the land, has let science and subsidies squeeze out all sense of the earth's magic and has surrounded the stones with a field of turnips. Turnips! It's hard not to conclude that the stones are dead. Whatever magic which inspired the superhuman effort to erect them is spent.

But go right up to one and you can't fail to sense some of its latent power. Very well, I know that it's only a stone, a pale yellow sandstone stained with the ubiquitous patches of black lichen, flecked with chips of grey quartz and sudden starfire of mica,

37

ordinary stone but invested with a purpose which renders it totally extraordinary. You can list the possibilities as to what that purpose might have been, starting with the rational and proceeding into the wilder regions of the occult. The three stones seem to be in a line - if you ignore the slight westward displacement of the middle one. (There was a fourth stone according to the record of the Tudor antiquarian John Leland who visited the site between 1538 and 1540, but this is said to have been toppled by treasure hunters and eventually dragged away to form the foundations of a bridge across the River Tutt just to the south in Boroughbridge.) A glance at an OS map will reveal that a line drawn through the stones to the NNW will pass through the henge at Nunwick, two and half miles north of Ripon, and through the three giant henges at Thornborough, ten miles away. This line is parallel with the two remaining henges in the area at Hutton Moor and Cana and, of course, with the ancient Dere Street. So what can be the significance of this alignment? The first thing that occurs to you is that it is in the direction of magnetic north, making the stones some kind of giant waymarks. But why anyone should want to drag stones of up to 50 tons in weight nine miles from Knaresborough, which is thought to be where they originated, just to build a signpost, when much smaller stones would have done just as well, baffles belief. Then there are the suggestions that the stones have some sort of calendric significance connected with the agricultural activities of the people who erected them around 2200 BC. Unfortunately there is no evidence of any summer solstice alignment, the nearest such astronomical event being, according to Aubrey Burl, the southernmost summer moonrise around this time. Writing in the Yorkshire Archaeological Journal in 1991, Burl offers the respective declinations to the south of the stones and concludes that 'these are all so close to the southernmost summer moonrise…there must be a good chance that this was intended by the people who built the row'. Again, such a massive undertaking for predicting the movements of the moon when something more modest would have done equally well? Elsewhere there is the suggestion that these Neolithic people were interested in predicting lunar eclipses and that stone circles like Stonehenge and megalithic rows like those at Carnac were subtle astronomical observatories set out for this purpose. Robert Graves in his crazy work - he uses the word himself - on the origins of European myth and legend, 'The White Goddess', argues that Stone Age rituals involved the worship of a moon-goddess. You can already begin to feel the ground beneath our stones start to shake. And this is before we've met the ley line theorists who would explain the alignment of stones and henges along the River Ure in terms of magnetic lines of force or other telluric currents no longer felt or understood by the blunted sensitivities of modern man but vital to our ancient ancestors' control of their environment. In a word, that they were geomancers, adept at harnessing the hidden forces of the earth which were somehow amplified by these huge stones. Indeed, there are still those sensitives around today who claim to be able to feel the spiral forces generated by the stones, causing them to feel dizzy in their presence or even flung to one side when they touch them. Worth a try, I thought. Stone-hugging is a purely innocent pastime, especially if performed in the interest of scientific experimentation. My hands firmly clutching the megalith, my cheek pressed to its gritty surface, eyes closed to shut out the clamour of the passing world, I can report feeling no sensation whatsoever except one of distinct uneasiness at the thought of being spotted by a suspicious housewife polishing her china in Druid's Close and ready to pick up the phone and ring the mental health authorities.

But if today the stones are dead so far as any physical sensation is concerned, they live on in the imagination. And this is the only way we can respond to them. This is why they inspire so much wild guesswork as to their purpose. There are no signs, no scrawls or patterns discernible in the stones to give any clue, no indication that the men who erected them had yet learnt to compress their thoughts and emotions into symbols to convey their feelings. It is an age before literacy, when art had moved no further perhaps than personal adornments and weaponry. So we are left to think of the giant stones and circles themselves as art, as an expression of feeling, enormous religious feeling. Only on such a scale could early man express the giant feelings that came at him out of the sky, out of the constellations he observed, the mysterious but vital movements of the sun and moon, the life and death cycles of the seasons. These were matters of enormous consequence, requiring an enormous response, in giant stones, the stuff of the earth itself. And they were a shout to the sky, to the universe, of the arrival of man himself, of this creature without precedent, without, to his knowledge, any history. A shout of raw spiritual exultation in himself and the great mystery of life into which he had been placed. These stones, I suggest, are the dawn of man's self-awareness, awareness of his own centrality and strength, strength enough to tow hundreds of tons of stone across the land, bed them in the fecund earth that sustained him and raise them as a symbol of his own response to the overwhelming mystery of creation. These stones and circles are his cathedrals.

There are six large circles or henges northwest of the Devil's Arrows, all of identical size at around 250 metres in diameter and within a space of ten kilometres. They are said to be the fifth largest of their kind in Britain and the largest outside Wessex. The most celebrated and best studied are those at Thornborough where there are three henges in a NW SE alignment, 550 metres apart and extending for 1.7 kilometres. The Thornborough henges have been dated to the Neolithic and early Bronze Age period around 1750 BC or later. Evidence of a curcus or rectilinear banked and ditched enclosure passing through the central henge and belonging to an earlier period of the fourth millennium BC is suggestive of a processional avenue leading to an earlier circle on the same site. The notion that the circles had a ceremonial significance is endorsed by the absence of flints and other finds in the immediate vicinity, leading archaeologists to conclude that they were sited away from human settlements because of their sacred nature. Virtual reality models of Thornborough have superimposed images of the Bronze Age night sky to explore the idea that the henges were specially orientated towards the stellar constellations.

This is all fascinating stuff, but what are the henges like today? It will come as a shock to today's curious visitor to see how time and modern man have treated these ancient monuments.

The best preserved of the North Yorkshire henges is the central of the three Thornborough henges. The circle is enclosed by irregular mounds about 15 feet high. Where the grass is broken you can see the stones and pebbles from which the mounds have been constructed, the moraine from the nearby River Ure which characterises this alluvial landscape. Inside the encircling mound is the shallow ditch from which the material has been removed to form the bank. If the ditch was outside you might conclude that the circle was defensive, but it's not. The perimeter bank, you'd infer, is for keeping things in not out. A charmed circle? A sphere of influence whose potency and sanctity is protected by the encircling bank? The effect of the inner ditch is to raise the ground towards the centre of the circle so that the midpoint is the highest point of the inner circle. The two mounds to the south form an entrance to this amphitheatre.

It's high summer and the banks are strewn with poppies, harebells, pale mauve scabious and yellow ragwort. It has been left uncultivated inside the circle, a sea of wafting golden grasses. Swallows swoop and switch on the wind. A rook complains. Skylarks trill and plummet. You can stand in the middle and, slowly turning, inscribe the surrounding circle with your gaze, following the undulations of the bank. Round and round until the earth around you slowly begins to spin. You are at the heart of the circle, the same circle whose shape is the pattern of the petals of the scabious flower or the dark heart of the poppy. The circle that is the fringed bowl of the sky, that is the motion of the earth, the moon, the sun and the stars, that is the spin of the galaxies. The endless circular dance of creation. The spiral force at the centre of the universe which the ancients recognised when they carved its symbol into stone. You can stand here and be caught briefly in its mesmerising spin, in the eternal dance of creation. You can feel what it is like to be at the centre of things again.

Is this it? Is this what these giant circles are about? A celebration of

41

man's position at the centre of things? Because if they are, sadly, today we have lost our way. We have wandered out of the circle, away from the heart of the mystery. Reason, technology, urbanisation, the seduction of relentless consumerism which threatens our very existence on the planet, have taken us away from nature and her cycles of harmony. So, in a fearful Faustian pact with the demons of so-called progress we have turned our backs on the magic and mystery of life, exiled ourselves from the knowledge which the builders of these circles understood. No wonder the Thornborough henges are threatened with destruction. The elevators and machinery of a gravel extraction plant hang over the site to the west. They are moving ever closer, eager for planning permission to dig up the henges for more ballast for the next motorway, so that we can drive further and faster away from the heart of the mystery.

The northernmost of the three Thornborough henges is the most atmospheric. It is hidden by a dense copse, a tangle of undergrowth and tall, crowded trees. It is as if nature, sensing the loss of these sacred places, has intensified her efforts to conceal them from the destructive hand of modern man. You enter off the lane from Nosterfield through a gap in the undergrowth and are immediately plunged into a sanctuary of intense greenery. Sycamore and beeches thick with ivy arch overhead. Bracket fungi project like grotesque corbels seeming to support the thick overhead canopy where the wind roars and the leaves flap with alarm. Sunlight, in a sickly green flickering haze, struggles to break through. Underfoot, bone-dry elderflower branches crack and a black puffball bursts like mummy wrappings. The bank and ditch are visible and I begin to walk around the inner ditch which is much more pronounced than in the middle henge. It is full of dog's mercury and the occasional cuckoo pint with green berries on a bare stem - both poisonous plants, I can't fail to notice. There's something over-green about this wood, promiscuous, as if everything was in the thrall of a strong natural spell. It is a timely reminder when I'd started thinking of circles and natural harmony, of how nature, left unchecked, can be frighteningly and overwhelmingly chaotic. This rampant vegetation is an insight into

42

what the great forests of pre-history must have been like when Mesolithic man first stepped onto these shores. The rankness, the sheer intensity of the forest's fertility, each species' fierce opportunism which spares no space from invasion, from the relentless imperatives of growth and reproduction, the wild circus of birth, procreation and death. The circus, the cycle, the circle, the only constant in this chaotic explosion of life. And yet, ironically, while these henges may have been a celebration of the great natural cycles of creation, they were also a refuge from the rampant forces of nature. Post holes discovered on the outer bank suggest that a palisade or timber fence enclosed the henge, keeping the wilderness in check, the first requirement of a civilisation: to protect its citizens from the wilderness around them in order to allow them to develop the civilised arts of meeting and settling their communal affairs or worshipping their gods.

Next I visited the two henges further south at Hutton Moor, starting with the southernmost, referred to by some as Cana, though I've not come across the name on any of my maps. You strike out towards it off a country lane by some bedraggled farm buildings. The walls were once neatly coursed with round stones and a terra cotta pantiled roof but are now collapsing under buckling brick pillars. Piles of bleached pallets and rotten straw bales moulder inside the buildings which open onto a neglected courtyard. But the place is still in use because round the back is a tall, unpleasant-looking, skin-coloured chemical silo. It bears a logo which underneath boasts: 'The Queen's Award to Technological Achievement'. What it contains, God, or the Queen, only knows. The only evidence of agricultural activity is a long parabola of water from an irrigation pump spewing out in broken waves onto a field full of potatoes. There hasn't been any rain here for weeks and underfoot the soil is fine red sand which drags drily at your feet as you walk. Yellow balls of chickweed hang on for dear life. Swallows skim over a field full of dry and brittle-looking pea-like pods, presumably rapeseed. You wonder at the future of trying to grow such things here if global warming continues. The field where the henge should have been is green with unripe corn, the edges of the field scattered with poppies like flecks of blood. A slight camber to the field is all that is left of the henge. Also, a tumulus, marked on an earlier map, has been ploughed away. Modern agribusiness, like quarrying for aggregate, is no respecter of our archaeological past in this part of North Yorkshire.

Another day and the summer further advanced with still no rain to speak of and I visited the other henge at Hutton Moor with better fortune. The tumulus marked on the map at the side of the path is still there. It is about 40 feet in diameter, only a few feet high but conspicuous enough to be recognised as a round barrow. Today it is covered with silvery grasses that shimmer and shift in the breeze under a blazing blue sky, drawing a numinous veil over the occupant's identity and all the details of his life. The vast expanse of this flat arable land stretching between the Pennines and the Cleveland Hills has absorbed his memory like the land absorbs the sky and like nature will ultimately absorb us all. Further along the track and there's a barley field. It's like exotic silvery-gold fur, stirring and rippling in the wind. I can't imagine spraying it with anything the Queen might award for technological achievement, it's so pure. 'That's why,' the modern agri-barons will tell us, 'Because we've sprayed it. Killed every bug that breathes!' So it becomes a very sinister 'purity', drenched in toxic residues. As if to warn us off, the field is flanked with a phalanx of tall thistles. A small but stately colony of dark-blue monkshood stands nearby. I quote from my wild flower book: 'Monkshood: extremely poisonous, only a small amount may cause death within a very short time.' I don't think the monkshood can be responsible for the death of the rook which lies in our path. His wings are spread sacrificially. His beak open like callipers in one last silent croak. The pale feathers behind the gape have been plucked out by something and contrast with his oily black body. Black and white. Good and bad. Nature make no distinction. Her only concern is the continuation of the cycle, the uninterrupted circle. The henge is in an empty field of short, stubbly grassland on the edge of a wood. Again, the sweeping, curving rise towards the centre but so shallow this time the bank is almost levelled out. A few

44

more ploughings and it will be gone forever, its purpose no longer a mystery because the mystery is no longer there. The OS map says nothing but simply, 'Henge (site of)'. On the way back to the road a hare blocks our path, reared upright, ears bristling, sounding the air. Eventually he lopes off nonchalantly into the corn. Hares love henges. I once counted close on twenty inside the middle henge at Thornborough, larking about. It was March. It can drive you mad wondering about the power of henges.

The last of the six great henges which almost wrap themselves in the sinuous folds of the River Ure north of Ripon is at Nunwick. Nunwick is for the most part a desultory collection of farm buildings, bleak, bleached, anonymous sheds with grey asbestos roofs where the moss browns and curls in the dry late summer heat. The absence of activity around these buildings is disconcerting, unsettling. You feel you've strayed into a ghost village. There's a bus stop where you can travel into Ripon two and a half miles away but I notice that the buses only run at breakfast time and teatime. In between stretches an eight hour limbo. Stop off at Nunwick as I did and you can become trapped in its inertia. A farm dog barks out of duty or hunger. Some sparrows flap and flurry in a hawthorn hedge, fussing over whatever it is that excites sparrows before suddenly departing. In the distance the muffled explosion of a shotgun briefly breaks the afternoon truce with the warm sun. Nothing for long disturbs the torpor of time, the stationary tide of history. If this was Spain or some other Mediterranean country you might think it was siesta time. But this is North Yorkshire in the twenty-first century where mechanisation and consolidation of ownership have bled agricultural areas like this of all vitality, of all human imprint. Where a century ago we might have expected to see fields of busy figures, the sound of voices, laughter even, now the monotonous hedgeless horizons are empty save for the dust of a distant tractor or harvester tracked by a mournful litany of crying seagulls. Modern agriculture has imposed itself upon the landscape as never before, draining it of interest and character. The fields are the agricultural equivalent of a Tesco supermarket. Beasts that once grazed in them now spend their short lives cooped up in sheds, being unnaturally fattened off protein supplements. Fields that once were an intimate jumble of hedges and hollows, wooded knolls and imposing trees that have witnessed the passing of centuries, are now bare and monotonous highways for tractors and their paraphernalia of lethal chemical dispensaries. A vast complacency has settled over areas of the English countryside like this which have been monopolised by large-scale modern agriculture. They seem to say: 'We farmers and what we do are the only things that matter. There are few if any footpaths because people are not welcome. There is no extraneous vegetation because we have no interest in wildlife unless it be to shoot it. And there's no history because history cannot be sold to make a profit.'

And so it is with Nunwick's Neolithic henge. It has been ploughed out and levelled to make room for a field of spring wheat almost a mile wide. I spoke to a landowner and he made it abundantly clear that he thought that this was the best thing for these troublesome antiquities. He applauded the activities of the gravel diggers at Thornborough. And I don't think his views are in any way uncommon, not to judge by the parlous condition of these Ripon earthworks. That there was a henge here at Nunwick at all, we must rely upon the word of those who have flown over it. From the ground only the wheel marks of a tractor hint at how the land rises to the shallow heart of the circle. If you didn't know about it you'd never notice anything. And I wonder if anyone does? As I stand looking out from the edge of the huge field the traffic on the road from Tanfield slides past: motorists returning from a late lunch, a B&Q van delivering kitchen furniture. Overhead, jet planes from a nearby RAF base drill corridors of noise through the sky. Today stamps its flat, dead hand on the mysteries of yesterday. That mixture of awe, wonder and poetry which we feel in the presence of the great mysteries of antiquity and gives a profounder dimension to our lives, here at Nunwick is erased forever.

Whatever the disappointments of henges obliterated by modern agriculture, it is useful to replace them by marking them on the OS map, so that with all six laid out before you, you can spend some time speculating upon their location. Given the scale of effort applied to their construction, why were so many built in such close proximity? You don't get mediaeval cathedrals built side by side in threes like the henges at Thornborough. The conclusion drawn by many archaeologists is that this area was regarded by Neolithic man as an especially sacred landscape, as special in its own way as the Wiltshire landscape around Stonehenge. The existence of so many ceremonial circles would suggest that people came in great numbers from all over the North of England and that they were places of pilgrimage. But what constituted the sacredness of this area? Again, a look at the map shows how close they are to the River Ure. In fact, they are all between the Ure and the Swale, enjoying the fertile alluvial silts of those rivers and their flood plains, a richness which contrasts markedly with the barer millstone grits of the Pennines and the Cleveland Hills on either side. So were the activities within the henges associated with a celebration of the landscape's life-sustaining nature? And did river-worship play as much a part in their ceremonials as the more obscure notion of moon-worship some have associated with the special alignment of the henges?

With no scientific explanations as to what made things grow best and with what imbued one harvest with plenty and another with dearth, early man would be left with nothing but his instincts to account for things. The coming and going of the sun, the spectacular presence in the night sky of a full moon, earth and rivers with their potential to sustain or deny life, have throughout man's early history led him to invest these natural phenomena with religious significance, with a god-like status which required his adoration and appeasement, his service in the construction of monuments and theatres of worship and sacrifice in acknowledgement of their power over his life. The best we can say of these North Yorkshire henges is that it is to this numinous instinct that they belong.

The other megalith of comparable stature to Boroughbridge's Devil's Arrows here in the North is the one at Rudston in East Yorkshire, five miles west of Bridlington. In fact, the Rudston monument is taller than any of the Devil's Arrows, standing at just over 25 feet high. It is as wide at the base as a man's outstretched arms, is sculpted to a blunt point, and to prevent the kind of fluted weathering that has eroded its North Yorkshire neighbours, it has been fitted with a lead cap. This gives it the appearance of a terrifying giant, helmeted warrior. The stone is scarred and pocked as pumice. It is grey gritstone and not the local chalk of the Yorkshire Wolds, leading to speculation that it was either brought here from the Cleveland Hills to the north or else found its way here by means of the Ice Age glaciers. But quite the most astonishing thing about the Rudston monolith is its position in the graveyard only feet away from the church of All Saints' Rudston. Now I know that people will tell you that the early Christians built their churches often on sites of pagan worship which, they point out, was a shrewd move on the part of the founders to ease the transition from one form of worship to another; and there's plenty of evidence up and down the land to show that these sites often coincide. But there is something so shockingly raw and nakedly brutal about this crude pillar of stone - phallic, some would say - that I find it hard to believe that at some period in the church's history the people have not moved heaven and earth, so to speak, to get rid of it. (Christian zealots burnt and cracked many of the Avebury stones in Wiltshire to destroy what they regarded as heathen artefacts.) It seems to me that the Rudston monolith is the very antithesis of everything which the Christian religion is meant to stand for. Christianity celebrates the gentle, forgiving and compassionate side of man's nature. The stone epitomises everything that is harsh, unrelenting and aggressive. It is a symbol of the power of earth not Heaven. In fact I'd go so far as to say that the megalith, despite being only half as tall as the church's Norman tower, dominates the church, dwarfs it, not in size but in sheer vitality, in elemental charisma. No wonder the worn faces of the carvings on the mouldings over the church windows look down in such mute dismay. This, I'm afraid, is an assertion of the power of primal energy, of action, not prayers, of aggression and war, not love. They'll tell you that the monument gets its name from the cross, the 'rood' stone, and that it was a rallying point for early Christian missionaries converting the pagans. But rud also means red, the red stone or blood stone, a place of sacrifice or other such sanguinary ritual. If it was ever adopted as a Christian icon, I suggest that it shows a singular failure of imagination to appreciate the stone's fundamentally pagan essence.

The rest of the stones in the graveyard, the headstones, seem untroubled by their incongruous neighbour. In fact, they seem to lean towards it almost submissively, as if acknowledging its ancient power. One in particular, only a few feet away from the monolith, catches my eye. Its inscription tells me that it is the grave of Elizabeth Ann Simpson who died at the pitiful age of only four months. A cracked bell in the church tower sets up a discordant chime. Somewhere in a nearby copse a pheasant crows derisively. I find myself reflecting on the choice between a Christian god of love that permit's the death of a four-month old child and the cruel indifference of an agnostic nature. And the word Hobson's comes to mind.

The old paganism still has its devotees. People have been leaving candles at the foot of the monolith and in the cracks and holes of the ancient stone they have pressed coins and left fruit to rot. A couple have brought their infant child and are holding him up towards the stone's grey face. He screws his eyes and clenches his fist in a tiny salute. Who knows what hold these ancient stones still have over us?

The Yorkshire Wolds contain an unusually large concentration of burial mounds, or round barrows. They pre-date the henges of North Yorkshire and are seen by some as their precursors. One such, Duggleby Howe, 16 miles west of Rudston on the road to Malton, is a Neolithic burial mound 36 metres across and, by my reckoning, six metres high. A very impressive earthwork. It is said to be at the centre of an enclosure 370 metres in diameter, though I was unable to detect any of this circle (largely because I hadn't heard about it at the time of my visit and therefore wasn't looking for it). You can't mistake the conical mound as you drive past on the road just south of

Duggleby village. The barrow is set upon rising ground outside the village and draws the eye away from the collection of dull and undistinguished houses set around a crossroads. It is a focal point for an emotional intensity where otherwise there would be none. You find yourself reflecting on the fact that this burial mound has dominated this spot for over 4,000 years. How do the people in the village feel when they allow their minds to wander towards their ancient neighbour? In the small hours of the night, perhaps, as they lie restless in bed, are they ever unsettled by thoughts of what may have happened here? Of what attended upon a cult of the dead? For it is thought that monuments like this, containing the bones of dead ancestors, were scenes of ritual and sacrifice to propitiate the spirits of the dead in order that fate might deal more kindly with the living. It is a practice so alien to the modern mind, so preoccupied by the humdrum considerations of modern life, that it cannot fail to disturb.

Duggleby Howe is set at the edge of a field where crops have recently been planted. Green shoots force their way through brown earth littered with splintered chalk. The chalk feels smooth and soapy to the touch and I'm handling it because scattered amongst it are fragments of flint which I can't resist inspecting in case they should turn out to be arrowheads or worked tools. Always on these expeditions you are on the lookout for something which may have the imprint of our early Northern settlers, some actual tangible link with our ancestors, instead of all this reaching in the dark inside your own head to get closer to them.

It is an autumn afternoon on my very first visit to the Yorkshire Wolds. The day had begun with thick fog shrouding the landscape and it has left a legacy of diffuse mist which a watery sun does little to dissipate. It generates a stillness, a strange sense of being cut off from the rest of the world, something I later began to recognise as a particular quality of the Wolds landscape with its empty, undulating chalk hills and sudden secretive dry valleys. The burial mound is covered in the dense brown vegetation of dead and dying thistles, nettles and briars. But at one side, to the west, there is a sudden explosion of autumn colours. Deep red haws, like clotted blood, shining black elderberries and, most remarkable of all, two crab apple trees laden with fruit, one lemon-yellow, the other bright red, the apples filling the air with autumn sweetness. What fruitfulness for a place of fractured chalk and flint, of old bones and ceremonial death. I climbed to the top of the mound to scan the brown-bellied swell of the surrounding slopes and watch the sunlight struggle through the mist to burnish the chalk-filled fields. Someone has, inexplicably, driven a wooden stake into the dead centre at the top of the mound and nearby a mole has fossicked a sliver of flint. But that apart, Duggleby Howe lies undisturbed, seemingly the very core of the afternoon's stillness. But like the rest of these Wolds barrows, it has not always been left undisturbed.

It is a precious quality of the human mind that events and experiences which when they happen can seem relatively unremarkable, will grow and blossom with time into something rich and strange. And so, long after I'd left Duggleby Howe behind, it began to exercise a power over my imagination. Here was a mound of earth and chalk, set in a landscape whose modest, even shy, appeal brings few visitors, passed every day by local folk, minds more likely set on the potato harvest than the doings of history, yet throwing up for me a multitude of unanswered questions clad in an aura of ever-growing fascination with the lives, and deaths, of these our early Northern ancestors. I allowed my preoccupation to become so public, talking about it whenever I could, that friends would ask: 'How are things at Duggleby Howe?' or 'Been to Duggleby Howe lately?', suspecting, probably correctly, that I'd never really left there.

And so I turned to the pages of the Yorkshire Archaeological Journal for some enlightenment. My nearest volumes were at the public library in Skipton. Unfortunately the two shelves of thick volumes lack an index. The nearest one, I was told, was at Northallerton. So to look for any reference to Duggleby Howe I had to sit on the floor in the reference library (Didn't you know the books would be on the bottom shelves?) and pore through the contents list of every volume to stand any chance of finding what I was looking for. And it was here that I met the Reverend Dr William Greenwell.

Dr Greenwell was a minor canon of Durham Cathedral in Victorian times. But his ecclesiastical duties must have been less than demanding because from 1864 he undertook the excavation of 234 barrows in the North of England as well as Wiltshire. And his methods were nothing if not thorough. In the book he published regarding his findings, 'British Barrows, a record of the examination of sepulchral mounds in various parts of England', published in 1877, he reveals in a footnote his methods of excavation. Not for Canon Greenwell the quick dip into the centre of the barrow of the impatient bounty hunter. His technique was to drive a trench the whole width of the barrow from south to north through the mound. In many cases, he reveals, he has turned over the whole mound. It may sound like the Victorian equivalent of setting to with a JCB, but Canon Greenwell's book reveals him to have been a meticulous workman. Very little inside the barrows seems to have escaped his eagle eye and his accounts of his finds are both scholarly and exhaustive. By far the largest area of exploration is the Yorkshire Wolds, so I turned eagerly to see what he'd managed to find in Duggleby Howe. But I was in for a disappointment. His only reference to an excavation at Duggleby was one at Duggleby Wold which was a barrow measuring 74 feet in diameter and six feet in height, only a third of the height of the mound I'd stood upon. I find it hard to believe that such an intrepid barrow rifler wouldn't have had a go at something of the magnitude of Duggleby Howe. But it seems that he, for whatever reason, didn't. For the record, his excavation of the lesser earthwork at Duggleby Wold revealed at its centre a flat-topped conical mound of chalk rubble on top of which, on a bed of charcoal, were the remains of a man, according to Greenwell, 'in a very decayed state'. Close to the body were two flint flakes, four flint chippings, three quartz pebbles and, beyond the head, four stake holes, identified as the remains of a platform which once supported the body.

People looking for sensational discoveries of lavish and valuable grave goods in the round barrows of the Yorkshire Wolds will be in for a disappointment. On the contrary, there is something almost pathetically commonplace about the worldly goods bequeathed to the earth and posterity by our early ancestors. Typically there would be a drinking cup decorated with chevrons applied to the wet clay with a bone instrument or even a thumbnail, flint tools such as knives, arrowheads and scrapers, or, in rarer cases, a stone axe hammer with a perforation for a haft, a whetstone, a flint and steel - which was a piece of flint scraped along a nodule of iron pyrites to create a spark with which to make fire - and perhaps an antler pick. What is particularly interesting is that most of these tools show no sign of wear and Canon Greenwell concludes that they must have been made specially for the burial for use in the afterlife. Articles of personal adornment are pitifully scarce but where they occur might include buttons made of jet for fastening garments around the body. Rings and necklaces of jet or bone are equally rare. So are bronze items, but where they do occur are usually knife blades which have been riveted to ox-horn handles. Undoubtedly the use of bronze and flint overlapped in this late Neolithic period to which Greenwell ascribes the Wolds barrows. But he suggests that bronze would not have been so readily procurable. The Wolds settlers were to some extent isolated from the rest of Britain because of being surrounded by low-lying swamp and the land being largely wooded. As a consequence they had little wealth in terms of gold, bronze, amber and glass found amongst the grave goods in other areas like Wessex. They may not, he concludes, have reached the same height of civilisation.

But despite this apparent backwardness, the care bestowed upon the burial of the dead, with the attendant tools and adornments, is an indication to Greenwell of an incipient civilisation, albeit a heathen and superstitious one. His excavations often reveal carefully placed circles of stone around the buried remains or inhumations. Greenwell suggests a reason for this: 'They were intended to prevent the exit of the spirit of those buried within rather than guard from disturbance without. A dread of injury by the spirits of the dead has been very commonly felt by many savage people. Nor,' he adds, 'is such a fear unknown in our own times and even amongst ourselves. Worship of ancestors,' he concludes, 'is always associated with fear. The propitiation of the dead with the view of diverting their displeasure and warding off the danger of their inflicting injury is widespread in the history of religion.'

Of the many hundreds of human remains Canon Greenwell uncovered in the barrows of the Yorkshire Wolds, both inhumation and cremation occur. Sometimes burnt as well as unburnt remains appear within the same barrow, although cremations represent only 21% of burials. Of the inhumations, he observes that the bodies are almost wholly placed on their side with their knees drawn up towards the head, in what we would call the foetal position. This is not through lack of space because some of the graves he found were as much as ten feet in diameter. But he doesn't believe this foetal position arises from any anatomical knowledge but is more likely to symbolise the sleeping position common to people afforded scant protection from the cold. That is, in death they were put to rest. He notes that while there is no pattern with regard to the compass position of these heathen remains, as you would get in early Christian or Saxon burials, from the bodies he found placed on their right side pointing west and those on the left pointing to the east, he concludes that generally the dead were placed in their graves facing the sun. And as far as the cremations were concerned, the burning of the bones was often incomplete, indicating to Greenwell that the use of fire was a form of ritual purification, rather like the use of water in modern Christian baptism is a substitute for complete immersion. It is speculation like this which makes Canon Greenwell's work so interesting to the lay reader. I doubt any modern archaeologists would be prepared to stick their necks out in such an entertaining way over matters which remain only speculative.

But there are some features of the Wolds barrow burials which to Canon Greenwell point to a condition of little more than savagery amongst the population. He says, 'It can scarcely be questioned that it was the habit to slay at the funeral and to bury with the dead man, wives, children and others, probably slaves'. This gruesome conclusion he draws from instances of the burial of two sexes -

assumed to be man and wife - in adjoining graves, plus the remains of children in graves which, to Greenwell's careful study, were clearly contemporaneous. This begs the question: How were they slain? It is a question, perhaps surprisingly, which the ever-curious Greenwell never addresses. Instead, the second half of his book is handed over to an eminent Victorian pathologist, Professor George Rolleston. It is his job to examine the skulls and bones and try to draw conclusions about the intelligence and ethnic background of our Wolds ancestors. It is fairly turgid stuff, often intelligible only to a craniologist. It is also comical in some of its conclusions so far as the modern reader is concerned. For example, Dr Rolleston asserts that small or 'ill-filled' skulls are an indication of 'feebleness' in their owner. But with regard to the damaged skulls and whether or not they were as a result of violence inflicted through human sacrifice, Dr Rolleston prefers to think the better of our ancestors and conclude that any damage he found was a result of pressure from the earth above or else subsequent disturbance from later interments. Which gets us nowhere in answering the question: If they killed off the family of the chief at the time of his death in order to bury them all together, how did they do it? I'm no pathologist, but I don't suppose strangulation or even throat cutting would show up in a skeleton that had been in the earth for 4,000 years or more. I'm probably thinking here of the sacrificial remains of Lindow Man discovered in a peat bog in Cheshire in the 1980s. Owing to the unique conditions of preservation, he was found to have been garrotted with a cord around his neck. He had also had his throat cut and his skull bashed in for good measure. But this was relatively recently, only 2,000 years ago, in more civilised times! But the authors of 'British Barrows' offer no answers to how the family met their end and are clearly too well-bred to indulge me in my modern taste - or lack of it - for grisly speculation.

But one extraordinary practice does emerge from Dr Rolleston's study of an infant skull excavated by Canon Greenwell from a barrow at Rudston. It showed evidence of the artificial deforming of the skull in infancy in a deliberate attempt to alter its shape in order to give it a more 'eminent' or 'commanding' appearance in later life, a condition more favourable for tribal leadership. And, according to Dr Rolleston, this would seem to have involved the wearing of some sort of 'deforming apparatus' by the child before the age of two. And if that sounds barbaric, what are we to make of Dr Rolleston's assertion that the practice had lasted in parts of Southern France and Normandy even into his lifetime!

After finding numbers of large barrows in which the principal burial was that of a child, Canon Greenwell infers that these early Wolds settlers lived lives that were tribal under a hereditary rulership. Just how he squares this with the slaughter of families following the death of a chief, I don't know. But the fact that so much effort went into the construction of a barrow when the burial was for that of only a child, remains a riddle. For example, at Rudston, one of the many barrows is 100 feet in diameter and nine feet high. He records that the principal interment was that of a child 'scarcely a year old' in a wood-lined grave. Scattered nearby were the bones of a young female, 'possibly those of the mother'. He concludes that the child was 'the offspring of the chief of some powerful tribe destined, if life had been spared, to rule in his turn over the people whose bodily toil contributed to the erection of this gigantic funeral memorial'.

I visited a barrow of comparable spectacular size to Duggleby Howe near Burton Fleming, just three miles north of Rudston. Willie Howe is completely covered in trees, beech, ash and hawthorn, which nevertheless can't disguise the man-made symmetry of the structure. The branches which overhang the surrounding arable land have been lopped to allow the tractor as close as possible to the monument, as if the farmer resented every square inch of soil taken up by this unprofitable thing called history. In fact, Willie Howe is marooned in acres of large-scale agribusiness. While I was there, tractors drummed and whined as they clawed the potato crop from the earth. Climbing through the brambles and lopped-off branches to the top of the mound, I was in for a sudden shock. The barrow was like a doughnut. The middle had been scooped out to ground level. As I stood in what must have been the secret, sacred heart of the barrow, from the thick undergrowth a wren scolds me for my intrusion. But this grave had been ransacked long ago. A mature ash tree rises from its centre. (Weren't ash trees held to be sacred once?) I can't believe that this clumsy failure to restore the barrow after excavation was the work of Canon Greenwell. In fact the only reference made by Greenwell in 'British Barrows' to Willie Howe is in a footnote when he refers to it as the largest barrow of his acquaintance, partly opened by Lord Londesborough when 'no interment was discovered, nor was the centre reached'. Nevertheless, it is a strange experience to stand where the body may once have rested, perhaps on a wooden platform surrounded by grave goods. The soft, brown brash creaks and crackles underfoot. Thorn trees fan out overhead as if to try and shelter the wounded grave, belatedly protecting its secret. The sky peers through the arching branches, over-bright in this darkling place. Prying perhaps? But then earth and sky are old enemies and the sky has always resented the earth her secrets.

And then I notice the snails, glued to the undersides of the overhanging branches of the ash tree. Scores of them, reaching high up into the topmost branches, each creamy-yellow shell marked with a perfectly symmetrical brown whorl, a miniature simulacrum of the spiral earth-force, that mysterious symbol that adorns so many Neolithic remains, from the cups and rings carved on the stones of Rumbalds Moor near Ilkley to the large standing stone of Long Meg near Penrith, the symbol which Canon Greenwell had recognised on many of the stones covering the urns or forming the cists of these prehistoric burials, the spiritual imprint of these Neolithic people, capturing their instinctive understanding of the endless circular pattern of nature, from the infinite spiralling galaxies to the life-cycle of the humble snail.

But who had been responsible for scooping out the heart of Willie Howe so many years ago? It turns out that Canon Greenwell had a rival, an even more intrepid barrow rifler. In the decades towards the close of the nineteenth century, J.R. Mortimer excavated more than

300 barrows, all within the Yorkshire Wolds. Whether he'd had a go at Willie Howe, I don't know, I was too busy being astonished at the sheer number of barrows to be found in the Wolds. The news required a complete revision of a long-held impression I'd had of the North of England being a sparsely populated and ill-favoured region so far as Neolithic settlements were concerned compared with the archaeologically rich areas around the ridgeways of southwest England. And one site which seems to have been pre-eminent here, comparable even to Avebury or Durrington Walls in Wiltshire, was Duggleby Howe. I didn't think it would be long before I'd be returning there.

J.R. Mortimer excavated Duggleby Howe in 1890, exhuming the remains of 10 adults and a child. Above these interments he discovered no fewer than 53 cremations. That Duggleby Howe was a really important sepulchral site only emerged clearly in 1971 when, viewed from the air, it was revealed that the mound was at the centre of a circular ditch 370 metres in diameter and enclosing a ceremonial area of over 10 hectares. You begin to understand the comparison with Avebury and Durrington. And situated as it is at the head of the Great Wold Valley, close to the spring head of one of those rare exceptions to the Wolds' dry valleys, the Gypsey Race, you can begin to see links with the great ceremonial henges of the Ure flood plain to the west around Ripon. The absence of any burial mounds associated with the latter, along with the more accurate dating of finds associated with the science of modern archaeology, incline archaeologists today to the view that Duggleby Howe is indeed a precursor to the Thornborough henges, and with the many round barrows of the Yorkshire Wolds can be dated to the third millennium BC. Alas, Canon Greenwell placed the barrows he uncovered at a period around 500 BC. With none of the extensive records of pottery and tools at his disposal to help date his finds, to say nothing of the technique of carbon dating, the Canon was hopelessly awry. But nevertheless, his accounts of his explorations and discoveries are far more appealing and accessible to the layman than many of the turgid papers of the modern professional archaeologist. He did, of course,

58

belong to the age of the enthusiastic amateur and, instead of looking nervously over his shoulder for the approval of his academic colleagues, he is unafraid to indulge in a little exhilarating speculation. I will always visualise him, quite fancifully, of course, atop one of his barrows in his dog collar, his cassock billowing out in the wind, hopping excitedly from one find to another like a jackdaw at a bird table. Let's leave him as he pauses to gaze out over the landscape above Rudston. In his book he describes the view from the Wolds ridge with its line of barrows following the crest of the hill, the plain of Holderness falling away to the south, behind him the undulating chalk hills of the Wolds and in the valley just to the north the mysterious Rudston megalith rising out of the churchyard. It's a view the Neolithic settlers must have been so familiar with that after reading about it, it had me hurrying back the hundred and odd miles from home to savour the Wolds one last time.

Nowhere could I find a suitable vantage point south of Rudston where I could take in the panorama described by Canon Greenwell. At the highest point of the whole Wolds you can never get beyond 800 feet and so you can't ever get the elevation which we from the hilly and mountainous regions to the west enjoy. I ended up on yet another of Canon Greenwell's barrows. It was just north of the Roman road from Kilham to Bridlington at South Side Mount, a shallow mound almost 200 yards across but only four or five feet high at the centre. As we approached, deftly picking our way along the tractor tracks to avoid treading on the ubiquitous turnip tops whose green leaves held their droplets of thaw from the overnight frost (I confess to a lasting confusion between the immature turnip plant, Brassica rapa, and the young rapeseed, Brassica napus, and where I have confused them, I apologise) we put up a huge hare who casually loped away. He'd been lying amongst the yellow bents and dead thistles of the mound which we surmised must have been his home. He was the first of our afternoon's magical encounters. Rudston and its megalith were invisible in the valley below, masked by a copse of sycamore trees planted as a windbreak. Nearby, a strip of maize plants had been left to topple and die and a flock of 50 or more chaffinches were having a field day picking at the corn cobs shrouded in their pale yellow mildewed hoods. Could the crop have been left unharvested for the birds? Yes, but not the chaffinches. Pens as well as drums full of seed were stationed along the edge of the copse. This was pheasant country, the birds reared and cosseted for the guns.

Under a dove-grey sky broken by patches of pale blue we crossed eastwards into a plantation. Someone had been busy here lopping the trees and leaving the brushwood around as cover for the game birds. It was heading towards twilight now and a stillness was settling over the forest, broken only by the sudden whirring of wings and splutter of alarm as pheasants abandoned their roosts at our approach. Deep amongst the trees we found our final barrow, betrayed by the unnatural swell in the forest floor. Like Willie Howe, the centre had been scooped out. Greenwell or Mortimer? Whoever was responsible, nature had once again done her best to conceal the violation. A dense brash of leaves and broken branches thick with green moss littered the floor of the hollow, with trees pushing upwards to hide the ravaged tomb. A scattering of spent shotgun cartridges seemed to sum up the value some people today place on such sites. Nevertheless, it felt dark and secretive as the night drew in and I didn't want to leave, not without some sort of epiphany, some sudden insight which would bring me closer to these Northerners of Neolithic times who I'd spent so much time thinking about. And it came in a brilliant and unexpected way.

As we left the barrow and passed through a clearing in the wood, three roe deer suddenly crossed our path. One moment they were there in front of us, their coats dark and shadowy, a white chalk-like dab on their hind quarters, next they were gone, dissolving into the landscape, leaving us with a sense of something not quite real, something not of this world but almost ethereal. And they left behind their gift. A talisman.

It was my wife, Margaret, who spotted it. In a molehill at our feet, glinting, catching the last of the daylight in its opalescent surface, a flint. An inch and a half in length and worked to a fine point, it was a chisel-shaped transverse arrowhead - I'd seen one that was identical in an illustration of the finds from Duggleby Howe. At last here was the tangible link with our ancestors, not the dead but the living. Because to feel the cool, smooth flake of the flint and observe under the translucent sheen the blue marbling, like veins under the skin, to run your fingers along its ragged edges and press the point into the softness of your flesh until it hurts, testing the arrow's lethal purpose, this was as vivid and real an encounter with the hunters who roamed this region 4,000 years ago as if, through some sudden kink in the smooth continuum of time, we'd brushed past one of them in the twilight of the forest.

It was a fitting finale to my excursions into the Yorkshire Wolds, something to take away and treasure. Something to evoke the spirit of ancient standing stone, henge and barrow and, when the memories start to fade, revive the exhilarating sense of mystery and magic which is the enduring legacy of our shadowy Northern forebears.

3. THE BRIGANTES

I may have lamented the lack of vantage points in the Yorkshire Wolds but there can be no such complaint about the western Pennines. The next stage in our quest for our Northern ancestors takes us back beyond the limestone uplands of Malham Moor to the second highest of the Three Peaks, Ingleborough. At 2,373 feet it is a rugged bulk of millstone-capped limestone flanking both north Ribblesdale and Lunesdale like a giant anvil. It rakes damp clouds and harbours peevish mists like the elemental thing that it is and yet, astonishingly, its summit was once the settlement of men. Ingleborough was once a hillfort of the Brigantes, that confederation of Northern tribesmen who dominated this region in the middle years of the Iron Age. They were Celts, a new ethnic ingredient in the melting pot that was to become the Northerner.

The Celts had migrated here from Western Europe during the first millennium BC. They brought with them a rich culture: a large pantheon of gods and goddesses and a skill in metalworking which enabled them to express their feelings and convictions through art, in other words, a rich iconography. What became of the native Bronze Age people with their round barrows and henges and poignant poverty of grave goods which we've been looking at, we can only guess. But the Celts were a belligerent lot, glorying in battle and hot-headed heroism, so we can surmise that integration may not always have been a peaceful affair. But the warlike Celts were to meet their match in the superior organisational skills and discipline of the Roman army after the invasion of 43 AD, though not without some periods of heroic resistance. It is to these events which we now turn with our first focus of attention on the dramatic bastion of Ingleborough.

The name Brigantes, some people will tell you, comes from the

Celtic expression 'the High Ones' and refers to their proclivity for choosing high places as their fortresses. The first usage of the name derives from classical writers and may simply have its origin in the way the Romans viewed these troublesome natives, as brigands or outlaws operating from the wild fastnesses of the Northern hills. But my preferred explanation comes from Anne Ross whose detailed knowledge of the Celts throws so much light on their everyday lives. She believes that the High One referred to in the name Brigantes is the Celtic goddess Brigit or Brigantia, the patron deity of North Britain. Her feast day, celebrating some sort of pastoral festival, perhaps the coming into milk of the ewes, was the first day of February. So it was about that time that I made my first trip up Ingleborough in almost 30 years to sample the conditions our Celtic ancestors might have met with around 2,000 or more years ago.

Anyone who takes to our Northern mountains in February probably deserves everything the weather throws at them. The forecast was for showers and sunny intervals and when we left the village of Ingleton to make the climb from the southwest it was dry and the cloud seemed to be breaking up. But before we'd crossed the common a misty drizzle began and as we trailed up the walled track that makes the first mile and a half of the climb so interminably dull, the rain began to thicken. It would be a mistake to say the mist descended; we were climbing into it, low cloud saturated with rain and stirred by a chill wind. Trees, ragged escarpments of blackened limestone, suddenly loomed. Occasionally a figure returning from the summit materialised, fuzzed at first to giant proportions by the mist before shrinking back to normal and hurrying past. A farmhouse, the last outpost of civilisation, next to a field scattered with dismembered vehicles, and then we were climbing more steeply beside a rushing river which left the track muddy and treacherous with wet, worn stones. By now the sweat from our bodies had linked up with the penetrating rain to leave our clothes sodden and our bodies cold. Weather like this laughs at normal hiking gear. What passes for waterproofs in most circumstances become blotting paper. Because of the mist and rain there was no view, no sudden perspectives to

64

compensate for this miserable trudge. It was a stark reminder of how unglamorous these Pennine mountains can be. How principally they are governed by weather, harsh, wet, cold weather. Each line of latitude is a rung on the ladder towards the extreme, the inhospitable, where life can only hang on: the brown bents between the rocks, the mealy grey lichen, moss that takes on an unnatural vividness against the surrounding greyness. And soon, you and your companion are no longer speaking. An alien environment like this engenders introspection, you take shelter inside your own head. You are like the Arctic explorer who is convinced he is being followed or the Everest climber who begins to see extinct beasts, strange phantasmagoria. You are out on the edge and anything can happen. So you are glad when cheery groups come past making plenty of noise and fuss, and you stop and chat and declaim against the outlandishness of the weather, and everything is normal again. But, apart from a cursory nod, you don't speak with the loners as they hurry past with their heads down, stuck inside their hoods with their own secret thoughts. You know they don't want you to speak to them because these mountains are their therapy against the damage done by a troubling world, their only hope of salvation. And then there are the solitary runners whom you soon learn to hate as they bound past on their steel ankles pursuing their merciless schedules - hate because their superhuman fitness belittles your own puny achievement as you wheeze and grimace your way upwards.

And then to finally break your spirit comes the false summit. You are convinced you've reached the top when you arrive at some stone steps and with one final agonising effort you climb them, only to discover yet another ridge rising out of the mist ahead. And the breeze which you felt when you set out is funnelling round the edges of the hill and has been transformed into a shrieking gale. And the rain is so heavy you might as well be walking underwater. And your body is so wet and numb with cold you believe you are in the first stages of hypothermia, so all you want to do is to sit down there on the stones and cry. Because you hate this place and you only ever want to see it again from the bar of the Crown at Horton-in-

Ribblesdale or from 20 miles away on a picnic site on the banks of the River Lune. Never again up close like this, like staring a crazed heavyweight boxer in the face.

But the miseries you can encounter on these Northern mountains are not the whole of the story. Sometimes during these intense physical privations there burns within you a bright, hard flame of exhilaration. The very act of pitting yourself against the unrelenting brutality of nature generates within an equally stubborn resistance, a resolve to be undaunted by whatever nature throws at you. It is as if an age-old instinct that drove us as a species down the long and difficult path of evolution to become masters of our environment clicked back into place. Suddenly you're alive again and fighting in a way that you've forgotten under all the cosseted indulgence of modern life. And you realise why it is that people do crazy things like run up mountains or row the Atlantic or trek across the polar ice. It is an intensity of existence which must become addictive. And you wonder if it is how our early ancestors, with their short lives and scant creature comforts, must have lived all the time.

On the summit - you'll have to take the word of others not me, because on that February day we barely saw our hands in front of our faces - there are the remains of Iron Age round houses and round the edges of the plateau what's left of a 14 feet thick defensive wall. They all show up clearly on aerial photographs. So was the settlement on Ingleborough a permanent township - some connect it with Rigodonum, the headquarters of a Brigantian princeling - or was it only inhabited in times of war, an outrageous act of Celtic bravura, a symbolic gesture which was a piece of psychological warfare which proclaimed: 'We live up here, so don't mess with us 'cos we're hard!' Who this show of strength was aimed at we can't be certain. Whether it was the Brigantes warning off other local tribesmen before the confederacy or whether it was adopted at a later date as a centre of resistance against the invading Romans, either way, we can be sure of the efficacy of the gesture. I'd be inclined to the latter view. The logistical difficulties of getting regular provisions of food and water to the summit to sustain a community for any length of time would surely operate against Ingleborough ever providing a permanent settlement.

It is at the foot of Ingleborough below its eastern flanks where more orthodox examples of Celtic settlement may be found. From Ribblehead running south along the western side of the Settle-Carlisle railway at Gauber Pasture and Colt Park the OS map reveals a series of settlements along the escarpment. Archaeologists have identified Celtic fields as well as the remains of round and sometimes square dwellings. The natural limestone boulders and exposed pavements that dominate the landscape make man-made structures difficult, if not impossible to recognise. It's Malham Moor all over again. For the amateur like me, impatient for the past to spill out all its secrets at once, it's a frustrating affair. I wonder that the National Park, with all its fondness for signpost and notice boards, doesn't see fit to give us a few clues as to the exact whereabouts of these ancient settlements. But then I suspect that they don't want people tramping around all over our history, albeit that it's the only way to forge any real links with the past. To sit as I did upon a lump of limestone near Washfold Pot, the stone mottled with grainy lichen of a grey-green and black and pocked with cavities where the rainwater stands tinged with a strange red deposit, there's time to reflect, let the mind unwind. Coils of cloud spin off Ingleborough while a watery sun struggles to break through. Across the valley another millstone bastion, Pen-y-ghent, crouches lion-like, both serene and menacing, confident of its giant status amongst these Pennine hills. I reflect on the nature of hills and mountains and our ancestors' love of them as tribal totems. Hills arrest the eye in a landscape, they don't allow it to proceed unless you have fully given them your attention, paid your respects. And so for the tribe they became a focus, where what was important to them could be concentrated. So these hills were the places to bury a chieftain or were tribal headquarters in times of conflict. Even today, the place where I was born takes its name from the principal hill, Pendle. It may be rarely, if ever, visited by many of those who live in its crowded southern valley but it is their totem, their icon. Its outline is on their boundary signs and is the borough's official insignia. It is not allowed to fade from the tribe's consciousness even though in an age of fragmented allegiances we may laugh at the idea of tribes. The name Pendle is from a Celtic word, pen, a hill. So what is Pen-y-ghent? Hill of the giants?

But whether you find the remains of these Iron Age settlements or not doesn't really matter. The experience of merely wandering around this landscape is deeply satisfying. You can store mental and emotional images like a squirrel stores nuts. They'll come in handy during those bleak, spiritually hungry times that constitute so much of modern urban living. On the way back to try once more to locate the settlement at Colt Park we stopped at Ribblehead station. Across the railway line is the old Ribblehead limestone quarry. The bare, scalped rocks are much as the retreating ice must have left them 12,000 years ago. A conservation group is attempting to recreate the conditions that vegetation and wildlife met as they first began to recolonise the area. It's a slow process and there's not much to see. Better to ignore the cloudy rock pools and bare scree of the quarry and let the eye range east across the landscape following the line of the Roman road from Lancaster to Bainbridge over Cam Fell to where the summit of Dodd Fell has turned flaxen pale in the winter sunlight. Or follow the course of the Ribble as it twists and turns on its journey south before Pen-y-ghent captures the eye again and leaves you struggling for metaphors to describe the still but powerful landmass, reclining perhaps like some naked muscular warrior. Our own dying Gaul?

Then follow the direction of the railway north to where Whernside rises, wrinkled with gullies. But it is something else which takes the eye this time, something man-made. The Ribblehead viaduct sweeps in a graceful arc across the valley. It is a heroic structure in keeping with the landscape; man making his own contribution to the grandeur of his surroundings. He's also made a religious contribution. There's something cathedral-like about that magnificent arcade of 24 arches. It is a giant step away from the mute worship of the forces of nature of our Celtic ancestors. To drive a railway straight up the rugged spine of England is a celebration of man's power over his environment. Some would call it the hubris of the Industrial Age for which we are only now beginning to pay the price. But it is hard not to be astonished by the sudden sight of the viaduct springing across the valley at Ribblehead. To think that it is not many years ago that they wanted to close the line down, making the expense of repairing the viaduct an excuse. Heathens. The wind funnels down the valley, whispering through the great stone and brick pillars, ghosts of the thousands who built the line and lived out here on the wild moors in shanty towns or else gave their lives and rest today in the tiny churchyard at Chapel-le-Dale.

Moving south from Ribblehead station on the Ingleborough side of the railway line, we can't resist a last attempt to discover the Celtic farmsteads. First there's Gauber High Pasture and then Colt Park, in all around 200 acres of fields where spelt wheat was grown up to an altitude of 1,100 feet. You can buy spelt flour these days and it has a rather coarser, grittier texture than normal wheat flour. It makes a more robust loaf, the sort of bread more favoured in Mediterranean countries. In fact, on the packet of spelt flour I sometimes use there's a recipe for Roman army bread. There's a clue here to the Roman interest in our region beyond mere military conquest. After the Roman invasion and the initial resistance of local tribes like the Brigantes, the Celts probably settled down to trading with the Romans, the local cereals providing just one native resource valued by the conquerors.

Celtic husbandry was by no means confined to cereal growing. Animal bones discovered at the Brigantian fortress of Stanwick, six miles north of Richmond, show abundant evidence of the rearing of cattle, sheep and horses. It has been suggested that a tiny bronze horned bust found at the Brigantian township of Aldborough may be associated with a cult connected with the fertility of herds of cattle. Certainly Roman writers depict the Celts as forever feasting off great haunches of animals roasting on spits, which may be where our reputation as a nation of beef-eaters, 'rosbifs', as the French would have it, has its origins.

Anne Ross uses Irish legend as well as classical writing and archaeological evidence to create an intimate picture of everyday Celtic life. Despite the popular image of the Celt as short, dark and swarthy, she suggests that their ideal of beauty was that of a fair-skinned people with fair or red hair and blue eyes. They were proud of their appearance (Archaeologists have recovered many of their mirrors, combs and razors) and rouged their cheeks and dyed their brows with berry juice. Both men and women plaited their hair, often washing it in lime to bleach it. The men shaved their cheeks and grew enormous drooping moustaches. Their clothes, tunics worn over trousers, were also dyed and they were much given to wearing ornaments such as gold neck torques, bracelets and brooches with enamelled inlays, decorated belts and battle helmets, all cunningly fashioned with typical Celtic motifs of subtle interweaving patterns and animal likenesses by their renowned smiths. But just in case you are inclined to believe that this all smacks of effeminacy, Ms Ross is careful to point out their notorious belligerence. Few feasts, fuelled by ale, could conclude without a brawl and bloodshed, usually sparked by some perceived insult or other. Their sense of both personal and family honour was paramount and they thought it was better to die a hero in combat than live a dishonourable life. They seem to have invented sledging, hurling insults at their enemy before charging into battle in a terrifying tumult of shouting and horn-blowing. Sometimes they cast off all their clothes, not out of mere exhibitionism but to show how they despised death by scorning any armour or protection. No wonder they fell like flies before the well-drilled and disciplined Romans. Albeit terrifying, they were a clamorous rabble bent on seeking immortal renown through individual and uncoordinated acts of heroism. There seems to have been a streak of wild romanticism about our Celtic ancestors.

The Celts removed the heads of their enemies and took them away as battle trophies. For them the head had a sacred significance and severed skulls have been found in many of their shrines. There is a skull in the Yorkshire Museum at York which was found in a ditch at

70

one of the gates to the Stanwick camp. A defeated enemy whose head had been hung there? Few museums of pre-history are without their stone-carved Celtic heads, instantly recognisable in their stark Mongoloid simplicity. The Celts conferred talismanic qualities upon the human head. Stuck on the walls of a house or the gates of the fort, the heads of your enemy would, because of their magical qualities, protect you from the forces of evil. Irish legend contains stories of heads which stay alive after death and sing or tell stories. The Celts were intensely superstitious. They performed acts of propitiation to keep on the right side of the dangerous supernatural forces which could run riot in their world. Thus the proliferation of votive shafts, holes dug into the ground as an entry to the Otherworld of the gods where conciliatory objects could be thrown. It must have been a nerve-wracking business being an ancient Celt. When you weren't at risk of losing your life in war or some post-prandial barney under your own roof, you lived in abstract terror of the malign supernatural forces which ranged around you. And we talk of the stresses of modern life!

Here in Upper Ribblesdale there was no need to dig a shaft for your votive offerings. Acid water and limestone provided the perfect entry into the underground Otherworld. As you stand near Washfold Pot just south of Colt Park you can hear the invisible water singing in the earth beneath your feet. Piles of broken rocks fill a hole where a farmer, careful for his sheep, has thrown them. But look down between the stones and you can see the water churning in the darkness. And at Washfold Pot itself, a dark, square mouth gapes. Hart's tongue ferns spill green into the daylight and an ash tree has taken root. Access to the Otherworld is everywhere, the boundaries with this world slender, almost non-existent. I'm sure that's how the Celts must have felt. Their gods, like all believers' gods, are immanent. And so, across the way, between Colt Park and the railway, we step into a long, narrow grove. It's fenced off, again to keep the sheep from falling into the grykes, for the floor of the wood is a limestone pavement but one which is teeming with green life: thick moss, ferns whose exquisite fronds are of maiden-hair softness,

71

and so many colours of lichen, their tiny scaly trumpets pointing skywards. But there is so much moss and lichen that the trees - ash, thorn and hazel - have become choked with it and many of them have fallen, stifled into twisted and tortured shapes that blindly grope their way across the black mouths of the grykes until to walk any further becomes dangerous. Not that I want to go any further. This is a place of bad magic with a repellent, claustrophobic and menacing feel. And it has me thinking of those other religious sites of the Celts and their Druid priesthood, the sacred groves. But not until I'm safely over the fence into the open.

It is the Roman, Pliny, writing in the first century AD in his 'Natural History' who gives rise to the enduring image of the Druids, the Celtic priesthood performing their religious ceremonies in order to keep in check the hostile forces of the Otherworld. They are, of course, oak groves where, he tells us, on the sixth day of the moon the mistletoe is cut by a white-robed Druid with a golden sickle and two white bulls are sacrificed. Other classical accounts tell of ritual human sacrifice, the victims sometimes burnt to death in cages made of branches, the origins of the barbaric practice fictionalised in 'The Wicker Man'.

There is scant archaeological evidence for centres of mass ceremonial gatherings amongst the Celts compared with the massive henges and stone avenues of earlier times. I wonder if this is because Celtic society was highly divided. There was a powerful aristocracy of kings and their client nobles, protected by the Druidic priesthood, but the vast majority were slaves and were of no account, with few possessions and little involvement in religious ritual. This also perhaps explains how a hillfort like Ingleborough might be serviced and maintained. With large numbers of slaves to build their defensive walls and ferry provisions and creature comforts to and fro, the aristocrats who lived there need hardly be troubled by the pitiless weather which had baulked our attempts to explore the summit of the mountain.

Iconography reveals some of the many gods and goddesses venerated by the Iron Age Celts. As well as many of the carved stone heads that have been found, there are images of horned gods, particularly the hunting god, Silvanus. Nemetona was a goddess of the sacred grove, often represented as a triad, three being a sacred number to the Celts, often seen as derived from the three phases of the moon: waxing, full and waning. The Druids were known to measure their months and years by the moon. The importance of the moon to our early ancestors takes us back to the alleged lunar alignment of the Devil's Arrows. Here, perhaps, is some continuity of belief between the Celts and the people they seem to either have displaced or absorbed from the Bronze and Neolithic times. Moreover, the moon god is female. To understand why our most important gods should have shifted from being female to male, Robert Graves in 'The White Goddess' points to a change during the first millennium BC from a matriarchal culture that worshipped a supreme goddess, to a culture dominated by the authority of the patriarch. So far as our early religions were concerned the matriarchal cult was seen as all-important because it was the female who brought life and fertility. Males were perceived to play no part in procreation. Only with the arrival of the Greeks and Plato where the emphasis was placed on rationality and male domination, even to the elevation of love between males, was the female demoted to the level of subservience placed upon her later by the Christian Church, a position which led to her subsequent inferior role in our culture in general. Graves argues that as a result, society has since developed away from the intuitive, poetical and happier mode of existence as inspired by the female muse and her symbol, the moon, to a male, sun-inspired rationality responsible for most of the world's ills. It's a powerful and attractive argument, especially when you examine the historical, male-driven development of the human race through epochs of war and scientific advancement to today's world of scientific and rational materialism. Suppose we had followed the female route to a society based on creativity, poetry and maternalism? How much happier and more harmonious would our lives be today? Would our retreat from nature and the subsequent environmental crisis facing our planet have ever occurred?

Across the valley from the 'sacred grove' of Colt Park and further south down Upper Ribblesdale the caves of Langcliffe Scar above Settle furnish plentiful entrances to the Celtic Otherworld. Excavations at both Victoria Cave and Attermire, half a mile further south, have uncovered dragon-shaped brooches in enamelled bronze as well as silver and gilt objects from Celtic craftsmen of the Romano-British period. That they were votive offerings to different local gods seems clear. No one wealthy enough to possess objects of such refined workmanship would be living in caves. An extraordinary collection of chariot parts was discovered in Attermire Cave. How they got there up a steep scree and then half way up a cliff face can be explained by a rare type of Celtic burial generally confined to East Yorkshire, a chariot burial reserved for some esteemed tribal warrior. When following in the footsteps of the Reverend Greenwell, I'd visited Dane's Grave, two miles west of Kilham near Rudston. This is a Celtic cemetery where warriors were buried inside a barrow along with their two-wheeled chariots and seems to have been unique to a Celtic tribe which migrated from Arras in Northern France during the fourth century BC. I still haven't recovered from the shock of discovering that a private landfill site had been allowed to develop around the area. Access is only possible by creeping through a clutter of breeze block and corrugated iron sheds hiding some sort of waste-disposal activities and then climbing over a mountain of mud and rubble. But even then, what is clearly a most important archaeological site has become an impenetrable thicket of nettles, brambles and rampant moss-choked elderflower trees. This, as my wife Margaret observed at the time, is heritage as a no-go area and we were forced to retreat, abandoning any attempts to respond to the sense of awe such antiquities should properly inspire. Alas, it's a familiar story. Many areas of the North where important discoveries have been made are then left to nature with the apparent indifference of the authorities. Few heed the words of Sir Thomas Browne in 'Urne Burial':

'Time hath endless rarities, and shows of all varieties; which reveal old things in heaven, makes new discoveries in earth, and even earth itself a discovery.'

Langcliffe Scar, stretching from the Malham Road over Cowside to Attermire Scar, is riddled with caves, the main ones to reveal historical findings being Jubilee, Victoria and Attermire. They make an excellent afternoon's excursion for the lover of rugged limestone outcrops and sudden expansive perspectives. Jubilee, the northern-most, has two entrances. The wind sweeping from the west across Upper Ribblesdale frets away at the cave mouths but once inside you are met with a sudden clammy silence broken only by the sporadic drip of water. Overhead, boulders jam the roof space menacingly and everywhere the rock is cracked and broken. Rocks that have fallen litter the muddy floor but footprints show that the dangers have not deterred the visitors. The rock is rough with lichen and seems to sweat with percolating groundwater. I go as far as I can until the daylight disappears. There is further access to one side but I haven't brought a torch so can go no further. (I never was much of a boy scout - too impulsive and not well enough prepared.) Victoria Cave further down the Scar is much larger and more celebrated. Here be monsters! The bones of rhinos, hippos and elephants, dragged in by scavenging hyenas have been identified. They belong to the warm interglacial period of the Upper Pleistocene around 130,000 years ago and were covered by several feet of glacial mud and debris. And when the ice finally retreated 12,000 years ago, hibernating brown bears took up residence. Early man also left his imprint with the discovery of an Azilian harpoon made of antler and viciously barbed. The cave was discovered in 1837 after a dog was sent into a small hole after a fox. This is according to a helpful illustrated notice outside the cave. The discovery of a bronze fibula led to a subsequent excavation which uncovered further brooches, bronzes and Roman coins from the Romano-British period, all indications of the notion that the cave was a religious site. Following the activities of the excavators and the removal of many tons of material, Victoria

Cave is now a gaping hole which, if you are prepared to ignore the signs about the dangers of falling rocks, as many are, you can clamber about inside. The number of other foxholes which are visible throughout the escarpment makes you wonder if there are other caves and further discoveries to be made along Langcliffe Scar.

The third well-known cave site is at Attermire further down the Scar. Access here is more problematic. On my first visit I attempted to climb from a point on the path directly below the cave entrance which is up a steep scree and then a climb of 20 or so feet up a cliff. The scree is a shifting sea of fractured rock which slides around underfoot with the sound of someone shuffling giant dominoes. Every step upwards was followed by a slide backwards and it had me heaving and wheezing into the coronary danger zone. When I arrived at the top below the cliff face I had to sit down to recuperate. The vantage is stunning, with views right down Ribblesdale to Pendle Hill and beyond. Below, the landscape no longer quite lives up to its name of Attermire because it's been drained for sheep to graze. Nevertheless, it's covered with patches of brown reed beds broken by zigzags of dry stone walls. Below Victoria Cave is a sheltered cirque beneath the lower fells which is crowded with sheep that have been brought down from the wilder heights ready for lambing. They stand about rather aimlessly, in thrall to biology or maybe economics. It's thought the Celtic farmers were pastoralists, moving their stock from one grazing ground to another. Today there's a battered caravan in one corner of a field where, I presume, the shepherd can take refuge in his long overnight lambing vigils. Looking back up the cliff to the cave entrance I realise I'm not going to be able to make it up there or, if I did, I doubt if I could get back down without the assistance of the rescue services. It's the bane of the elderly, the mind outreaching the abilities of the body. Then I realise there's a narrow ledge leading right to the cave and all I need to do is approach it from further along the Scar where only a minimum of rock climbing will be called for. I make it onto the grassy ledge and am soon at the mouth of the cave. The opening is a longitudinal split in the rock-face. At the entrance the limestone has a reddish appearance, giving it the warm look of sandstone. But it's a bronze-coloured lichen, another colour to add to the baffling variety of this humble, primitive plant, this hardy co-existence of algae and fungus. I move inside the cave through a narrow rock defile which will just take the width of my shoulders. The lichen here is a pastel green which traps the rags of disappearing daylight and glows eerily. Then it's into the muddy darkness.

There's a black passageway to one side where, for a moment, the wind from somewhere up above seems to grumble like someone muttering in their sleep. Then the silence returns. Were there others besides our warrior and his chariot remains buried here? Others who still lie here down these black passageways under this mud and rock? Or was the cave mouth sealed after his interment, after the votive offerings of bronzes and other precious objects were left here? As a portal to the Otherworld it should be scary in here, given what we know about the unpredictable nature of the Celtic gods. But the votive offerings have done their work and I feel only the clammy silence and hear only the drip of water, like the slow drip of time itself. Besides, the old gods are dead. Aren't they?

Outside I hear the first curlew of the year, her plangent notes spilling over the marshes of Attermire. Night is closing in upon this vast prehistoric landscape. The hills begin to brood, whale-grey in the flagging light. I watch the last lick of sunlight drain from the west, saffron-yellow. The wind which has nagged and fretted all day begins to drop. I will pass the black mouth of Victoria Cave again soon, where darkness lives and hides countless other undiscovered mysteries.

I like to think that our rugged and independent Northern ancestors, the Brigantes, stubbornly resisted the suave colonialist arrogance of the invading Romans. But politics always dilutes the romance of history. Shortly after the invasion of Claudius in 43AD, Queen Cartimandua, with her consort Venutius, allied herself to Rome. This means that the Brigantes did not join the rebellion of Boudicca in AD 61. Only after the divorce of Cartimandua and a subsequent power struggle did the Brigantes, under Venutius, take up arms against the

Romans in 69AD. Venutius was ultimately defeated by Petillius Cerialis and the Ninth Legion, being either killed at his tribal headquarters at Stanwick or else driven into exile in the western fastnesses of the Pennines or the Eden Valley from where the Brigantes continued their resistance through guerilla warfare. A programme of fort-building by the Roman governor Agricola throughout the North meant that in effect around AD 80 almost the whole of Brigantia was garrisoned and the region was under Roman martial law. Native Brigantes would have been enlisted into the Roman army or commandeered for the vast programme of road-building. Taxes would have been levied against the native tribesmen and many would have moved to the civilian settlements, or vici, in proximity to the Roman forts, there to provide services, not least perhaps the sale of home-grown meat and cereals and the manufacture of clasps and jewellery associated with the fine work of Celtic smiths. By the end of the first century Brigantia had been pacified.

Like so many figures of the distant past Cartimandua and Venutius slide in and out of history like ghosts. All that we know about them comes through classical writers like the Roman historian Tacitus who describes Cartimandua as 'powerful in lineage'. Does this explain why a woman is found in charge of a tribe whose territory stretches from the Don to Hadrian's Wall and possibly from coast to coast? The construction of the vast Neolithic henges and substantial barrows we have visited in North and East Yorkshire implies a powerful aristocracy commanding wealth and manpower. The remains of children in some of the East Yorkshire barrows suggest a hereditary system of rulership. Was such an organisation of society still in operation amongst the Celts who found themselves facing the Roman armies? Or did sheer prowess as a warrior count for more than lineage in the leadership stakes? Fortunately, Cartimandua probably possessed both. Women seem to have rivalled their men in strength in Celtic tribes. The Roman writer Dio Cassius describes Boudicca as 'huge of frame and terrifying of aspect and with a harsh voice. A great mass of bright red hair fell to her knees'. And Tacitus, when he records how Setonius Paulinus invaded and destroyed the Druid stronghold of Anglesey in 59 AD, paints a terrifying picture of frenzied native women dashing around in black 'like the Furies, with hair dishevelled, waving brands'. In a society which worshipped many female deities for their control over nature and success in war, and also took its tribal name from a goddess, a female warrior leader would present no cultural difficulties for the Brigantes.

But where was Cartimandua's seat of power? Some scholars believe it to have been somewhere in the Vale of York, but until inscribed stones or other epigraphic details are found, there can be no way of telling. We know that Aldborough, at a crossing of the Ure just east of Boroughbridge, was a Brigantian tribal centre. Known as Isurium or Isubrigantum, Aldborough may have been settled by the Romans shortly after the conquest and have provided a focus for a tribal settlement. Unfortunately there is no evidence for a pre-Roman settlement at Aldborough, although its proximity to the Devil's Arrows and the Ure henges, as well as the discovery of a bronze bust of a horned cult deity there, makes for attractive speculation for pre-Iron Age activity.

Keen to explore Aldborough for myself I made the journey across the Pennines only to find the site shut up for the winter. It is closed and padlocked between the 30th of September and the 1st of April. So too bad if the promptings of your historical curiosity don't coincide with the tourist season. When I rang the offices of English Heritage in York, who are responsible for the site, I was told that many of their sites were closed throughout the winter. They didn't seem to know why except that it may be due to their being dangerous during bad weather conditions. But Aldborough village which surrounds the site is the most sedate and tranquil of places. I can't imagine intemperate weather conditions ever daring to assail it. No, I think it's more likely to do with them not being prepared to pay the wages of a pensioner to sit in the small museum at the gates and take the £3.50 entrance fee out of the peak season. And this from the same government department which threw billions of pounds at the Olympic Games.

79

In a thoroughly rebellious mood I looked for ways to breach the defences of Isubrigantum. The trouble is that wherever you go in Aldborough you are not very far away from vigilantly twitching curtains. I made a detour away from the houses and nipped over a fence only to find myself in a pinewood. Every tree trunk was thick with ivy leaves which shone in the winter sunshine and the glades were full of snowdrops. This calmed me down a bit but I was still no nearer my target and my courage was ebbing. I was still deep inside neighbourhood watch territory and for all I knew my progress was being monitored. Mobile phones were probably already ringing to alert English Heritage's version of the Praetorian Guard. So I gave up and promised myself to return when winter and insane bureaucracy lifted their siege.

Instead, I wandered northwards towards the River Ure. It's late in the afternoon and all day the frost hasn't thawed in the deep herringbone tractor tracks that score the green lane which runs towards the river. The land is flat and the river snakes. Tall banks protect against flooding. Where I stand the river is 40 or 50 feet wide, muddied with light brown sand and tinged with algal green. The current is strong and purposeful yet the surface slick is smooth enough to mirror the reflection of trees that line the banks. A solitary fisherman sits gazing at his own navel, his hands clasped like a man at prayer. There's a tidemark of flattened bents where the river, in angrier mood, has threatened flooding, spreading the fine reddish silt which gives the region's soil its richness. The river is a bringer of fertility but also a bringer of flood and destruction. Nature, life on our planet, is always a fine balance between narrow parameters: just the right distance from the sun to create that critical band of temperatures which makes life possible; an atmosphere with the precise proportions of oxygen to carbon dioxide; rivers like this, balanced between fertile renewal and fatal inundation, plenty and starvation. I'm sure the Celts and their predecessors were aware of this and, like many today, ascribed it all to divine ordinance. So many swords, shields and daggers from the period have been found in rivers like this, intended as offerings to their fitful gods. As if drawn by some hidden undercurrent that can still tug at the mind over 2,000 or more years, I vow one day soon to follow the Ure back to its source, past the sacred henges and high up Wensleydale to Lunds Fell on the very edge of the Cumbrian border. A pilgrimage to the birthplace of this river god.

An English Heritage site which you will find open all year round (perhaps because they haven't yet found a way to make us pay to see it) is the Iron Age fortress at Stanwick north of Richmond. A helpful map of the site located on the outskirts of Forcett village suggests that Stanwick was the seat of power of the Brigantian queen, Cartimandua. But most scholars reject this, arguing that it is too far north, situated as it is on the fringes of Lower Teesdale. What everyone does appear to agree about is that here is where Venutius, who superseded his one-time wife Cartimandua as leader of the Brigantes, met his Nemesis at the hands of the Roman army under Cerialis in 72 AD.

The extraordinarily extensive four miles of fortifications, with ramparts up to 16 feet high fronted by deep ditches, indicate that Stanwick was an important Brigantian settlement before the Roman invasion. But excavations at the site in the 1950s by Sir Mortimer Wheeler, who older readers will remember as the flamboyantly moustachioed wag of early television programmes, uncovered luxury goods imported from across the Roman Empire as well as Roman roof tiles. To account for this, Hartley and Fitts suggest that buildings within Stanwick were built by the Romans on behalf of the Brigantian aristocracy. Presumably this was during the period after the invasion when the Brigantes accepted Roman rule and before the subsequent ill-fated rebellion of AD 69 and the rout of Venutius. Whatever the history of Stanwick, its huge size makes it well worth a visit to comprehend the sheer extent of Brigantian tribal organisation.

The first thing that strikes you about Stanwick is the muted normality of the location. This is rural England as you might expect to find it anywhere down the island's eastern flank. It is flat, sporadically wooded and intensively agriculturalised with acre after acre of remorselessly green, weed-free fields, pleasant but nondescript to a hill or mountain man raised off more passionate landscape. The camp's situation is the very opposite of the dramatic bravura of the Ingleborough hillfort. It suggests a different side to the Celtic nature from the turbulent warrior: the placid agriculturalist wanting to be left alone to get on with his cattle-rearing and corn-growing, happy to be left out of the turmoil of history with its wars and conflicts. (The discovery of many cattle bones and the size of the fortification suggest that the defensive structure enclosed fields for stock-raising and other farming activities.) But this is an impression which only lasts until you spot the earthworks, the broken grassy banks that range round into the distance, enclosing a huge area of 750 acres. For when you climb these banks, at their best-preserved just south of Forcett off the lane to Carlton, and see how high they are and how the defensive ditch plunges down from stone-faced ramparts to make them virtually unassailable, you then realise an important historical truth: that peace and tranquillity is often only bought at the cost of lavish defensive security.

Violets are growing in the banks of the ramparts today, rich purple violets and pale-petalled primroses. The celandines are coming into bloom too, yellow starfire bursting through the debris of last year's leaf-fall. There will be bluebells later on, to judge from the glossy leaves greening into life. The ramparts here are thickly wooded and a short distance along the top you come to what looks like a viewing platform with a short wall where you can look down into the defensive ditch. Cut into the ditch below is a rectangular pit walled with rock on two sides and with steps on another leading down into a pool. On the map by the roadside this is described as the 'guardianship site'. Is it a votive pool or shaft where offerings to the gods who guarded the camp were cast? We retrace our steps along the top of the ramparts to return this time along the ditch to inspect the guardian site. The water is murky with submerged branches and dead leaves. You can feel its cold breath rising from the surface where the sky trembles in the reflected tracery of the overarching trees. Otherwise it is still. I'm tempted to say uncannily still, but that would be to hint that the guardians of this place may not be dead. We have long turned our backs on such primitive superstitions. Today's votive offerings lodged at the pool's edge are a cartridge case, a coke can and some plastic wrappers. Children, no respecters of spirits, have hung a rope from a tree so that they can swing out across the ditch. We are no longer at the mercy of these petulant gods. To be sure of a good harvest today all we need to do is throw on some more fertiliser, spray some more pesticides. To protect our cattle from disease all we require are a few injections provided by the pharmaceutical industry. The riches of modern technology have rendered nature obedient to our will. Only the landscape of the mind is made poorer by the disappearance of these gods.

Further along, nearer where the ramparts cross the road, we come across two men lurking in the undergrowth by the ditch. They're looking out onto a field of seedlings where they've set up a motley collection of decoys. They are armed with shotguns. They tell us they're protecting the crop of oilseed rape from pigeons which, they say, can do an awful lot of damage. We take their word for this and, as they're anxious to see the back of us, we leave them to it. A few minutes later a pigeon flies overhead, spots the decoys, and foolishly changing direction is drawn irresistibly towards them. Our hearts in our mouths we wait for the roar of the gun. When the blast comes we expect to see the bird cartwheeling to the ground in a flurry of smashed feathers. But no, they've missed, and our feathered friend turns sharply and flies away, living to peck another day. We let out a wild cheer. Isn't oilseed rape the stuff they use to produce nasty hydrogenated fats which are said to be slowly killing us? Isn't it the pesticide-hungry, nitrate-leaching crop that is already making the London to Edinburgh train journey pass in a sense-numbing glare of canary-yellow monotony and is destined to invade every corner of our rural landscape in a way Julius Caesar could only dream of as we use it as a biofuel? Long live the pigeon, the last bastion of British defensive resistance against the Euro agri-invaders. The Brigantes would have been proud of them.

4. ON THE EDGE OF THE ROMAN EMPIRE

When the Ninth Legion sacked Stanwick in 72 AD, the rebel Brigantes would have fled westwards across Stainmore into their Pennine fastnesses. Brigantia was pacified due in no small measure to the extensive network of roads, forts and signal stations which were built to enable the Roman army to maintain a tight military grip upon the natives. To follow the route of the Roman Ninth Legion across Stainmore today is an act of faith in your own historical imagination which nevertheless reaps tangible and exciting rewards. The course is along the modern A66 from Scotch Corner to Brough, which in essence provides a spectacle of something which is hateful about the modern world. It is a world in transit, cars and articulated lorries driving at motorway speeds, foot down furiously racing to the pounding of rubber against tarmac which is the unending drumbeat of an army bent upon the conquest of the clock. Whereas the student of our past and the romantic who travels this way sees only files of plumed helmets and burnished breastplates or streams of ragged native warriors on the run, and wants only to dawdle, turn back time and stop to examine every shred of evidence of what happened here 2,000 years ago so as to vivify those mental pictures of the past which can so enrich our present lives.

And so it can be a frustrating and sometimes dangerous activity to explore and stop off at the forts, signal stations and marching camps which line the A66. Travelling from east to west, the first two destinations present no problems because they are off the busy trunk road. They are the forts at Greta Bridge and Bowes.

Behind the Morritt Arms at Greta Bridge on the lane to Brignall there's plenty of rumply evidence of the Roman fort in the grassy field. You can clearly see the bank and ditch which defended the fort platform from the south. To the north and east the River Greta and a small tributary entwine the fort in a protective embrace. To get onto the platform there's a well-disguised footpath over the wall by the river bridge. It takes you into the field - more like parkland, dotted with handsome beeches - where you can climb the steep bank from the river to where the fort once stood. The platform is full of tantalising bumps and submerged stonework where rabbits have been burrowing into the foundations, and it pays to examine the soil they have thrown out. I soon found traces of what I took to be Roman pottery, very dark in colour and one piece in particular clearly from the rim of a vessel. By extrapolating the arc I reckoned it formed a cup of three inches in diameter. A Roman drinking vessel which had once touched the lips of a thirsty legionary who had marched the dusty road from York?

Bowes Roman fort is disappointing. The site is dominated by the keep of the mediaeval castle which sits upon the northern half of the fort platform, borrowing the stone and leaving only a largely featureless rectangular mound with just a hint of geometrically-shaped foundations beneath the grass. The keep is cold and bare, square and gaunt in structure, its walls scarred with ragged and protruding masonry and its windows yawning gaps. It was built between 1171 and 1178 as a defence against the Scots who under Robert the Bruce created mayhem in Yorkshire. But it is the events of more than a millennium earlier which concern us here.

Looking out westwards from the site of the Roman fort at Bowes to where the trans-Pennine traffic trails up the dual carriageway, you can see how the fort was positioned to guard the eastern approaches to the Stainmore Gap. There's a bare, inhospitable feel to the landscape in this direction and a cold wind sweeps down the pass. It's beginning to feel more like true frontier country. To the south the hills rise onto Scargill Moor. I'm informed that this was Roman hunting country. The Roman officers were fond of hunting as a means of passing the time in their long northern vigils and two shrines to a hunting god, Vinotonus, have been found on the moor. Clumps of sparse conifers straggle the hillside, leaning under the force of the wind that frets its way through Stainmore like a nagging draught through a gap in a door. Northwards you can see nothing for the rooftops of the modern village of Bowes, but even if you could, it wouldn't give you an uninterrupted view because the fort is set too low down to command a proper view of the Teesdale valley to the north. From the top of the ridge, a swift and determined enemy could be down on the fort in a matter of minutes. So perhaps the perceived threat was seen as not coming from the north but from the west through Stainmore or the southwest from Ingleborough and the other Brigantian strongholds. The first fort at Bowes was raised by the Roman governor of Britain, Agricola, around 78 AD and like all the early Agricolan forts was a timber structure on earth ramparts. Like the fort at Greta Bridge and the one at Bainbridge further south, it was the governor's response to Brigantian insurrection and enabled him to throw a cordon around the troublesome and remote western regions before pressing on northwards to deal with the Scottish tribes. Only later, under the Emperor Trajan (98 - 117 AD) were the northern forts strengthened, their earth and pallisaded ramparts replaced with stone.

It would be naïve of me to suggest that the Roman garrisons were reliant upon their own visual sightings of the native tribesmen to warn them of an attack. They had an elaborate system of signal stations to pass on details of enemy movements and a short journey along the A66 will take you to the site of one of them. It is just opposite the Bowes Moor Hotel and entails a hazardous crossing of the dual carriageway to get to it. The remains consist of an earth rampart contained within a ditch, though the dense ground cover of heather, moss and reeds makes it difficult to recognise. There would have been a timber-built tower inside the enclosure where semaphore signals could be passed from station to station along the road to the forts. Did they warn exclusively of imminent native uprisings or were they sometimes used for more mundane purposes? 'Got any decent olives left? Ours have gone off.'

As I stand on the foundations of the signal station a grouse pokes an inflamed comb above the heather. I am engulfed in wild moorland. The clouds hang grey and heavy, slate-like above the earth, a landscape pale with dead bents and dun stains of heather, gashed with black peat hags and hidden bogs. This must have been a dreaded place to a soldier of the Ninth, the Hispania, reared in the warm, dry foothills of the Sierra Nevada. Northern Britain: uncouth, outlandish, on the brink of Ultima Thule, the most northerly region of the known world, a place of myth and legend and unknown terror. No wonder they asserted their civilisation so determinedly, brought it with them like a light against the darkness: their roads through the cleared forests, meticulously drained and metalled; their buildings of mortared stone with frescoes, mosaics and hypocausts; their communications network like this signal station. But places like Stainmore must have been a continual reminder of what they were up against, how thin the veneer of civilisation they had brought with them. And if you doubt that, look how comprehensively it was to collapse when they left after 400 AD. Even today Stainmore exudes an innate wildness, a natural hostility. As I step unwarily across the heather my pulse is suddenly set racing as a grouse explodes into whirring, cackling flight from under my feet. Overhead, black-headed gulls are fretting and quarrelling. I discover a log which has been laid across a dyke, and nailed to it under a mesh tunnel is a wicked-looking spring trap set for some unwary animal, possibly a stoat. This place is full of hidden tensions, ancient unresolved struggles for survival. Nature and the landscape will guarantee that it is never civilised. Is this why the traffic rushes past so furiously, racing for the Stainmore Gap, a bolt hole from the terrors of the wilderness, where the Eden Valley and the cosy, familiar world of civilisation beckons?

As I take my life into my hands and recross the road, dodging the thundering lorries, I observe a modern replacement for the signal station, a mobile telephone mast. And I cannot reconcile myself to the thought of all that babble of modern mobile phone conversations cluttering the ether and driving away the whisper of those fragile ancient ghosts that still hover about this place.

Right at the top of the pass is a Roman marching camp. It is to be approached with the utmost terror as you make a u-turn on the dual carriageway (Is this allowed?) about a mile west of the Bowes Moor Hotel and return to the lay-by at Rey Cross. The cross is the top section of a pre-Norman boundary stone erected around 950 AD to mark the border between English Northumbria and the Scottish kingdom of Strathclyde - or so a notice tells me. It also reveals that local tradition says it was erected on the burial place of Eric Bloodaxe, last Viking ruler of York killed nearby in 954 AD (I'm tempted to say while crossing the road). From the cross you have to walk back westwards along the roadside verge to reach the camp. It's 350 yards of torture as you pick your way along a corridor of human detritus - discarded cans and plastic bottles and torn and flapping polythene - buffeted by the slipstreams of passing lorries and choked by their exhaust fumes. Drivers look at you as if you were an escaped madman. They're right about one thing. I am trying to escape, from the twenty-first to the first century, and I'm seeking out the place where the fabled Ninth Legion once camped.

At last there's a gap in the fence where a gate leads off the road into an enclosure. It is hidden from the road by snow fences because this is the summit of the pass where wind and weather is whipped into a fury of release as it finally shakes itself free of the highlands which have impeded its progress off the Atlantic. There's no question of not being able to recognise this earthwork. The walls of the northern ramparts are almost six feet high and the square enclosure could have contained a whole legion of five or six thousand men. This is where the Ninth, under Petillius Cerialis, erected their leather tents as they swept westwards harrying the Brigantes after they were defeated and driven from Stanwick in 72 AD. I sit on one of the many lichen-blotched gritstone boulders that litter the site. The earth around is full of red sand scuffed up by the countless rabbits that have taken over this place. Perhaps if I'd time and patience I might discover that they'd scratched up one of the dice or gaming pieces, along with coins, buckles, breastplate and harness fittings and spurs, like those I'd seen that morning at the Bowes Museum in Barnard Castle. But I root and scrabble until my fingers are stained red with the sand, all to no avail. The past does not relinquish its treasures so readily. I must content myself with listening to the falling cry of the curlew and reflecting that the Roman soldiers must have listened to the same sad notes.

High above Brough on the very western edge of the Stainmore Gap is, to my mind, the best and most exciting of the A66's Roman remains. This is Maiden Castle, a Roman fortlet that housed probably 50 or so men. Its triumph has got to be its vantage high above the Eden Valley. You have shaken off the sombre hostility of Stainmore and the view is your reward for all the privations of the journey. How the Roman foot soldiers must have felt when they reached this point I can only guess. If they had not been pagans I would say it was like entering into Eden. With shafts of evening sunlight flooding the valley below, it comes as an epiphany, a sudden revelation of light, air and huge perspective. Spring fields flush with fresh green growth, intimate pastures generous with hedgerows and trees, stretch to the horizon where the Lakeland fells are only a distant, hazy shadow. It is a welcome home after a long and arduous journey, a welcome as warm and inviting as a kettle on the hearth and the smell of fresh-baked bread. It is, I suppose, if you were forced into exile far away from your native Northcountry, the thing you would miss most about the landscape: those journeys down from the hills into your home valley, out of hardship into comfort, from the harsh and hostile into the familiar and comforting. It is one of the basic antitheses upon which life and happiness is based. It is something we seemed to understand better in the past than today when pleasure is often too readily and easily available. We seem somehow to have forgotten that the deepest pleasure is often born out of some measure of hardship. Like light and darkness, they need each other, just as our valleys needed the turmoil of the hills, the tumbling violence of water, the groaning and cracking of ice and glacier to create the valley's peace and benevolence. Out of strength comes forth sweetness, and there can be nothing sweeter than the view of the Eden Valley from the summit of the Stainmore Pass.

I don't suppose for a single moment that the Roman soldiers felt any of this. Any relief that they may have felt after the long uphill slog must have been tempered by the thought that in the Eden Valley lay the heart of Brigantes country. The pleasures of the view would soon be overtaken by a sense of apprehension that they were now entering enemy territory. This is where Venutius was thought to have fled to set up his guerilla headquarters. Two thousand years ago this was a war zone.

To get to Maiden Castle which guards the western approach to Stainmore you need to cross the main road again onto its north side. You'll not find any signs to help you, but the place to cross is at the exit to Brough where you'll find a gate and a field track running parallel with the eastbound carriageway. A five or six minute walk up the track will take you onto the hill where the fort - perhaps better described as a fortlet - stands. The square defensive stone banks are unmistakable, with two clearly visible gateways in between. The inside is full of reeds where you can see the exposed outline of internal buildings marked by lines of ruined masonry. You get a real sense of a functional structure. At 1,400 feet it is the perfect lookout over the Eden Valley and the mountains to the south. With the moorland landscape around you, perhaps largely untouched by 2,000 years of time, it's not difficult to look at the world through the eyes of a Roman foot soldier. Pity that there's nothing to tell you it's here apart from a broken signpost in the middle of the fort, so the traffic below thunders past oblivious to this marvellous window on the past.

Before following the route of the legions north from Stainmore to Hadrian's Wall it would be well to return south to examine another first century fort established by Agricola to police Brigantia. This is the auxiliary fort at Bainbridge in Wensleydale. All the forts we've visited so far were auxiliary forts, that is to say they were meant to house a thousand men who were auxiliary troops, soldiers who were not Roman citizens but were recruited from the different provinces of the Roman Empire. There was nothing to stop native Brigantes enlisting with the auxiliary, much as it conflicts with my own romantic notion of our native Northerners resisting to a man the forces of Roman imperialism. Just as some natives chose to remove to the civilian settlements that grew up around the forts, so others would join the army in order to enjoy some of the benefits brought by the superior level of civilisation of their conquerors. Bainbridge fort is 20 miles south across the high fells from Stainmore. If they were connected by road over Tan Hill I can find no evidence on the map, though the signal station at Roper Castle is on the way south and might give a clue as to the location of a road. The road to Bainbridge from the south is much more discernible. It travels from the Lune Valley past Ingleborough to Ribblehead and then northeast over Dodd Fell and down into Wensleydale. As you stand at Gearstones on the Ingleborough to Hawes road you can follow the course of the Roman road with your eye as it climbs over Cam End. You get a real sense of the essence of these ancient roads that follow direct routes over open moor and mountain. They pursue their unswerving course, undaunted by the sheer scale of the topography they are bent upon conquering. In this they perfectly embody the Roman spirit of conquest, a force as powerful and unrelenting as any force of nature. Even today, unelevated like the A66 to modern needs but mere tracks for walkers seeking the loneliness of the hills, they are a signature on the landscape of this once great power and its terrifying sense of purpose and determination. You begin to see what the poor Brigantes were up against and how Rome successfully ruled our island for three and a half centuries. And yet, looking out, this huge, empty country ranged around you, the Three Peaks etched against the sky behind, the yellow moor grass rippling at your feet like a restless sea, the only sounds the wild note of the curlew and the wail of newborn lambs for their mothers, you can't fail to feel a sense of sadness. Today it seems to condense around the sight of a single solitary figure walking northwards up the track ahead and now the tiniest dot in the distance, insignificant in the immensity of his surroundings. Soon he will be gone over the horizon, as will all of us. Even the might of the Roman Empire crumbled to dust. As the Edwardian poet, Edward Thomas, wrote:-

'Roads go on
While we forget, and are
Forgotten like a star
That shoots and is gone.'

The sight of the fort at Bainbridge must have come as a relief to the foot soldiers marching over Dodd Fell and down into Wensleydale. After the harsh hilltops with their gritstone ramparts, the dale spreads placidly below, resting in the warm spring sunshine. The fort lies on a hill at the other side of the village. It's a fine strategic site, looking out north to the Askrigg fells and commanding a view both west and east along Wensleydale. We asked the farmer who was busy tagging his newborn lambs in a barn at the foot of the hill for permission to explore. He displayed the typical Dales mix of shy friendliness. The fort is grassed over with only occasional areas of exposed stone. For many years the site was a training camp for archaeology students of Leeds University. All that remains of this today is a concrete apron where they had their hut. I had attempted in vain to obtain Brian Hartley's account of their excavations in the late 1950s but the volume dealing with it has disappeared from the University library. The same paper has gone from the city Central Library too. What on earth could it have contained? Something that someone didn't want us to know about? My fanciful brain full of silly conspiracy theories, I trawled the grassy platform of the fort. Again the rabbits had been busy, scratching into the stonework of the defensive wall. After Agricola a series of stone forts occupied the site until the end of the fourth century and it was from one of the walls that the rabbits had uncovered evidence of this constant rebuilding. Lumps of lime mortar had been exposed and a fragment of wall plaster decorated with green and orange paint. You could see the brushstrokes. Part of a fresco perhaps from the praetorium or commandant's house. This was a thrilling discovery and one for which I will ever look kindly upon the rabbit fraternity, even those in my garden who make toothy inroads into my vegetable crop. I also discovered a sizeable lump of galena which made me wonder whether the fort had a workshop where local lead was smelted. The other interesting thing was that, standing on the fort platform and looking back across the River Bain to where the Roman road climbs south, you can make out the outline of rectangular earthworks on the grassy slope above the village. Was this the site of the civilian settlement? However, an aerial photograph I've seen shows evidence of the vicus at the side of the fort. How I wish the student who had made off with Vol IX of the Proceedings of the Leeds Philosophical and Literary Society - a more likely explanation than any conspiracy theories - would return it so that I could confirm some of my speculations.

Evidence of rebuilding at forts like Bainbridge in addition to fire damage has led archaeologists to speculate about uprisings by the Brigantes against the Romans, especially in 196 and 197 AD. The native Britons are thought to have taken advantage of the civil war at that time, when Septimius Severus took on Clodius Albinus in Gaul, Albinus, then the provincial governor of Britain, having removed many of the 50,000 troops stationed in Britain to fight in France. This left forts like Bainbridge seriously undermanned and hence vulnerable to native attack. Only after the defeat of Albinus and the capture of Britain by Severus, who established the imperial capital of Rome at York between 208 and 211 AD, did matters settle down.

But this begs the question, where were the Brigantes rebels hiding out all this time? I assume it must have been a classic case of guerilla warfare like we've seen in modern times in Vietnam or Iraq or even in Ireland during the Troubles, where ordinary-seeming village communities harboured extremists and nationalists. So when the uprising of 196-7 AD occurred, might we not expect warriors to emerge from the Celtic settlements like those I'd been searching for at Colt Park at the eastern foot of Ingleborough or other settlements that you can find marked on an OS map of the Dales region? I shouldn't put it past the Romans to have had their own intelligence service, with soldiers 'acting on information received' issuing from their forts to exact retribution on the villages, especially after the sacking of forts like Bainbridge and the massacre of the garrison.

The traveller amongst these hills and dales today will find it hard to imagine them ever being the scene of such drama, or of all the resentment, suspicion and discord that would infect the local communities under an army of occupation. The massive permanence of the natural landscape belittles the skirmishes of history. Driving from Kirkby Stephen down Ravenstonedale after a visit to the A66 forts and seeing the precipitous eastern edge of Wild Boar Fell capped in mist, offers a perspective which dwarfs the ambition of even the mighty Roman Empire. I have a particular romantic attachment to Wild Boar Fell. I suspect it consists of all those vague, unspoken and often unanalysed feelings which constitute our love of place. It belongs to the realm of poetry rather than prose and we are therefore often content to leave it undisturbed by reason and just enjoy its hazy, warm thrill. I first came across Wild Boar Fell in childhood pictures of the Settle-Carlisle railway, the most exciting of which showed Scotland to London expresses thundering up to Aisgill summit drawn by powerful steam locomotives billowing smoke. The Fell was always there, crouching in the background like some great resting beast, a reminder of the hostile terrain the builders had had to drive the railway through and symbolising their formidable achievement. Then the extraordinarily named valley in Wild Boar Fell's shadow, Mallerstang, a name with such a wild, mysterious and exotic ring to it that it seemed to belong to the world of mediaeval romance, of knights and quests and good and evil in mortal conflict. And I suppose that impression was helped by the story that the fell got its name from being the scene of the last wild boar in England to be hunted down there. And when later on I discovered the ruins of Pendragon Castle at the foot of the fell, the emotional pentangle was complete. This was a place of true magic.

I decided to visit Mallerstang as part of my still unfulfilled resolve to trace the River Ure to its source. For on Lunds Fell overlooking the Mallerstang valley and Wild Boar Fell is Ure Head where the river begins its journey south and east down Wensleydale and past the Thornborough henges and the Devil's Arrows and into the Ouse. It's also a watershed, for within a few yards of Ure Head are the streams and gills which turn the other way, northwards, and become the River Eden. If there ever were such things as river gods, this was their birthplace.

The journey takes you north from Garsdale Head up the Kirkby Stephen road. You then take the track at Shaw Paddock onto the fell side, on the eastern flank of Mallerstang. As you leave the track on Lunds Fell you begin to see where the newborn rivers get their strength. The hillside is a giant sponge. Your feet sink into cushions of soft moss. There are reed beds where bog-brown water lurks and trickles. The green sphagnum moss and fresh shocks of moorland grass contrast with the brown peat-ridged drainage ditches dug by the farmers. And soon we hear the river itself singing in a gill about 50 feet deep as it swirls and skirmishes with the rocks, splashing down tiny waterfalls and gurgling into rock pools, its sweet song mingling with the call of the curlew and the weep-weep of lapwings in the home fields in the valley below. Overhead the skylarks flap and glide, making short, stubby waves in the air. For some reason they seem curiously silent at this time of year. All the time our slow progress up the hill is monitored by the brooding presence of Wild Boar Fell from where the wind is brewing, sending the pale reeds into a shiver of excitement. And now, higher still and the gill with its river passenger has gone, absorbed into the flat bulk of the moortop where the clouds press. This is Ure Head, birthplace of the sacred river.

It begins to rain, fine, misty rain borne on the sudden wind which springs across the valley from Wild Boar Fell where the clouds hang in heavy, Fauvist blocks which seem to mirror the grey bulk of the fell itself. And this triggers a recollection of reading somewhere about a unique phenomenon of this area, the helm wind, described as a kind of cyclone revolving on a horizontal axis and issuing from a cloud like a helmet which forms over the mountain top. Perhaps this was a nascent helm wind, just practising, flexing its muscles. Whatever it was, it seemed to add to the strangeness, the otherworldliness of the area. And I wondered if this atmosphere was the legacy of the Brigantes, an imprint on the ancient landscape of their rich and subtle inner lives with their belief in magic and gods and natural harmonies, a whispering echo of the spirits themselves clinging like gossamer threads to these once-sacred places. But then a goods train pulsed up to Aisgill summit on the railway line below and moments later the air is split with the roar of a fighter aircraft sweeping like a grey dart down the Mallerstang valley, shattering such thoughts and sending the old gods shrinking back into obscurity.

The further east of the Pennines you go, the greater evidence there is of the native Britons accepting Roman rule. There are much fewer manned forts and instead of Brigantian hillforts we begin to see the emergence of Romano-British townships like those at Catterick, Brough-on-Humber and Aldborough. I knew it wouldn't be long before I'd be obliged to return to Aldborough, a mile east of Boroughbridge and an important crossing of the River Ure in Roman times. Excavations in 1961 revealed a walled town of over 50 acres. Beginning as a first century Roman fort it soon developed into a fortified town built on the Roman grid pattern with a forum and lavish Roman-style town houses with mosaic floors and hypocausts. There's a good chance it could have had an amphitheatre located somewhere outside the town walls, but none has been found. The aristocratic Brigantes of this region were happily adopting their conquerors' sophisticated life-style - if such a phrase can be used to describe gladiatorial games and the slaughter of animals for public entertainment. Further into the region and the number of Romano-British villas, like that at Rudston, attest to the further integration of the local Britons into the Roman way of life. Interestingly, there's no evidence of these villas further west than Gargrave in Craven, and this is out on a limb.

I'm afraid there's precious little to be seen of the remains of Isurium Brigantum, largely because today's village of Aldborough sits on top of it all. It's after the first of April so the padlocks have been removed from the English Heritage site. What there is to see is a disappointment, in my view not worth the entrance fee. What you get is a cosy stroll along concrete paths between neat fences through the narcissus-filled borders and conservatories of the back gardens of well-heeled village England. It is as if the conservative aspirations which drew the Brigantes here into the fold of comfortable Roman society were still alive and well in Aldborough. It is about as removed from the passionate fastness of Ingleborough and Wild Boar Fell as a Celtic feast is from a vicar's tea-party. After its excursion through the blossomed back gardens the path leads into a meadow of lush greenness where cows graze that are so clean they could have been shampooed for the occasion. Here, side by side are two small pantiled buildings, one of brick the other stone, each containing a mosaic floor upon which the visitor is graciously allowed to gaze through heavy iron bars. The mosaics are small, grey, dusty and thoroughly unspectacular. Underwhelmed, we returned to the small museum at the site entrance only to find nothing whatsoever on display. We were informed that they'd recently had a break-in and all the items had been stolen. They had, however, fortunately been recovered but they hadn't had time to replace them in the museum. So we had to content ourselves with reading all the labels whilst staring at the empty display cabinets and guessing what 'a jasper gemstone depicting a hare in a chariot drawn by a cockerel' may have looked like. There should have been Samian tableware on display and bone fan handles, all the so-called high status consumer goods the Romanised Brigantes had sold their Celtic birthright for. When I attempted to negotiate a refund on my entrance fee I was politely told by the attendant that it would not be possible because 'the high-ups won't allow it'. I had a mind to reach for my Roman curse tablet - something I'd spotted in the well-stocked Roman museum in Ribchester - where I could scratch a message to the gods on the lead surface requesting the assistance of Jupiter to bring down eight thunderbolts on the heads of the 'high-ups' of English Heritage.

No excursion around the Roman fortifications of the North can fail to include a visit to York. York was one of only three legionary forts, capable of billeting 6,000 men, in the whole of Britain. The others were at Chester and Caerleon in Gwent. You can begin to discern the thorough, systematic, grid-iron approach, to conquest employed by the Romans here in the North by the positioning of their forts and their connecting roads. To the west, their road was a bit like today's M6, only it ran north from Chester to Carlisle through Ribchester, the Trough of Bowland and Overbarrow. (I explore this road in my book, 'Real Lancashire'.) While to the east, the main south to north road took roughly the direction of the modern A1(M). Trans-Pennine links joined up these N-S arteries: from Manchester through Ribchester, Elslack and Ilkley to York; further north, from Overbarrow across the Pennines to Bainbridge and Wensley; and further north still, along the A66 corridor. The route along Hadrian's Wall we will come to later. You soon begin to see how these roads, with their connecting strings of forts, were the highly organised way the Imperial Eagle quartered the troublesome Northcountry.

The legions first arrived in York around 71 AD. It was the IX Hispana led by Petillius Cerialis marching up from Lincoln to deal with the Brigantes united under Venutius. Before this the York area was occupied by a scattering of Iron Age farmers. The garrison at York occupied a 50 acre site where today the Minster now stands. It was on an easily defended tongue of land between the Ouse and the Foss. The civilian town, known as the colonia, was to spring up later on the other side of the Ouse to the south. The Ouse was, of course, navigable from the sea and this was no doubt vital to the subsequent development both of fort and colonia Not only did York become the capital of the North of England or Britannia Inferior (Inferior?) but under the Emperor Septimius Severus it was the home of the Roman imperial court between 208 and 211, and in 306 AD it witnessed the crowning of the great Constantine as Emperor. York's illustrious past must make it an obvious choice of capital should the devolution of the North ever occur.

Ignoring for the time being the rest of the city's incredibly rich history, one of the great joys of walking around York today is the knowledge that you are treading on so many undiscovered Roman remains. This is brought home to you by a visit to the Minster, for here you get a chance to go underground by stepping down into the undercroft. Because the central tower of the Minster was ready to collapse, between 1967 and 1972 extensive work was carried out to shore up the foundations. In so doing the workmen unearthed the basilica or headquarters of the legionary fortress. You can stand deep under the mediaeval cathedral and touch the four feet thick basilica wall with its base for one of the hall's columns. That people do this can be adjudged from the smooth and rather greasy feel to some of the stones. However, it must be said that establishing any emotional contact with the great tide of events that followed the arrival of the legions in York - the VIth Victrix replaced the IXth after their withdrawal in the second century - is not made easy. Despite a sonorous notice which announces, 'You are only a few metres from where world history was made' and two replica plaster busts, one of a frowning Vespasian, the other of Septimius Severus with hair and beard like a nest of worms, to say nothing of a welcome from a cardboard cut-out of a centurion, any attempt to create an atmosphere of historical gravitas falls rather flat. Perhaps it's the distracting roar of the air conditioning or all the probing halogen spotlights that conspire to keep the spirit firmly rooted in the present. In fact, the undercroft is more a monument to the wonders of modern structural engineering than the glory that was Roman York. You are surrounded by smooth, grey reinforced concrete and row upon row of shiny, giant, stainless steel nuts and bolts whose job is to drag the wandering mediaeval foundations of the church above into a state of obedient stability. There are even glass expansion plates to indicate the slightest fraction of movement. It is indeed a tribute to today's civil engineers which, despite the halogen lamps, put the wall opposite, built by the soldier masons of the IXth Legion, into the shade.

It pains me to report that the centrepiece of the Minster's Roman archaeological treasures is not the restored wall paintings from one of the headquarters rooms or any of the finds like the wolf's head key handle recovered during the renovation work, but the remains of a drain. It is proudly watched over by a replica plaster cast of Constantine the Great, whose face is flat to the point of hollowness and shines like a greased pig. The drain is built of carved stone slabs and took waste water from the fortress into the River Ouse. A notice rather unnecessarily observes, 'It shows the excellent engineering skills of the Romans'. Indeed, it is as fine a sewer as I have ever seen. Others clearly think so because they've thrown hundreds of coins into it, which I for one found surprising since we'd already been charged £4 to visit the undercroft. With an additional entrance fee being charged for the cathedral, it will not surprise the modern visitor to the Minster that these days the sound of the church organ is drowned out by the ring of cash registers.

I make no apologies for banging on so often in these journals about the price of admission to so much of our historic heritage. For the not so well-off parents to have to fork out not inconsiderable sums of money to educate and inspire their children about history at a time when our schools are manifestly failing to do so, is nothing short of a national scandal. Why should access to our historical birthright be the prerogative of only the well-off? If we can afford to lavish billions on sporting extravaganzas such as the Olympic Games, to say nothing of our own independent nuclear arsenal, why can't we set aside more for the subsidy of free access to our historic treasure houses? And if the Church can't take a lead in this, on moral grounds alone, how can we expect others like English Heritage and the National Trust to do so?

Less than half a mile west of the Minster lies the excellent Yorkshire Museum. In recent years they have begun to charge for admission but with the enlightened proviso that once you've paid you can return as many times as you like for a year for nothing. And anyone passionate about York's extraordinary history will certainly want to return again. And as far as observing remains of Roman York, you won't have to disappear underground. In fact, as you approach the museum which is in beautiful gardens, a natural haven away from the relentless tide of traffic across Lendal Bridge, next to the ruins of St Mary's abbey, you pass the spectacular remains of the legionary fortress walls, strengthened in the third century and comprising a multangular corner tower overlooking the river Ouse.

This is as good a place as any to stop, away from the bustle of the city, and prepare to make the mental journey across almost two millennia. For your musings I recommend you step inside the fortress walls and rest upon one of the many stone sarcophaguses scattered around the inside of the multangular tower. These tombs, some with their lids jauntily strewn aside as if their occupants had just nipped out for a stroll round the town, are an admirable location in which to reflect on the passage of time and begin to resurrect some of the details of a lost civilisation.

The fortress wall is a time chart. Above rest the stones of the mediaeval walls of the city with their cruciform arrow slits. Beneath lies the Roman stonework, 15 feet or so of it, which includes, on the inside, a decorative layer of terracotta tiles. The stone walls were cut into the banks of the original earthen ramparts, with wooden palisades which would have constituted the original fort built by Cerialis for the IXth Legion around 70 AD. Continual strengthening of the wall occurred throughout the Roman occupation, culminating in the present 10-sided tower thought to have been constructed around 300 AD and capable of supporting a launching platform for heavy projectile throwers like the ballistae. Today, on the inside, weeds and moss have invaded the wall and it manages to look rather dejected with crumbling patches where the stonework has collapsed. Mauve toadflax and yellow ragwort cling, and at the base the purple-coloured cranesbill grows. The pigeons strut about the parapet imperiously. We watch a song thrush cock his head to listen to the earth then suddenly jab to winkle out a worm. A magpie swoops down to see what he can plunder and the thrush flies off. The message is very clear: conflict is at the very core of nature. And the stones themselves preach a more melancholy sermon: all human life is transient. Even the great civilisations must disappear, while nature clings on, indifferent to human fate.

As you enter the museum you are greeted by a painted wall from the fort at Catterick. Excitingly, for me, the dominant green and orange paint was identical to that on the mortar I'd found at Bainbridge. A fat American tourist wearing an aquamarine t-shirt and carrying a bright orange rucksack, noisy and unselfconscious, loudly reads from every exhibit that takes his fancy, as if he'd discovered them all himself. He's clearly obsessed with ancestry. 'Makes you wonder how many of the Brits are related to these Romans,' he announces. And I've never thought of it like that. I've spent too much time siding with the Brigantes freedom fighters to consider just how many of us were a product of the inter-racial breeding which must have gone on wherever the Roman armies reached their brawny arms. Roman York, once the civilian settlement was established, must have been astonishingly cosmopolitan. Wherever the Roman armies went they enlisted from the conquered countries. There were Anatolians from the conquest of Asia Minor and Spaniards in the IXth Hispana. Septimius Severus was from Lepcis Magna in North Africa and I guess was dark-skinned. Constantine, proclaimed Emperor here in 306, was a Yugoslavian. And so on. At meal times it must have smelt like a North London high street today with all the takeaways going full tilt. Exotic isn't the word. And after that, if the local girls were half as attractive as the 'golden-haired maidens' Anne Ross tells us were celebrated in many of the traditional Celtic love songs, well, say no more.

The Roman citizens of York come alive - if that's the right expression - in the tombstones on display in the Yorkshire Museum. The carvings may be battered and worn but they reveal the rich variety of humanity which populated a period of history which can sometimes seem so shadowy. Here's L. Duccius Rufinus, the standard bearer of the IXth, his legs looking too short for the rest of his body. (All that marching, perhaps?) There's the tombstone of Flavia Augustinia, wife of a veteran of the VIth Victrix, the length of life of their children recorded with pitiful precision, her son living for just one year and three days, their daughter for one year, nine months and five days. And on a merrier note, there's the tombstone of Julia Velva, showing her reclining on a couch with a wine jar in her hand. A boy stands nearby ready to give her a top up. And there's even the tombstone of a Smith. He stands, hammer in one hand and tongs in the other and sporting a beard. We're told that the shortness of his tunic is indicative of his low social status. What's the Latin for, 'What's new?'

It's a wonderful museum whose artefacts bring alive those excursions I made to sometimes bare and empty locations. For example, there's the tiny bronze bust of a cattle god, no more than three inches from head to chest, found at Aldborough. It has a muzzle and horns and uncanny, round, craterous eyes, a tiny but potent symbol of the importance of cattle to the Brigantian way of life. And there's the human skull from Stanwick with a great chip out of the front from the death blow. The poor victim, two teeth missing, still seems to be grimacing at the blow. A caption asks, 'Was he a Roman or a Brigantian and was he a victim of the battle around 72 AD?' But it is the iconography that's most fascinating, the sudden creative visualisation of those abstract notions of Celtic gods on which I've speculated. There's a ceremonial mask from Catterick found near a fourth century temple. It's made of clay with holes which may have been used to fasten it over a priest's face as he enacted some sort of religious ritual. Blunt horns protrude from the top above gaping, round eye sockets and the thin, lipless gash which is a mouth, giving it an appearance of terrifying vacancy. The blind stare of an empty universe. The stuff of nightmares. It is a lasting image which accords with the hours I've spent in empty, windswept henges and beneath bare standing stones, speculating upon what may have happened there. So I'm glad when the images are not so scary and you could laugh at them. Like the relief of a googly-eyed Celtic god with a drooping moustache and hair that flared out as if caught in a gale for all eternity.

Many of the things you read about and lodge in the mind only as inert historical facts spring to life in a museum like this. For example, I'd read that York was renowned for the discovery of burials in gypsum, a lime-like substance which can turn to plaster of Paris. But when you see the results of one such burial, with the imprint of a mother, her dead child placed between her legs, the impact is as powerful as it is poignant. The Romans always buried their dead outside the walls of the city and photographs of excavations show skeletons scattered randomly as if they'd all been suddenly struck down by a Star Wars death-ray. Contrasting with all this death, votive offerings indicate how obsessed the Romans were with fertility and potency. Tiny phallic amulets seem to have been regularly carried about by the Roman soldiers and it is not difficult to see what must have been on their minds as they made the long march north from York. Examples of Brigantian craftsmanship reveal how much demand there must have been for the local smiths who set up their workshops in the vici. There's a Brigantian sword found at Thorpe Rudston with a bone handle and ornamented bronze studs inlaid with coloured glass. And found in a ditch at Stanwick, a sword with a scabbard of ashwood from the early first century. The compass-drawn circles set in ellipses which provide the decoration make the sword seem to have eyes, giving it a life of its own just like the magical swords of myth and legend. Pity it's only a replica and the cultural imperialists down in London have seized the original. There's also an image of a horse's head from the metalwork of a harness which, with its long muzzle and slit eyes, like the Uffington white horse which guards the Iron Age hillfort on the Oxfordshire Downs, achieves its striking effect through the barest minimum of lines, making it as modern-looking as any work of abstract art. But perhaps it's the public works of art by the Roman craftsmen that catch the eye most. There's the splendid life-size figure of Mars from the fourth century, with its crested helmet, breast plate and greaves. His spear arm is missing and his general martial appearance is marred only by a somewhat fleshy lower jaw and full lips, rather too sensual and dissipated for the god of war, I think. And then, overhead, there's the wonderful inscription taken from the Eboracum fortress gate with its magnificent lettering, incisive as if it had been cut yesterday, recording the gate's construction in stone by Trajan in 107-8 and carried out by the masons of the IXth Legion.

By the time of the Emperor Trajan it appears that most of Brigantia had been pacified, perhaps the only exception being the mountainous western regions of the Lake District. Here, at Hardknott, lie the remains of the best-preserved Roman auxiliary fort in Britain outside Hadrian's Wall. It dominates the mountain route across country from the Roman port of Ravenglass over to the fort at Ambleside, then to Brougham near Penrith and linking up with the route from the east via Stainmore. All the mystery and confusion that lay under the bare grassy platforms that is all that is left of forts like Bainbridge and Greta Bridge is lifted at Hardknott, where the walls of the headquarter buildings still stand to a height of two and a half feet, giving a real feel for how the forts were organised. All the buildings at Hardknott have been helpfully labelled and there is a plan of the layout, nothing of which detracts from the sublime isolation of this mountain fortress. You climb up to the fort from the eastern approach road which winds down dizzily from Hardknott Pass and the first thing you meet is a levelled area which was the parade ground. Square-bashing was really a vital part of the Roman army's preparation for war and one wonders whether the native tribesmen ever bothered to do the same. I think that we can conclude that with the Celtic flare for individual acts of glory and heroism rather than well-drilled discipline, the answer is no. Alas, in such humdrum planning and not in deeds of derring-do lie the successes of history.

Hardknott fort was built during the reign of Hadrian (117-138) by troops from Dalmatia, today's Croatia, to house a cohort of 500 men. Curiously, there's a line of slate half-way up the three metre thick outer walls, showing where the Victorians had a go at rebuilding them - one colonialist empire refusing to be outdone by another. Through the east gate and the first buildings you meet are the granaries, the piers that held the wooden floor and raised it off the ground to keep the grain dry still visible. Then in the centre of the fort is the main roadway, the via principalis, separating the praetorium or commanding officer's house from the principia or headquarters building. One room to the northwest was a temple where the standards of the garrison were kept. The barracks for the troops were wooden buildings set inside the walls on the north and south sides of the fort, and there were four watchtowers at each corner. So much for the layout. But it's the setting of Hardknott that really impresses. It has been compared to Mycenae, the Greek hilltop citadel of Agamemnon. Walk up the via principalis - and I challenge you not to adopt the hint of a Roman swagger - and out through the north gate. Suddenly the ground plunges away 1,000 feet into Eskdale. Across the valley the Scafell range of mountains link arms like four mighty giants out for a stroll. Today it is warm and the mountains lie still and peaceful, smeared in a blue mist and soundless save for the distant craak of rooks in a wooded ravine on Harter Fell to the south. The call of a cuckoo drifts upwards from Eskdale which is lush with new green growth. The hazy sunshine, the vast, all-enveloping presence of these mountains, invest the whole scene with a dream-like quality, a sense of slipping out of time. Who were these people who built this place? Men or gods? Did it ever really happen that a race of men more civilised than anything that was to come for almost 2,000 years, marched half-way across the world to an island of savages to build stone castles in the sky amongst all these empty mountains?

It was of course the business of war and conquest that brought them, the nasty human business of subjugation through fear. And just to emphasise how little distance we've come so far as that is concerned in all those years, the peace is shattered as a jet fighter bursts screaming out of the mountains, sending shockwaves bouncing from every peak. Jet planes or marching spears glinting in the sun? Different maybe, but both just as deadly. After all, there are no degrees of deadness.

Returning to the road through the southern gateway, built from red sandstone which must have been transported here and contrasts with the grey Borrowdale rocks which comprise the rest of the fort, you pass the bathhouse with its circular hotroom. I don't know whether the camp commanders were like fastidious landladies, but Roman bathhouses seem to be always outside the forts, as if the grubby soldiers, after a long day's marching, were not allowed in until they'd had a good wash - or, in the case of the Romans, sweat and scrape down. Nine miles down Eskdale at Ravenglass there is a Roman bathhouse which still stands to an astonishing height of around 12 feet. Walls Castle is said to be the best-preserved Roman ruin in the North of England. Three of the building's arched doorways are still standing and the plaster rendering is still attached to some of the red sandstone walls. A niche in one wall of what is thought to be a dressing room, would perhaps have held the image of some deity or cult figure. Given its wonderful state of preservation, there is remarkably little fuss made over this ancient monument. No mercenary turnstiles, regimented walkways or awkward opening hours, just a ten minute stroll along a pleasant lane lined with birch trees, flushed today with red campion underfoot and speckled with white wood sorrel. You are surrounded by the parkland of the Muncaster Estate where doves coo and the crow of the pheasants echoes through the woods. Then suddenly, in a gap in the trees, the Roman bathhouse is there, a red wall of stonework rising up like the neck of an ancient dragon. And knowing its great age, you feel a shiver of excitement. You have been allowed to make the discovery yourself and it's a genuine thrill to find so much of it still standing. And you begin to wonder whether people have always felt this way, this sense of awe, respect and mystery in the presence of this ancient, long-gone civilisation, and that this is what has kept it free from molestation. And you can't help but praise the wisdom of those today - English Heritage, by Jupiter!- who have left it like this and not turned it into the sort of penny peepshow that so much of our historical heritage has become.

Across the way from the bathhouse is the flat, grassy platform of the fort with its deep ditch surround. It has never been excavated, though the railway builders cut it in two when they drove the railway up the coast to Whitehaven and beyond. From here you can see the slow curve of the River Esk as it trails out into the estuary and the distant sea. And you can see how this must have been an important supply port for Hardknott and the forts across the mountains.

And now there's just one final journey to be made across the Roman North of England, and that's to the greatest fortification of all, Hadrian's Wall.

What part the Brigantes played in the decision to build the Wall is open to speculation. Trouble with the natives had flared again at the beginning of Hadrian's reign in 117 AD but it was with the tribes of southern Scotland, the Selgovae and Novantae. Hadrian's predecessor, Trajan, had set up a series of forts along the Stanegate, the road between Carlisle and Corbridge, but they were hardly adequate to deal with a concerted Scottish attack. And if the Scots were to unite with their southern neighbours, the Brigantes, the fragile Roman hold on the North was under serious threat. So it was in 122 AD Hadrian ordered the construction of 76 miles of wall between the Tyne and the Solway, with further defences down the Cumbrian coast. If you look on a map, this is the narrowest part of England, referred to sometimes as the Solway-Tyne isthmus. In effect it was the nearest they could get to a natural frontier, a frontier that would serve a highly symbolic function. Here were the limits of the greatest Empire in the world, and it was not so much about what the Wall was intended to keep out to the north but the civilisation and its unparalleled achievements to the south which it was keeping in. And so Hadrian's Wall needed to be the immense undertaking it proved to be. It has been calculated that over a million cubic yards of stone had to be quarried. In addition to a wall 20 feet high and 10 feet thick, it included 12, later to become 16, fully-fledged forts, castles every mile and watchtowers in between. It was a linear garrison for 12,000 soldiers, or around a quarter of all the Roman soldiers in Britain. That's how important it was to Rome. And again if you look at the OS map, you will see that the frontier did not only consist of a wall with a deep ditch in front. Behind the wall, anything up to half a mile away in some places, was a vallum, another ditch flanked by earthen banks constituting a further barrier 120 feet wide. And so, sandwiched in between wall and vallum was a formidable militarised zone, full of military installations and buzzing with armed soldiers, a no-go area for anyone but those strictly approved of by the occupying forces. Remarkably, and as a tribute to the skill, organisational powers and persistence of the Roman military, the Wall took only six years to complete. But no amount of statistics or poring over maps is a substitute for a visit there, where it is in the context of the landscape that the Wall announces its most beautiful and spectacular achievement.

To witness the Wall in its most dramatic of settings we began our excursion at Steel Rigg, about two and a half miles west of Housesteads fort. It's after 6.30 on a May evening and the place is deserted, a rarity for the Wall in the summer months. From the car park the Wall beckons across a short field. Here it is on level ground and almost suburban in its meticulously coursed and bonded neatness, each stone carefully dressed. Everywhere it has been extensively restored but nevertheless, this first sighting is a real excitement. And when you turn to look eastwards to follow the line of the Wall as it snakes into the distance, hugging the contours of the escarpment high above the waters of Crag Lough to the crags beyond Housesteads, you are captured by its magic and want to walk every inch. But the lateness of the hour means we must tailor our ambitions and content ourselves with getting to know some of the Wall's details.

The facing stones are of grey gritstone grizzled with lichen. It's a quartzose grit which makes it fine-textured and it came from local quarries. A quick look at the map reveals scores of disused workings. The core of the wall was filled with rubble set in puddled clay. The discovery of lime kilns near Housesteads shows that they also used lime mortar. Today lime mortar is evident in the grouting and where the interior of the wall is exposed. I suspect most of this is the work of restoration. At one point, close to the ground, I observe a mason's mark in the shape of a cross. The work of Victorian restorers? I don't think the Romans went in for mason's marks but just left inscriptions saying which legion built each section. The Wall was the work of the XXth Valeria Victrix, the IInd Augusta and the VIth Victrix, the legion which took over from the IXth in the legionary headquarters at York. How the soldiers looked forward to a stint building the Wall one can only guess. This evening the sunlight is struggling to break free of the clouds but a sharp wind never stops blowing off the Solway. The ragged escarpment to which the Wall seems glued makes it uncomfortably exposed, and the way it dips and twists, following the undulations of the land, must have made it a nightmare for getting heavy stones to the spot to say nothing of building to a height of 20 feet. As we breast one incline the Wall suddenly plunges away into another dip and there below is our first sighting of a milecastle.

A climb down a long flight of stone steps from the crag top takes us into the enclosure that was milecastle 39. It's about 30 feet by 20 with two gateways, one in the south wall approached through a break in the ridge, the other in the north wall leading out into enemy territory from where the 30 soldiers manning the milecastle could sally forth to deal with any hostile incursion or else use the 30 foot high watchtower to summon assistance from one of the larger forts nearby. Further structures, small turrets about 14 feet square, were positioned two between each milecastle, again serving as lookout and signal towers. As has been pointed out by others, the great virtue of this system was that the enemy could never know from which exit the Roman soldiers would emerge, hidden as they were behind the high wall: either from the milecastle gates or the larger gateways of the forts, or a daunting combination of the two. The intensive fort and signalling system must have guaranteed that the Romans could muster their troops to any place on the Wall within minutes.

If there is such a thing as psychogeography and places can be said to retain some of the resonance of the activities and emotions with which they were once associated, here is one such place. Stepping out from the northern gate of a milecastle into the vast swell of open country that lies beyond, you can't fail to feel a quiver of that apprehension which a Roman soldier must have felt at leaving behind the sanctuary of civilisation for the great wilderness of barbarity beyond. An Empire that stretched from the deserts of Arabia to here and which was predicated upon the rules of law, reason and social order, suddenly gives way in the thickness of a stone wall to the swamps and forests of the north Northumbrian wilderness where Celtic tribesmen acted only upon instinct and bloodthirsty savagery. Who could fail but to shudder? And to the

Roman soldier scanning the horizon for enemy activity from his watchtower, what would this landscape have looked like 2,000 years ago? We're told that Neolithic and Bronze Age man cleared vast swathes of the landscape of trees. But how much of the great forests would have remained? Presumably much more than exists today. Today only the conifer plantations darken the distant horizon, the rest is sweeping tracts of open country, a huge, empty canvas for the shifting images of light and shade. With the forests of old must have come only darkness, the darkness of fear, for they were concealment for an enemy full of brooding resentment and bent upon violent revenge for the seizure of their ancestral lands.

It has been calculated by Hartley and Fitts that something in the order of 12,000 acres must have been appropriated just for the creation of the militarised zone defined by the vallum. And any peaceful movement through the Wall of traders would have involved the payment of customs duty. Conquest always carries prerogatives which are hateful to the conquered.

From milecastle 39 the Wall now climbs to the top of Highshield Crags. Some rock climbers are tackling the crag which rises vertically from the tarn below. You can see the wisdom of the Wall following the high ridges: with such sheer cliffs there's no need for digging the deep ditch - on average 27 feet wide and nine feet deep - normally found on the north side of the Wall. Sitting on top of the crags, the jackdaws busy at their nests below, Northumbria stretches into the distance to Kielder Forest and beyond. You can begin to experience the sense of invincibility the Romans must have felt in their achievement. The wall is such a big idea and it deserved to succeed. It was only breached on occasions when because of internal strife within the Empire too much manpower was withdrawn. Now it's a place of peace to stand and sit and look out and dream of the great sweep of our Northern history, tortuous as the Wall itself as it journeys across the landscape and inscrutable as the messages written by the wind upon the turbulent waters of the loch below.

The next day we are up early for a marathon exploration of the central section of the Wall, the 15 or so miles between Portgate, just north of Corbridge, to the Vindolanda fort on the Stanegate, four miles east of Haltwhistle. This will allow us to take in the forts at Chesters and Housesteads in addition to the Roman bridge over the North Tyne at Chollerford and the Mithraeum at Carrawburgh.

There's nothing much to be seen at Portgate today but in Roman times it was an important gateway through the Wall because it carried the road to Scotland, Dere Street, the route that passes the henges on Hutton Moor and the Devil's Arrows, 70 miles further south on the way to York. Again, passing through the Wall on the way to Scotland must have seemed daunting, like stepping over a threshold into the dark. Soldiers returning from campaigns to try to subdue the Scots and those drafted into building the Antonine Wall on the Clyde-Forth isthmus, must have returned - if they were lucky - with tales of the barbarity of the Scottish tribes. Then there's the legend of the ill-fated IXth Legion, sadly probably not true but immortalised in fiction by Rosemary Sutcliff in her 'Eagle of the Ninth', which tells the story of the disappearance of a whole legion into the mists of Scotland never to return. I don't doubt that there would have been a barracks room mythology about the journey to Scotland and its attendant fears that would have raised the pulses of the soldiers marching out of the Portgate. Standing on the roadside beside the roundabout today as the A68 disappears northwards following the route of the Roman road, you can't fail to respond to the romance of the spot. Where the gate must have stood, the roundabout is crammed with may blossom. Despite the traffic the heavy scent of lilac blossom drifts from the hedgerows. In the fields the barley is beginning to ripen, moving in soft waves like silvery hair stroked by the wind. A blackbird sings his heart out in an ash tree, late of leaf and boding well for a dry summer if country lore is to be our guide. Only the rooks at their nests high in a sycamore, sounding harsh and quarrelsome, strike a note of discord, a reminder that ancient echoes of conflict still resonate beneath the placid surface of this landscape.

The road to the west of the roundabout, the B6318, follows the

113

course of the Wall. In fact, it is the Wall. When General Wade came along to try to put down the Jacobite Rebellion of 1745, he filched the stones from the Wall to build this, his military road. This means that for the next three miles there is no Wall. What you can see, quite spectacularly, is the ditch on the north side and the vallum to the south. At this time of year the ditch is full of broom bushes in bright yellow flower. In the past the broom was commonly thought of as a magical shrub from which the fairies spoke, something perhaps which the Romans would have appreciated with their veneration of the spirits of different places. And for a while it is the spirit of this, the North of England, which preoccupies my thoughts.

I leave the road and clamber down and across the ditch to get a better vantage of my surroundings. Both north and south the folding plains of Northern England seem to stretch forever. Southwards, where the shifting light probes the various textures of the landscape, of field, copse and moor, the distant Pennines beckon. North, under a sky of bright, broken cloud, the mountains of southern Scotland melt into a slate-blue mist, while east and west the Wall stretches out its arms to link two seas. For me, this is North. It is air and space and light and it is a boundless freedom of spirit reflected in and inspired by the exhilarating liberality of the landscape. It is both a physical location and an emotional state, you can't divorce the two, you never can with landscape you become involved with. And now the historical dimension adds its quota to this rich complexity of response. The more you get to know, the more that places like the Wall begin to reveal themselves, the deeper the emotional involvement. So in the end all that you can do is stand and stare like I was doing, in a state of enthralment, unable to turn away and leave it alone, wrapped in this warm, almost painful, soul-gnawing sensation of being at one, totally engaged with your environment. In love, I suppose.

Just a turn south of the B6318 at Brunton and you can view a well-preserved turret, one of the small, square towers, two between each milecastle, used as a lookout for enemy movements beyond the Wall.

The Brunton turret is about 14 feet square inside and contains a small altar base and stone threshold with a pivot hole for the door. Men probably slept in the bottom and climbed a wooden ladder to do stints on watch from the 30 foot tower. Today the view north is totally obscured by mature trees, oaks and Scots pine. You come away with the impression of how poky these turrets were, men thrown together in claustrophobic proximity, which must have been the story of daily life in the Roman army for most soldiers. A breeding ground for discontent, perhaps, and the factional conflicts like that in AD 196-7 which gave the native tribes an opportunity to rebel and left parts of the Wall in ruins until reconstruction in the early third century.

Before visiting the fort at Chesters we took the path southwest at Chollerford Bridge to view the remains of the bridge which took the Wall across the North Tyne. Here you can marvel at the size of the stones for the abutments, the platforms which supported the arches of the bridge across the river. The 600 kilogram stones lie scattered around like giant's playthings. You can see the hollows where the cranes were positioned and the holes in the stones into which were let iron fittings to attach the lifting ropes. The ruins of the bridge lie where time has left them, some still in the river, others in the shade of two oak trees. Small birds are nesting amongst the scattered ruins today, all the immense effort and energy of man long dissipated while the forces of nature are perpetually renewed in the endless cycles of life and the ceaseless flow of the river. Is this why the Celts, who celebrated the eternal cycles of nature in the circles and interlacing patterns of their art, were so little interested in such man-made structures and when the Romans left were content to return to their old ways of building in wattle and straw? Did they intuitively perceive the transience of all such human endeavour? Could they have predicted such poignant ruins?

At Chesters Bridge, if you are so inclined, you can play hunt the phallus. Somewhere amongst the masonry lies a stone carved with a phallus, on the lowest course of the abutment. Low and coarse? No. Apparently, the phallus, we are told, to the Romans wasn't rude but represented good fortune and protection against evil. Perhaps it was put there after the first Hadrianic bridge was destroyed by flood and replaced in the time of Septimius Severus, which are the remains of the bridge we see today.

Chesters fort across the river was home to a cohort of Asturian cavalry. These auxiliaries were recruited from Spain for their skills in horsemanship. I can't help but feel a slight personal connection because troops of the same origin were garrisoned at Ribchester, the nearest fort to my home in Lancashire. In the small museum there is a gravestone showing one of the Asturians riding down a native Brigante. The rider is proudly and dismissively plunging his spear into the native who lies prone at the horse's feet and is depicted as short and ugly-looking with a big nose and ears. No doubt this very unflattering representation of the local tribesmen was a piece of Roman propaganda and doesn't accord with the picture of a proud and heroic warrior race painted by Anne Ross. There's another such gravestone of one, Flavinus, in the Abbey at Hexham. And later, in one of the Vindolanda letters, we will come across another example of the contempt in which the Roman soldiers held those natives who didn't readily submit to conquest and subsequent Romanisation. But ridicule is an important weapon in fighting fear, as the political cartoonist of the modern age demonstrates in his depiction of tyrants and monsters like Hitler. The massive effort employed by Rome to contain the native Britons shows that it held them in anything but contempt. The Wall is as much a monument to heroic native resistance as it is to the colonialist power of Rome.

The fort at Chesters gives an interesting insight into the Roman mindset. The first thing that really strikes you is the gridiron regularity of the barracks block, all straight lines and identical rectangular rooms. In fact, all the forts throughout the Empire were built to a similar pattern. There was no scope for any architectural experimentation, eccentricities or individuality. Once you've studied one fort, you've seen them all, one milecastle and one turret and the rest are just the same. The only variation is in their degree of preservation. It's therefore tempting to see the Roman Empire as a remorseless, mass-producing machine of conquest, driven by the ruthlessly rationalised imperatives of expansion; doubtlessly bringing advantages but at a terrible price in terms of conformity and standardisation. Dare I say, like today's giant supermarkets with their identikit buildings, standardised products and mission statement to eliminate all competition and conquer the commercial world? That's why, if you are a believer in individualism you can never warm to the Romans. You can admire their vision, their energy, their determination and self-belief, but when it comes to it you're always on the side of those they oppress: the gladiator up against it in the coliseum, the wretched Brigantian with his big nose and ears, dying under the cavalryman's spear. They are the underdogs, and in their imperfections, their awkwardness, their victimisation at the hands of fate, we recognise their humanity. But history is rarely on the side of the underdog, the vanquished. It is on the side of the conqueror and it immortalises them in the proud busts and gravestones which look down on us from their museum plinths. The Romans were never really very human. Look how their emperors thought of themselves as gods.

The museum at Chesters fort is wonderful. It contains hundreds of stone reliefs and sculptures from all the forts around. It is a veritable mason's yard of venerable stonework. A pantheon of stone gods look down in time-worn indulgence: river gods, war gods, gods of victory and goddesses of fortune. The Romans had a very practical arrangement with their gods. They were expected to do things for them. They remind me of the rather ridiculous practice of the Latin footballer of today who runs onto the pitch crossing himself. As well as sorting out the universe their gods are expected to answer their prayers and bring them victory.

Three and a half miles west of Chesters is the fort of Carrawburgh. It is as rough as Chesters is cultivated, just a grassy platform in a field grazed by sheep. The magnet which draws visitors is tucked away in a boggy dip to the west of the fort. It is the remains of a small, rectangular temple with three carved altar stones where cult ceremonies and sacrifices to the bull-slaying god Mithras took place.

117

The altar stones are replicas because the originals have been taken to a museum in Newcastle and the posts that supported the roof have been replaced by concrete pillars. But the building is still strangely affecting. One of the altar stones was hollowed out to contain a lamp which would illuminate the crown of fire radiating from Mithras's head. He was thought to have slaughtered a bull from whose blood sprang the rest of the life in the universe. It is a resurrection myth which incurred the displeasure of the early Christians who are understood to have desecrated the temple in the fourth century. Roofless, the sunlight streaming down onto the grass and daisies which now grow in the once-shadowy aisles where the celebrants crowded, it is hard to imagine these dark, blood-letting ceremonies taking place here. And the constant stream of sight-seers makes it doubly difficult. We are cornered by a garrulous Geordie who insists upon telling us about his travels in Tunisia where, he told us, the Roman remains are much more spectacular and well-preserved. 'Compared to them, this is a laugh,' he told us. We tramped back up the hill to the fort platform where we recovered our naïve enthusiasm by spending an engrossing half-hour fossicking amongst the mole hills and rabbit holes. Under the grassy covering we discovered hidden wall courses and the remains of the fort's gateway. Curiously, to discover things for yourself in this way is much more satisfying than having acres of stonework exposed before you, neatly tied and labelled, for a monetary donation. To judge from how well the molehills had been rifled, many people who visited Carrawburgh that day seem to have felt the same way.

The Roman soldier was free to worship any god he wished provided he fulfilled his obligations to the cult of the deified emperors and the guardian spirits that watched over his unit's standard. This meant that the Romans often adopted the native Celtic gods. In the museum up the hillside at the ever-popular fort at Housesteads, three native cowled gods gaze glumly from a wall relief. They are the genii cucullati. Found in the vicus or township attached to the fort, they may only have been worshipped by the native Celts. They have the bearing of a conquered race, expressions of lugubrious resignation on their worn faces, their tiny feet protruding from their lumpy, mud-coloured cloaks, like bored children standing around in oversized parkas. These cloaks were the cucullati, a traditional Celtic dress no doubt invaluable for keeping out the mean weather associated with this exposed section of the Wall. Finds from the Housesteads vicus give an insight into the dubious pleasures of life for those natives who had thrown in their lot with their oppressors. They include taverns and gambling dens as well as a workshop for minting illicit coins. Housesteads was built for the first cohort of the Tungrians, who were from Belgium. Their accommodation boasts the best-preserved latrines in Roman Britain. As if the surviving fixtures weren't enough, there's an artist's impression of the latrines in use showing Roman soldiers with their pants down happily chattering away to one another while squatting on seats over a channel of running water. Another smaller channel in front of them is used for washing sponges attached to sticks, instruments of personal hygiene one of which a soldier is waving in the air to make some important conversational point to his seated companions. What did I say about not leaving things to the imagination?

But the intimate details of the life of a Roman soldier are best revealed in the celebrated letters found at the Stanegate fort of Vindolanda, two miles away across the B6318 from Housesteads. The excellent museum at the site tells the story of their miraculous discovery, said by the British Museum at the time to be the top British ancient treasure. Fragments of writing tablets made from small squares of wood with letters either scratched on wax or else written in ink had been preserved in freak anaerobic conditions, enabling scholars to read unique descriptions of the daily lives of the people of Roman Vindolanda in the reign of Hadrian. There are details of food preparation, complaints about poor beer, New Year and birthday celebrations, stores and household accounts, the news of the capture of a deserter and intelligence reports. One such report declares that 'the Britons are unprotected by armour. They have many cavalry who do not use swords, nor do the wretched Britons

119

mount in order to throw their javelins.' The Latin expression used to describe the Britons is 'Brittunculi' which we're told translates as 'wretched little Britons'. More contempt for an enemy that the Romans were to build 76 miles of wall, scores of forts and fortlets, and use 12,000 soldiers to suppress, sometimes unsuccessfully.

But any final observations on Hadrian's Wall must be from the justifiably popular fort of Housesteads. Visitors come every year in their thousands to view it, climbing the Whin Sill escarpment to wander amongst the ruins and stand by the Wall to look out over the surrounding countryside. From here the Wall commands a view of vast tracts of Northern England. Only the trees high on the crags to the west where the Wall marches back to where we began at Steel Rigg obscure a full 360 degree panorama. At last there's a real sense of being able to reach out and draw the horizons together as the Wall itself does, bringing that sense of oneness with the landscape and its history in their whole numinous complexity. It is exhilarating, a spiritual tonic, and you can see it in the faces of the visitors as they return down the stony path from the fort. They've been uplifted and perhaps, like me, know better now what it is to be Northern, to belong here as a bird belongs to the sky and a fish to the water, not in a way that can easily be described but in a way that is intuitively and instinctively right. And perhaps they can feel proud, knowing that despite the protracted efforts of the greatest civilisation in the world, we, here in the North, were never really conquered by the Romans. After 300 years and countless lives they finally gave up and went home.

5. SAINTS AND MONSTERS

Some historical knowledge of a place, however scant, can transform the way we feel about it. Take Goldsborough, a tiny village on the North Yorkshire coast a few miles North of Whitby. You can stand on the hillside above the sea and imagine yourself in the most peaceful of idylls. All around you the cattle graze contentedly. Sunlight falls upon the yellow fresh-cut fields and somewhere a distant tractor drones soporifically. The fields are small and varied. Here and there one has already been ploughed, exposing the rich reddish loam of the topsoil. No suggestion here of the brutality of large-scale farming which is the curse of so much of eastern England. Here the landscape is on a human scale with small, intimate fields, walled and hedged as they have been for generations. Yes, there are the mighty cliffs of Boulby towering above the sea just to the north of Runswick Bay, said to be the highest in England at 660 feet. And the bare knuckles of the headlands are clenched defiantly at the invading sea. For the wind is not always the gentle breeze that it is today. You only need to look at the shape of the thorn trees in the hedgerows, permanently bent by the force of the wind. But today the sea is still, deepening blue as it melts into the horizon sky, the occasional container ship gliding barely perceptibly across it northwards towards the Tees estuary. Like the hamlet of Kettleness below, ignored by the hordes who invade the popular resorts and villages nearby, Goldsborough seems to have been sunk in slumber forever.

But begin to unearth the stones that disturb the evenness of the pasture here beneath your feet and Goldsborough starts to tell a far different story. It was once the scene of an incident which symbolised the violent transition from the civilising order of Roman rule to the anarchic land grab of the Anglo-Saxon invasion.

In 1931, two archaeologists, William Hornsby and John Laverick, were searching for the missing link in a chain of five Roman signal stations stretching from Huntcliff, close to the Tees estuary, down to Filey. During the fourth century the Roman north was plagued with pirate raids. Angles, Saxons and Jutes, from Germany, were looking to plunder the rich settlements of Yorkshire. The Roman villas, like those established in the Ryedale Valley, had to be protected. To do so, the Roman army at the fort at Malton and the Roman coastal shipping patrols based in the Humber and the Tees needed warning of enemy naval incursions. The signal stations were fortified towers, up to a hundred feet high, capable of relaying such warnings.

Hornsby and Laverick eventually found their missing station about half a mile from the sea on the hillside vantage I have just described. It consisted of a ditch protecting a fort with a stone wall four feet thick, four turrets and a gateway leading into a courtyard from which rose the stone beacon tower. Extensively charred timbers and the collapse of the tower walls indicated that the station met its end in a violent conflagration. Protected by the fallen wall in the southeast corner of the tower was the most sensational of the two archaeologists' discoveries. They found two male skeletons face downwards against the wall, their skulls shattered. Beneath one of them, 'the skeleton of a large and powerful dog, its head against the man's throat, its paws across his shoulders. Surely,' they concluded in their report, 'a grim record of a thrilling drama, perhaps the dog one of the defenders, the man an intruder.' And they ask, 'Had the marauders come in the dead of night or during the din of a storm? Or perhaps when a sea fret blanketed everything in a fog?' I find it a chilling rather than a thrilling scenario, one which, as I say, completely contradicts the peaceful scene today, suggesting that this was once a place of intense anxiety, of terrible insecurity, of lives lived under the shadow of sudden, violent murder. Indeed, it was the threshold of the Dark Ages.

For the forensically inclined the skulls of the two men can be inspected in the Whitby Museum amongst the fossils and the giant marine reptiles glued to the walls like giant flying crocodiles. Both skulls have jagged holes around the left temple. (Indicating blows from a right-handed swordsman, eh Watson?) The trusty dog is nowhere to be found.

A coin discovered near the feet of one of the skeletons was a silver siliqua minted during the reign of the Emperor Honorius, proving that the signal station had stood until at least the beginning of his reign in 393. We know that the stations were commissioned by Count Theodotius around 370, so they seem to have had a short life. This was because, towards the end of the fourth century, the Roman army was being continually stretched. Barbarians were attacking Gaul and pushing south towards Rome itself. The withdrawal of troops from Britain meant forts and villas were more and more vulnerable to attack. The Germanic tribes who had cast envious eyes across the North Sea were now in a position to realise their rapacious ambitions. Between 401 and 407 Rome had fallen to Alaric and his Visigoths. An appeal to Honorius fell on deaf ears and Britain was told to fend for itself. The Dark Ages had begun.

The term Dark Ages, whilst effective in conveying the idea of a time of singular barbarity, was coined more to indicate a lack of contemporary accounts of what life was like in fifth century Britain. No longer part of the Roman Empire, the spotlight of attention went out. Historians have to rely upon the account of a sixth century monk called Gildas, writing around 547, a century and a half after the Roman withdrawal. Gildas's is a catalogue of woes, of warring Romano-British factions, deserted towns and pirate raids. Shadowy figures from our Primary School history lessons emerge from the twilight. Gildas tells us that a British 'tyrant' called Vortigern introduced Saxon mercenaries into Britain to help in its defence. Not the brightest idea, because soon the so-called defenders had turned attackers. According to Bede, writing even later, the Saxon mercenaries were led by Hengist and Horsa. These promptly sacked the island. It's the start of a long and bloody struggle between native Britons and the invading 'English'. And from the shadows of this period emerges another figure, more, sadly perhaps, a figure of myth and legend than historical reality. Gildas writes that in the 490s a native Briton, perhaps a Romano-British tribal leader, emerges, winning a famous victory against the Saxons at a hillfort known as Badon Hill. This, says Gildas, is King Arthur.

But what has Arthur, with his traditional haunts of Camelot and Avalon, associated with the southwest, to do with the North of England? We'd certainly like a bit of him to add his glamour, poetry and magic to our own dark history. Well, we could be in luck. Another writer looking back at this period, Nennius, writing some time after 800, records 12 battles fought by Arthur. And Michael Wood in his memorable TV series of the early 80s, 'In Search of the Dark Ages', suggests that many of these battles may have taken place in the North in Cumbria, Rheged and southern Scotland. One in particular, the fight at Camlann, where Arthur met his end, occurred at Birdoswald, Roman name Camboglanna, the 'crooked glen' of the River Irthing.

Birdoswald is the Roman fort on Hadrian's Wall just over the Northumbrian border in Cumbria. It is an understated ruin, a bare outline or ground plan rather than containing some of the more detailed features of a Chesters or Housesteads. But venture beyond its southwest wall and the ground plunges down into a magnificent wooded glen with the loop in the River Irthing hundreds of feet below. Here, suggests Michael Wood, could have been enacted the last stand of King Arthur, his enemy not the Anglo-Saxons but rival British chieftains fighting over the ruins of Roman Britain. But Wood enjoys the thought of a real King Arthur here at Birdoswald only briefly before, with only the place name to go on, reluctantly dismissing the idea for a lack of evidence.

But if the dark events of the attack on the Goldsborough signal station can charge a peaceful spot with some of the terror of sudden death, so the very name of Arthur can invest the glen of the Irthing with some of the romance of the 'once and future king'.

In the grass above the wooded glen the harebells tremble in the late August breeze. Buttercups trap and distil the afternoon sunlight in their enamelled yellow crucibles, while purple clover stains the grass. The light splashes and dances on the blade-like leaves of an ash tree which rises out of the ravine above the army of trees which crowd the glen. The northern fells of the Lake District rise in the distance while the Wall marches inexorably eastwards across country from the ruined fort. Today it is hard to imagine this as a scene of battle, a place shattered by the discordance of war and dying. Insects murmur hypnotically. The sunshine dispenses drowsiness. It is a place of pure peace. If ever Arthur fought and died here I can't think of a finer place for his spirit to wander. A true Avalon.

One of the most poignant images to reflect the state of post-Roman Britain is to be discovered in the basement of the Bowes Museum at Barnard Castle. It is the Binchester Lady. Her body was found in the ruins of the Roman commander's bathhouse in the cavalry fort at Binchester near Bishop Aukland. She's an Anglian, or Anglo-Saxon, buried around the year 500. Did the recent invaders live in the ruins of our Roman forts and towns, witness to their steady disintegration? Nearby was evidence of a building used as a butchers, with animal bones, also rooms used for metalworking. Like today's motley industrial units sheltering in the carcases of our once-great textile mills, perhaps? Only, today we move on. Our early English ancestors seem to have suffered from a collective cultural amnesia, forgetting how to mix mortar and build in stone, returning to primitive Celtic tribalism after enjoying Rome's imperial system of government.

The Binchester lady is rudimentarily pathetic. She lies in the museum, a collapsed skeleton on a bed of gravel. Her skull is missing and seems to have been replaced by a mortared brick. Her body is sadly disarticulated, rearranged in a manner that whatever is left of her allows. Her rib bones form a grimy fan around her blackened spine. Her feet are turned in, looking for her missing toes. A shin bone has gone AWOL. A knee cap lies on its own like a stray pebble. And by her side, a copper alloy brooch, an amber bead necklace and two bone antler objects - the contents of her handbag. Even in the year 500 ladies never went anywhere without their handbags.

The Northern forts were the first to fall to the barbarians. The outpost fort at Bewcastle, 6 miles northwest of Birdoswald, built as part of the forward defences of the Wall, probably fell towards the end of the fourth century - in excavations there, no coins or pottery dated after 370 AD were found. From housing a cohort of a thousand men it sank into obscurity. Today the stones of the fort form the walls of the crumbling Norman keep built shortly after 1092. The intervening seven centuries seem as empty and uncommunicative as the landscape itself around Bewcastle. Driving along the quiet lanes through the pretty hamlets of the Irthing valley, it comes as a shock to glimpse through the hedgerows the sudden stark outline of the moors. The fields start to change from grassy green to reedy dun. A general bareness begins to prevail. In the distance, dark pine forests scratch at the sky. A sense of wildness is setting in. You know you are approaching some kind of edge, a bleak frontier tainted by the residue of a forgotten fear.

The Roman soldiers would have felt it. After all, this was a war zone, beyond the protection of the Wall. The fort, it's thought, was built over a native shrine to the war god Cocidius and altars to the god were found along with silver plaques. As we've seen, the Romans would have had every reason to fear the British tribesmen up here in their wild native fastness. But I'm suggesting something more than the fear arising from the likelihood of an ambush striking at a patrol from the moorland mists and forests. Perhaps, to our ancestors, whether Roman or Celtic, the landscape itself might appear intrinsically fearful. Not until relatively recently and the arrival of the Romantic poets have we begun to regard the wilderness in aesthetic terms, as a place of beauty and spiritual uplift. Before the nineteenth century cultivated people eschewed the wild outdoors as much as they did a suntan. Nature in its ruder manifestations was shocking to their refined sensibilities, so much so that the French painter, Claude Lorrain, popularised the use of a mirror so that the observer could turn his back on the landscape and only view it within the framed, and hence tamed, confines of the glass. The great and the good employed the services of a Capability Brown to neuter nature by designing gardens with views in which the formal and civilised values of man predominated over uncouth nature. It was the age-old instinct - though they wouldn't have thanked me for suggesting it - of the henge builders: shutting out the chaos of nature in a bid to impose some human control over a frighteningly hostile universe.

On my second visit to Bewcastle when, unlike on the first, the mist had lifted and the sun lit a warm afternoon, the only other people there were a party of two elderly couples who had set up their picnic table and chairs on a grassy mound outside the church. They were resolutely defying any suggestion of hostility within the surrounding landscape as they sipped their tea and nibbled their sandwiches, chattering amiably. 'Hear no evil, see no evil ….' Their incongruity struck me quite forcibly, particularly since I was struggling with my own distinctly uncomfortable feelings for the place. I could not rid myself of my first impression of Bewcastle as a bleak and abandoned spot. On that first visit, thick, grey cloud had hung about the moors and the pine forests etched a black line under the horizon sky. The crumbling walls of the featureless keep intensified the impression of abandonment. The church is bare and utilitarian, lacking warmth, though there is clearly an active congregation somewhere to judge from the exhibition in the small building in the churchyard with its pictures by local children of Bewcastle's long history. But for all that history, from the Bronze Age, through Roman to early Christian and mediaeval times and beyond, when reiving ravaged these border lands, it is clearly more like a place which time has finally had enough of.

Yet time's chill imprint is everywhere at Bewcastle. Within the churchyard, with its weird assortment of rickety headstones, many from the eighteenth century, memento mori abound. Here's Death depicted with his scythe and here's a skull and crossbones. And crude but horribly effective, here's a man throwing up his hands in terror as he sees the hourglass running out, the sexton's spade already at his feet. The dark drama of these stones suits the landscape.

But the graveyard's most celebrated tenant is the Bewcastle Cross.

127

It stands close to the church porch, a shaft 15 feet high covered in a profound nexus of carvings. There are convoluted Celtic scrolls of vegetation which twist and morph into strange birds and beasts as they climb the cross. There's cunningly interlaced knotwork. And struggling to emerge from the obscurity of the time-pitted stone there are runic inscriptions and names of long-dead Dark Age tribal kings: Oswiu and Alcfrith and their followers Hwaetred and Wothgaer. And on the west face of the cross, where the prevailing weather has been most cruel, three human figures emerge. One, a man holding a lamb with a halo round its head, is understood to be John the Baptist. Another is the figure of Christ standing on the heads of two prone beasts. And the third is John the Evangelist bearing an eagle. So here, on the fourth face of the cross, we have a radical new iconography. From the pagan images of nature with plants and animals locked in their endless cycles of procreation which fill the other three faces, we have the sudden appearance of the personification of redemption and resurrection. Christianity, the most important cultural influence in the history of western civilisation, has arrived in the North.

The Bewcastle Cross is Anglian, thought to date from around the seventh century. Roman Christianity spread to the North during the early years of that century, converting the Anglian settlers. But why here? Why should it have found its way in such a stunning manifestation into such, dare I say, God-forsaken parts? Into the dark and violent realm of the Celtic war god, Cocidius, here on the edge of the wilderness? As we shall see, the early Christian missionaries chose some of the most remote places to set up their monasteries and monastic cells, and there's a suggestion that one such cell may have existed here at Bewcastle. But I'd like to offer another, more psychologically exploratory explanation, something that could tell us about the underlying psyche of those Germanic invaders, the Angles, who settled here in the North and became the rootstock from which so many of us have come to believe we are descended.

To fathom the minds of people who wrote nothing down is an uncertain business. With the Neolithic people we can only look at their circles and standing stones, their baffling cup and ring marks

Malham Cove. An alien and primal power.

Malham Tarn. The hunting ground of Mesolithic ancestors.

Rudston. Pagan vitality which seems to dwarf the church.

Willie Howe. Trees try to hide the ransacked barrow.

Brigantes country. Looking north towards Wild Boar Fell.

Victoria Cave. The bones of rhinos, hippos and elephants have been found here.

Votive pool? Stanwick Iron Age fortress.

Scafell from the Roman fort at Hardknott, the North's Mycenae.

Chesters fort museum. A mason's yard of venerable stonework.

Mithraic temple, Carrawburgh. A place of cult ceremonies and sacrifices.

Looking northwards towards Bamburgh from Lindisfarne. 'The fusion of grey, still water and dove-grey sky conveys a sense of milky dissolution.'

Hexham's Saxon crypt. Once the visitors have gone you may read the stones' messages of mortality.

The Gosforth Viking cross. Carved figures wrestle for interpretation.

The abbey church at Rievaulx. 'A marvellous freedom from the tumult of the world.'

Selby Abbey, east window. To walk along the gallery in front must be like walking in heaven.

Hermitage. 'A brutal assertion of martial might.'

Derwentwater, where the lake water is a soothing stream of light which, nevertheless, still carries the memory of tragedy.

Axe factory, Stickle Pike. 'A gully of stone to send you surfing a thousand feet or more to a broken leg, or worse.'

and the contents of their burial mounds. With the Celts the task became easier because we had the writings of the Romans and the vestiges of Celtic culture which survive into Irish and Welsh folklore. When it comes to the Anglo-Saxons we at last begin to get their own literature, although this usually appears after their conversion to Christianity. As far as the pagan Anglo-Saxons were concerned we have the tantalising symbolism of grave goods like the objects found in the celebrated Sutton Hoo ship burial, known to date from between 620 and 640. This is thought to be the burial mound of the East Anglian king, Raedwald. But what is the significance of the so-called 'sceptre', a two-and-a-half foot long whetstone with decorations of heads and a bronze stag? The conclusion drawn by some is that the whetstone is a symbol of the king's power in a country torn by war and so dependent upon the sword and the loyalty of warriors to their king who in return for their arms offered them his protection as the gold ring-giver in the great mead halls of the Anglo-Saxon warrior aristocracy.

Written records, including runes inscribed upon rings, reveal this Anglo-Saxon society to have been a deeply superstitious one. Charms and spells were in widespread use, some carried on amulets in order to ward off sickness or danger. Witchcraft and sorcery survived even into the Christian era, a kind of double indemnity against what fate or the Devil might have in store for them: sudden warfare, inexplicable sickness and death. Life in Anglo-Saxon England was lived under a continuous and widespread threat.

The greatest example of the literature of the age, written some time between the seventh and tenth centuries, is the heroic poem 'Beowulf'. It is charged with fear and menace, driven by blood-feuds, the imperatives of revenge and the vicious cycle of blood shedding which dominates the era. For, like the Bewcastle Cross, it might have a Christian message imposed upon it but it is predominantly pagan. The poem is a celebration of the Germanic heroic tradition where prowess as a warrior in this life overrules any concerns about salvation in a life to come. And, of course, it has its mind-chilling monsters.

While Grendel and his mother might well symbolise the collective unease of a society riven by tribal warfare and sudden death, the monsters of 'Beowulf' are firmly rooted in the real Anglo-Saxon world. The poet tells us that they haunt the marshes and the desolate fens. They emerge from the misty moors and heaths to plague the protective sanctuary of the lofty mead hall, the very best that Anglo-Saxon civilisation can provide yet powerless in the face of the enemy. They come from beyond the pale, the waste places on the edge of civilisation. In Christian terms they are banished, the progeny of Cain. They are the demon exiles come from the outlands, nature's hell.

The landscape that is the lair of the 'Beowulf' monsters is a familiar one to the Northerner who seeks out the wild uplands of our region. When the moors are at their most hostile, on a day when cloud presses like a grave slab, the earth is heavy with trapped water and black, menacing rocks loom out of the mist to confront you - I am reminded of my day on Ingleborough - it is an archetypal landscape of fear. Almost fifteen centuries on and it is capable of drawing out the demons from the shadows of the race memory. Perhaps it was this, set beside its violent history, which triggered my unease at the dark hinterland of Bewcastle. And might it begin to explain the location of this early English cross? The thing to remember is that in its heyday the cross, with its magnificent carvings still fresh from the mason's chisel, would have been painted in bright colours. It would have been like a guardian beacon in this landscape of fear, a vast communal talisman against the besetting evils of the age, against the night terrors of our infant nation.

And yet, despite its sacred cross, Bewcastle could not rid itself of violence and murder. From the twelfth to the early seventeenth century the area was riven by border wars. This is the land of the reivers - in his translation of 'Beowulf', Seamus Heaney calls the monsters 'reivers from hell' - where farms were fortified and pele towers built against Scottish raiders. The pagan war god Cocidius was not so easy to extirpate. And some would say that he still survives into the present day, this time in the most terrifying of all his manifestations.

Take the Roman road - if you can find it - southeast from Bewcastle back towards Birdoswald fort, and where it begins to skirt the edges of Spadeadam Forest close to the Northumberland border, you will see something different on the horizon, something alien. Shuffling up to the dark edges of the forest, all the better to conceal their dark purpose from view, are the concrete silos and block houses of the Cold War. Here is an evil to make the mythical monsters of the Anglo-Saxons seem mere bugbears. It is the nightmare to end all nightmares. The mass extermination of all human kind through thermonuclear war.

Almost as if taking their cue from the indelible print of violence which has vitiated this landscape since man first took up weapons against his fellow man, Spadeadam Forest was chosen, back in 1954, to be the secret site for the development of this country's own medium-range ballistic missile capable of delivering a nuclear warhead. Known as Blue Streak, the missile was an expensive flop. Its failure lay in the fact that the rocket was fuelled with kerosene and liquid oxygen. Because liquid oxygen ices up, the rocket had to be fuelled before it was launched, meaning at least a 15 minute delay after any nuclear alert and hence making it useless as a rapid-response weapon. Because of its vulnerability to pre-emptive strike, the idea of concrete silos for the rockets was developed and RAF Spadeadam was chosen for them. The rockets were tested at Woomera in South Australia but after spending £84 million on the programme it was eventually scrapped in 1960 in favour of the American Polaris missile delivered from British submarines.

The Cold War chill still hangs about Spadeadam. The mouldering concrete installations amongst the dripping pine forests are reminiscent of a scene from a film set in some bleak Central European buffer state on the brink of catastrophe. The whole location whispers secrecy. Bewcastle's echoes of history are deadened by the appalling political machinations behind Spadeadam's philosophy of the unthinkable. Blue Steak may be dead and buried, its rocket parts entombed in museums up and down the country, but the strategy of mass-destruction survives in ever more terrifyingly efficient guise, hidden away in bunkers under the deserts of America or lurking under the seas around our shores. From the shadows of the forest you can hear old Cocidius snickering.

Despite a sense of dread I felt compelled to snoop. If you cross the Roman road near Spadeadam Farm there's a path that takes you across Ash Moss to Dumblar Rigg. These are the bogs and fens of monster country. Startled skylarks rise awkwardly from shocks of pale reeds. Your path is constantly impeded by ditches, spongy with moss where hidden streams chuckle. Dying thistles poke upwards, bruised purple heads broken by the wind. And then some nightmare derelict buildings come into view, bare cubes of slobbering, blackened concrete. A notice warning of some sort of radiation hazard stops you in your tracks. Beyond is a flagpole with a faded red, drooping flag still flying. There are some more modern buildings, huts with camouflaged trucks parked outside. The hum of a generator breaths a sinister sort of life into the scene. What on earth are they up to here now? What skeletons are being resurrected? I half expect an ancient black Wolsey to race up, like a scene out of some crazy old science fiction film, and a grim-faced Professor Quatermass to emerge dressed in a massive overcoat. But nothing happens and I see no one. As I turn away, deterred by the air of menacing officialdom, I'm left with one thought, one that must have run in the brains of our leaders back in the 1950s when this was all built, and for all I know still does: if you've got something nasty going on, stick it up North somewhere out in the wilds and hope no one will notice.

Across country near the east coast another fusion of Dark Age monsters and modern technological nightmares can grip the mind. The North Yorkshire Moors was the first stopping off point for settlers crossing the German Sea. The map is covered with earthworks and tumuli dating back to Neolithic times. In the Whitby Museum a special exhibition features Fylingdales Moor. In 2003 a moorland fire devastated the surface vegetation, exposing boulders covered in mysterious carvings. Some are geometrical, diamonds and triangles and crossed hatchings, others the typical Neolithic cup and ring marks dating from between 3000 and 2000 BC. Surrounded by so many of the museum's ammonites, where millions of years of time are petrified into a simulacrum of the creative spiral, one can't help but wonder if the ring carvings are a crude attempt to reflect an awareness of the same cosmic process. But tramp across the moors at Fylingdales and any such sophisticated notions take flight. This is archetypal monster country, if the 'Beowulf' poet is to be our guide: a desolate sweep of moor and boggy waste in which the superstitious minds of prehistory may have looked to talismanic stones to ward off the threat of evil. And Fylingdales has, like Bewcastle, its Anglian connection. On one of the Neolithic burial mounds, a Christian cross from the seventh century at Lilla Howe, with its own story of Dark age murder and heroic self-sacrifice.

The quickest route to Lilla Howe is to strike out eastwards across the moor from the A169 Pickering to Whitby road at Eller Beck Bridge. The path follows the beck, but it is a treacherous thing, as we discovered, as likely to lead you into some hopeless bog as to your destination. I have an uncanny ability to lose a path, even the most obvious. I put it down to an inherent waywardness of spirit. It often leads to drama and confrontation which the more careful wayfarers avoid. In the case of Fylingdales it is the MOD which the errant traveller is most likely to confront. The parallels with Bewcastle and Spadeadam are remarkable. Only instead of a Cold War flop, if what we read in the newspapers is to be believed, Fylingdales is central to today's early warning missile defence system. Its giant concrete truncated pyramid rises above the Palaeolithic moorland, a brutal watchtower to Armageddon. What progress mankind has made from the Roman signal station at Goldsborough, 10 miles to the north, as the missile flies. What giant strides towards oblivion! We're soon lost amongst the heather which is spiked with bleached reeds, the only indication that we've gone wrong being a sudden unwelcome efflorescence of official notices telling us that we're now in a prohibited area, that we have breached the official secrets act and military bye-laws will be invoked. I anticipate the imminent wail of sirens and the arrival of the goon squad pressing automatic rifles to our heads as we lie face downwards in the grass amongst the sheep droppings. Fortunately, before all this can become a reality, we spot Lilla Howe, a sudden eruption of the bare skyline, its cross shaft rising like a small tower. Realigning our bearings we rediscover the path and another twenty minutes finds us standing on the mound surrounded by a vast sea of empty moorland. Westwards the moor melts into the horizon. Southwest and you can see the Hole of Horcum, like the vegetation-covered crater of some giant meteor strike. Eastwards the sea glints beyond a swathe of pine forest. The cross itself is of grey-green gritstone, the shaft and cross all of one piece but with the arms of the cross broken so that they take on the appearance of ragged, jowled faces, an uncanny echo of the Easter Island statues. But why a Christian cross in such an outlandish places, and who was Lilla?

To answer these questions we can turn to Bede. According to the eighth century monk and scholar, the most powerful early king of the new settlers, the Anglians, was Edwin of Northumbria. Edwin lived in the early decades of the seventh century and his story encapsulates the violence and bloodshed of the age. Conflict raged on several fronts: against their implacable enemies the native Celts, against the British tribes of Scotland and Ireland over border territories, and against their own fellow Anglo-Saxon settlers over tribal expansion and leadership. Despite the advent of Christianity it is a dark period of internecine warfare where the fate of kingdoms is settled by the success or otherwise of individual leaders in battle. Set against this context of bloodshed, the Christian crosses of the period are a poignant symbol of the gulf between the ideal of what we would be and the reality of what we are, between the good and evil of man's nature.

Edwin was king of all the land north of the Humber, which comprised the two Northumbrian kingdoms of Deira and Bernicia which stretched as far north as the Forth. Upon the death of Raedwald in 624, Edwin succeeded him as ruler of the Angles south of the Humber too. But however great his power, in the violent climate of the times Edwin's position was still precarious. According to Bede, the West Saxon king, Cuichelm, sent an assassin to Edwin's court. Under the pretext of delivering a letter he drew a dagger from under his garment and attempted to stab the king. One of his thegns, Lilla, being unarmed, interposed his body between the weapon and the king, losing his life but saving the king's, who was only injured. To commemorate his loyal sacrifice, Edwin ordered the state burial of Lilla in a Bronze Age burial mound with the erection of a stone cross. This is the origin of the cross on Lilla Howe.

Today Lilla Howe is set in hundreds of acres of bare moorland, as I've said. Why should they have decided to bury Lilla so far away from any settlement? According to Bede, the assassination attempt occurred at the king's royal residence by the River Derwent. The source of the Derwent is about a mile away from Lilla Howe to the southeast, but the stream must take a long, meandering course before it reaches any kind of civilisation. Nor has archaeology revealed in the vicinity anything to compare with another royal residence connected with Edwin, at Yeavering, half-a-mile east of Kirknewton in the very north of today's Northumberland. Extensive excavations there revealed evidence of a timber-built hall about 90 feet long, similar to a mediaeval tithe barn. Like the great hall of Heorot attacked by Grendel in 'Beowulf'? But wooden structures have the habit of disintegrating, even without the help of marauding monsters, and the failure to discover the remains of any similar mead hall near Lilla Howe doesn't mean there wasn't one. But we are still left with the appearance of a Christian cross on a pagan burial mound and I believe that the best way of explaining this is again in symbolic terms and the Christian determination to convert the heathen heartland of the North, so dramatically represented by such wild moorland as Fylingdales, soaked in the superstition of monsters and demons and scattered with pagan shrines and the rough magic of inscribed stones. For Edwin himself had converted to Christianity in 627 upon his marriage to Aethelberht of Kent who brought her Roman chaplain, Paulinus, north with her. His mission to convert the

Angles began with the construction of the first church at York on the site of today's Minster and, according to Bede, he baptised people in the River Swale near Catterick, similarly at Yeavering where he washed them in the waters of the River Glen.

But the assimilation of Christianity within the heroic warrior culture of the Germanic people, where honour had to be defended by revenge and bloodshed, was never going to be a straightforward matter. The first thing Edwin did after recovering from the assassin's wounds was to march the full length of the country into Wessex and slay all those involved in his attempted murder, which included five West Saxon kings. Blood will have blood. His wars included the destruction of the Celtic kingdom of Elmet in West Yorkshire in revenge for a kinsman's death, the occupation of the Isle of Man, the invasion of Anglesey and North Wales and the besieging of Cadwallon, the king of Gwynedd. This last venture amply illustrates the saying that those who live by the sword shall die by it. In 633, in retaliation, Cadwallon, with his ally Penda of Mercia and an army of Britons, marched north, slew both Edwin and his son in battle and laid waste the whole kingdom of Northumbria. In recording this, Bede has nothing but contempt for the two British leaders, describing Penda as an idol-worshipping pagan and Cadwallon as only a professed Christian who in reality was utterly barbarous, sparing neither women nor innocent children and set upon the extermination of the entire English race. On the other hand, Bede has only praise for Edwin. His reign of 17 years is 'glorious', the last six years of which he laboured for the kingdom of Christ. It's not difficult to see that the monk is inclined to be partial to the converted Christian and overlook his manifest belligerence. He even goes so far as to insist that under King Edwin the North was so peaceful that a woman could carry her newborn babe across the island from sea to sea without any fear of harm.

The truth seems to have been a very different matter. Life in seventh century Britain, to borrow a phrase from Seamus Heaney's introduction to his strikingly vivid translation of 'Beowulf', was lived 'in an endless cycle of dread'. After Edwin, his cousin Osric rules Deira until, within a year, Cadwallon destroys him. But in the same year, Cadwallon himself is killed. The Christian Oswald rules Northumbria for the next eight years until defeated and killed by the godless Penda. And yes, you've guessed it, Penda is subsequently killed by Oswiu, who then sets about shoring up the ruins of Christianity in the kingdom. Names appear then disappear back into the darkness of the age, washed away by blood. But when a name survives in stone it begins to resonate down the dark corridors of history, vivifying the monotonous catalogue of slaughter and succession. The runic inscription on the west face of the Bewcastle Cross is understood to translate as: '…set up…in memory of Alcfrith a king and son of Oswiu. Pray for his soul.' A victory cross raised to mark the triumph of the North's seventh century Christian warriors against the dark forces of heathenism?

A journey to the northern limits of today's Northumberland is to brush shoulders with the shadows of these brutal and momentous seventh century events. It is also to enter the mists of the dawn of English Christianity. The growth of Christianity may have had a lot to do with the brief periods of peace and security afforded by powerful kings. The newly converted Edwin brought Paulinus to baptise his followers in the River Glen just north of his stronghold at Yeavering in the foothills of the Cheviots. Today, Ad Gefrin, as it was known, reveals nothing of the grandeur of an Anglo-Saxon settlement with a mead hall like the mighty Heorot of 'Beowulf' where the magnanimous leader might dispense gold rings to his faithful warriors. Under the shadow of Yeavering Bell, which rises with unnatural symmetry to over 1,100 feet, here was a settlement that dated back to Neolithic times. On the summit of the hill once stood the greatest of Northumbrian hillforts. But the site of the Anglo-Saxon settlement is on a sandy plateau between the hill and the river. Today they've built a somewhat bizarre stone structure by the roadside. It looks like a gateway and a notice announces, 'GEFRIN, royal township of the seventh century kings of Northumbria'. But the gateway is made of solid stone and there's no way through it. It is as if the constructors were preparing us for the disappointment beyond, because there's nothing whatsoever to be seen. Time and neglect have walled-up the past.

Entering by a wooden gate you are met by a bare pasture of yellowing grass. And that's it, nothing apart from one of those lectern-like notice boards which tells you that here was once one of Edwin's palaces and in 633 he was killed by Cadwallon, his apostate foster-brother who then burnt the place down and spent a year laying waste the whole of Northumbria. Historical antennae twitching, we wandered all over the plateau. Overhead an occasional glider slid eerily by like some huge, skeletal bird, emitting a tortured wail of sliced air. Yeavering Bell sulks, no longer presiding over a place of kings but only of quarrelsome rooks and bare grey skies broken by the brief appearance of a pale sun like beaten tin. It is a disturbingly empty valley, enclosed by a ring of silent hills. It is as if time were saying: 'You've had your share of events, of war and the coming and going of warriors and kings. Now you'll have nothing.' And we found nothing to disturb the bare monotony of the plateau. No evidence of Brian Hope-Taylor's exhaustive excavations in the 1970s of a massive timber hall, apartments for the king and his retinue, a wooden temple and a semi-circular moot area to seat a gathering of 150 people - details which first showed up in an aerial photograph which alerted archaeologists to the site but nothing of which has been preserved; no outlines of the buildings; nothing on which to hang a few poor threads of imagination and dream of men who sought glory in battle and salvation in Christianity; just cold hills and a silent valley and nature going about its endless business, careless of human affairs. Ironically, it is something the Anglo-Saxons themselves might have appreciated. No people understood better the transient nature of human fortune and a strong elegiac element permeates their literature. Take these lines from 'The Wanderer', a poem uttered by one who has lost his lord and his hall and is left to wander the earth in sorrow:

'Whither has gone the horse? Whither has gone the man?
Whither has gone the giver of treasure?

138

Whither has gone the place of feasting?
Where are the joys of hall?'

It seems that a nation riven so by war and its fickle changes of fortune and with such a heavy sense of mortality was ripe for the arrival of Christianity with its promises of eternal bliss.

After the death of Edwin, Oswald took revenge on Cadwallon and began his eight year reign. The Roman missionary Paulinus had fled back to Kent on Edwin's death and in 635 Oswald sent to Iona for the Celtic bishop, Aidan, who came to live at Lindisfarne. Roman Christianity was divided into diocese, but all the Celtic missionaries needed was an isolated site for their monasteries. This is the beginning of the great age of Celtic monasticism in the North. Almost a dozen monasteries were established on islands or close to the shore along the 130 miles or so of coastland between Coldingham, near St Abb's Head north of Berwick, and Whitby. Names like Jarrow, Monkwearmouth and Lindisfarne began to emerge from the sea fret of Northumbrian history and with them the haloed figures of Aidan, Cuthbert and Bede.

But why should the monks of the seventh century have chosen to make their homes on the storm-lashed shores of the northeast coast? Five hundred years later their successors, the Cistercians, were to build their abbeys in the most idyllic and naturally bountiful sites deep inland, fleshpots like Rievaulx and Fountains Abbey. When they first arrived on these shores, the Angles of Northumbria chose the basaltic fortress rock of Bamburgh to establish their stronghold. A sheer rock face provided a defence from any inland attack from their foes, the Celtic tribes, and the sea to the east afforded a means of retreat in the direst situations. Bamburgh became the seat of the rulers of the Northumbrian kingdom of Bernicia. As sponsors of the new religion they would be able to offer protection to the missionary monks. But as Peter Hunter Blair points out in his very readable book, 'Northumbria in the days of Bede', for many years after the Anglo-Saxon invasion, threats of war no longer came from the sea but from inland. The northeast shores would have become a place of safety. Until the nasty and unexpected arrival of the Vikings, that is.

But Lindisfarne, where Aidan brought his monks in 635 to build their wooden church and settle in their wattle and daub huts with roofs thatched with reeds, seems to me like the mirror image of the monastery on Iona from which they came. Each has the slenderest toehold on the mainland, with the wild ocean beating at their door. They seem to me to be the littoral equivalent of the crosses at Bewcastle and Lilla Howe. Exchange open moor for sea, the dry cackle of the grouse for the harsh cry of the seagull, the rush of wind across the wastes for the drum of the waves against the shore, and you are up against the same wild frontier, the same chaotic swirl of mindless and repetitive nature, the edge of the wilderness with all its associations of primal fears and race nightmares. It is no coincidence that the monsters of 'Beowulf' not only stride the moors and fens but also haunt the lakes and meres. Droves of sea-beasts come to attack the hero when he swims after Grendel's mother in the heaving depths of the lake. Moorland and sea fuse in the mind of the Anglo-Saxon poet as he presents the setting for the archetypal terrors which arise from the pagan wilderness. Perhaps the monks were not so much retreating from the world when they chose their wilderness homes as confronting head-on the very thing it was their mission to address: a state of nature, including human nature, without God, unredeemed and beyond the grace of salvation. They were following in the footsteps of Christ himself who retreated into the wilderness for forty days and forty nights to confront the Devil.

There is no wilderness to confront today's visitor to Lindisfarne. When the tide allows, you cross the two mile causeway across the flat and rather dreary dunes and marshes where on my visit the sky was as leaden as the ocean. Traffic is drawn to the narrow causeway from every bed and breakfast along the coast from Berwick to Seahouses, everyone aiming for the narrow time-gap when it's safe to visit the island without getting stranded there by the next tide. Warning signs show a four-by-four submerged to its roof in seawater. These rather cheered me up. The car park on the island soon fills up with buses and coaches and today's pilgrims start to traipse towards the mediaeval monastery or the gift shops and cafes, B&Bs and pubs: rowdy kids and shuffling grans, harassed mums and bored dads. Yes, I'm afraid the crowds have robbed Holy Island of all its holiness. Anyone expecting a mystical or religious experience to come lapping out of the sea or rising from the once-hallowed earth will be disappointed. But you can comfort yourself with the thought that it was always so with places of pilgrimage. Imagine Canterbury when Chaucer's rumbustious pilgrims arrived. And as for the commercialism, didn't the word tawdry arise from the tatty trinkets sold at the shrine of St Audrey?

It was the rich pilgrims attracted to the island that gave the monastery its wealth, commissioning the monks to produce such magnificent works as the Lindisfarne Gospels with their fabulous illuminated pages. I say fabulous advisedly. Look at a picture of the opening page of the Gospel of St Matthew and you'll soon start to notice strange beasts lurking amongst the interlaced infillings of the lettering: animal heads with horns, birds with curling beaks and staring eyes, plumed serpents emerging suddenly from the maze of interlocking, brilliantly-coloured knotwork. Perhaps you need to look no further than these glum-looking beasts trapped within the wonderful ornamental harmony of the Celtic knots and patterns, within the Logos, the word of God, to see the perfect symbol of how the new religion came to control the pagan universe and the chaotic forces of nature.

Unfortunately there are no illuminated manuscripts to dazzle the eye in the small museum on the way to the mediaeval abbey. But once you've handed over your money to the attendant from English Heritage who run the site, there are some lettered gravestones to see with Saxon names carved in runic lettering. There's Ethelhard and Aedberecht, and a woman's name, Osgyth, names written in thin, straight lines which threaten to dissolve but then seem to waver against the pockmarked sandstone, like ghosts striving to return from the grave to stamp their lost personas on our minds: 'Yes, I am Osgyth, and once I was alive like you.'

But we'll never know who these people were, and English Heritage is not interested in telling us. They're more interested in selling us stuff. So over half the museum is given over to the gift shop where you can buy a wooden Viking sword for the children to poke one another's eyes out with, or priory mugs. (Who's the mug?) There are tapestry throws for sale and mediaeval tunics with great red St George's crosses on to delight every football hooligan. And something from the monks: English Heritage Wassail fruity ale with, we're told, 'an underlying happiness'. And if that doesn't make you sick, how about an English Heritage baseball cap? A baseball cap, for the Saints' sake! In mediaeval times when the Church was at its most venal, they used to sell bogus relics. It was known as simony. I think English Heritage have reinvented the practice.

Outside I try to salvage some of the real Holy Island, the Lindisfarne of history where that first guttering candle of Christian faith was lit and kept alive in the storm of savagery and bloodshed. The real luminary of Lindisfarne was, of course, Cuthbert. He followed a generation after Aiden to become prior here in 665, a year after the famous Synod of Whitby brought the Roman and Celtic churches together over the matter of the date for the celebration of Easter which had divided them. Whether the tourists had started to arrive by then, I don't know, but not long afterwards Cuthbert sought the solitude which the monastery couldn't provide by moving out to the nearest of the featureless Farne Islands off the Bamburgh coast where he lived on a rock. Bede tells us that the island was the haunt of evil spirits but when Cuthbert came he ordered them to leave and the island became habitable. He goes on: 'There Cuthbert lived in solitude for many years in a hut surrounded by an embankment so high he could see nothing but the heavens for which he longed so ardently.' (From the Penguin translation of Bede's 'Ecclesiastical History'.) He died in 687 and when his body had been buried for eleven years, in order to place it in a new coffin, the monks exhumed it only to find that it had remained uncorrupted, 'so that he looked as if he were asleep rather than dead'.

On the ridge which looks down upon the ruins of the eleventh

142

century Benedictine priory is where the early Lindisfarne monastery is thought to have been located. Standing there, Cuthbert-like, trying to seek my own solitude, I watched the crowds coming back from Lindisfarne Castle. Time is running out before the tide returns to cut the island off and they're streaming past to their cars like extras from a disaster movie. Soon it begins to get quieter and during the lull some of the atmosphere of the island filters through. The curlews that have left their summer nesting grounds on the high Northumberland moors whistle hauntingly. The breakers on the edge of the bay are a distant murmur. The complaining sea mews are silent. Looking out to sea, the fusion of grey, still water and dove-grey sky conveys a sense of milky dissolution. A dream-like state begins to overtake the mind, displacing the world of people and traffic. Peace, of sorts, descends, and I find myself wondering: What did Cuthbert think about for all those years on his rock in the ocean staring at the sky? Can you spend so much time thinking about God? What is there for the mind to concentrate on? It's like catching smoke. A sense of God - if those moments when the disparate, jarring, baffling universe slips into place and you feel at one with it all, is to be called a sense of God - in my experience, just arrives unannounced with a sudden sunset, an exhilarating landscape. You bump into such moments during the course of life. You can't conjure them up by sitting on a mud floor staring at the sky. Can you? Maybe it was easier then, back in the seventh century, without so much nonsense clamouring away for your attention. So many distractions, so much anxiety. Indeed, my own pursuit of this subject was rapidly overtaken by the thought that there were only 15 more minutes before the tide returned and the causeway was flooded and I would be obliged to spend six more hours here until the waters retreated again. And I'd been warned that all the shops and cafes and pubs shut down. Nothing to do then but think about God and listen to your stomach rumble and feel your tongue dry out. Now that might bring me closer to what it felt like to be Cuthbert! But you'll not be surprised to learn that I was off like all the other lemmings, back across the causeway to the mainland. I had to find out what became of Cuthbert.

143

Durham Cathedral has the remains of Cuthbert's coffin in its Chapter Office, a unique example of Anglo-Saxon carved wood made in 698 to hold Cuthbert's exhumed body. In the sepulchral light, dimmed to protect all the precious objects on display, one can only marvel that these fragments of oak have survived. Some, as big as a foot square, have been reassembled to form the narrow, house-shaped coffin. The wood shines like bronze and the figures carved on it are etched black, as if burnt into the polished grain. They are Christ with the symbols of the four evangelists and the twelve Apostles. Their faces have something of that wistful look of stone Celtic heads but are more expressive, eyes less round and more almond-shaped, with eyebrow lines, some with down-turned mouths, looking decidedly glum in their piety, with none of the joys of the resurrection. And in the lambent, almost golden light of the grain, lightly scratched, emerge the names in Latin of the Apostles, that same spindly Anglo-Saxon runic lettering I'd seen on the gravestones in Lindisfarne. But this wood is somehow more magical than stone, perhaps because you know it's organic and therefore transient. And yet it has survived for over thirteen hundred years. And because you know that a coffin has been in contact with a body, it's all so much more intimate, almost uncomfortably so. In spite of our intensely secular age, Cuthbert's coffin can stir some of that raw sense of wonder that has made it an object of reverence to pilgrims down the ages.

Cuthbert's body is buried behind the high altar of the cathedral. Surrounded by stones polished by kneeling visitors is a vast slab of stone engraved with the simple Latin inscription, Cuthbertus. It has none of the simple impact of the wooden coffin but has been given the full panoply of this mighty Norman cathedral. Four huge pewter candlesticks stand guard at the corners of the gravestone. Overhead is a resplendent canopy showing Christ in glory in blue and red colours and drenched in a starburst of golden rays. Surrounded by a forest of intricately carved pinnacles is a fourteenth century statue of Cuthbert holding the head of Oswald with which he was said to have been buried after the king's head was removed when he was killed in battle in 642.

In sharp contrast is the shrine to the man who brought us our knowledge of St Cuthbert and the history of the arrival of Christianity to the North, the Venerable Bede. At the opposite end of the cathedral to the high altar, west of the nave, in the Galilee Chapel, is a setting of much greater light and air which befits the vision of a scholar whose influence spread far beyond the confines of a North Sea rock to the whole of civilised Europe. It is another hefty slab of stone, this time on a table tomb above which hangs only a single flickering candle. And on the wall beyond, written in beautiful gold letters, some of Bede's own words whose simple power outshines any amount of pious ornamentation.

Bede was born in 673 and at the age of seven began his education at the monastery of Wearmouth. A few years later he moved to the monastery at Jarrow where he was to remain for the rest of his life. During that time this wild, barbaric region of Northumbria, until so recently steeped in warfare and driven by blood feuds and tribal enmity became a focus of Christian enlightenment and scholarship. Two-way traffic between the monasteries at Lindisfarne, Jarrow, Monkwearmouth, Hexham, Whitby and York of scholars and priests exchanging books and manuscripts with other centres of learning throughout Europe, ensured that this part of the North of England achieved a level of scholarly and spiritual distinction unparalleled since that day. One story illustrates the drive of the individuals behind this extraordinary cultural flowering. At Jarrow, Bede's teacher was Abbot Ceolfrith. In the year 716 and at the age of 74, Ceolfrith set off on the long and perilous journey to Rome. With him was a copy of the great Northumbrian Bible intended as a gift for the monks of Rome. It was the painstaking labour of the Jarrow and Wearmouth scribes and artists, containing over 2,000 pages of vellum and weighing over 75 lbs. The book survived the journey and is preserved today in Florence. Ceolfrith did not, but died in France, in Burgundy. Bede's own contribution to this outpouring of scholarship was not only in the compilation of the Bible from many different fragmented sources, but commentaries treasured by scholars through to the present day, his lives of the Saints and his history of England upon which so much of our knowledge of the Dark Ages relies.

To visit the monastic church of St Paul at Jarrow is to run the gauntlet of modern horrors a universe apart from the pious and scholarly world of Bede's day. After emerging from the exhaust-clogged flue that is the Tyne Tunnel, following signposts that appear and disappear like a maliciously grinning Cheshire cat, you pass through a landscape which has still not fully recovered from the blight of nineteenth and twentieth century industrialisation and arrive at something called Bede's World. After Lindisfarne I was not ready for Bede's World. I am still not ready for Bede's World. So we passed it by through a fairly featureless modern park and went straight to the church. From the outside it is a nonedescript Victorian building with soot-blackened stones. Only the ruins of the Norman monastery to the south of the church promises something different. Giant electricity pylons stride past the east window like blundering louts, and through an arch of the monastic ruins you can glimpse the cranes and storage tanks of what remains of the shipyards. Aircraft hang low overhead, returning holidaymakers from cheap flights to Europe. Despite the surrounding trees and the soft cushion of autumn leaves, the roar of traffic is unabated. To imagine this to have once been the hub of Anglo-Saxon monasticism, what Simon Jenkins has called 'early Christianity's most celebrated shrine', is going to require the most serious stretching of the imagination. But step inside the church beyond the nave into the soft floodlighting beyond the modern rood, a wooden carving of a desperately emaciated Christ, and you are at once in the seventh century Saxon chancel. Above the chancel arch is the original dedication stone of 685. It says, 'Dedicated on the 9th of May in the 15th year of King Ecgfrith and the 4th year of Abbot Ceolfrith'. Suddenly, thirteen centuries have unfolded their locked arms to embrace you.

The stones of the chancel are Roman and could have come from the fort at South Shields. High in the south wall, the middle of the three small Saxon windows contains a circle of stained glass no more

146

than six inches in diameter. It is made of fragments of glass assembled from pieces found nearby. It is a rare example of Anglo-Saxon glass-making, a reminder of the flourishing of art and craftsmanship which accompanied Jarrow's outpouring of scholarship. For me, the glass, with its sudden transformation of the grey light from the Tyne beyond into pale yellows, greens and blues, epitomises the enlightenment which the monasteries of Northern England brought to an age of heathenism. It also symbolises the survival of such fragile beauty as places like this, through centuries which brought Viking invasion, the vandalism of the Reformation and the brutal industrial materialism of the past two hundred years.

Jarrow is not alone in its miraculous longevity. Thirty miles to the south, near Bishop Auckland, is Escomb, a rebuilt pit village. Here survives the oldest Anglo-Saxon church in England, dating from the last quarter of the seventh century. Contained within a unique rounded Saxon churchyard full of sycamore trees, it is surrounded by incongruous modern houses with their bright, blank Tyrolean finishes. Raw conviction set against modern pusillanimity. The church building looks like a gaunt barn left behind because some obstinate farmer has refused to go along with the modernisation scheme. But borrow the key from No 26 Saxon Way and unlock the chained churchyard gate, tread through the thick carpet of leaves past the Victorian gravestones heavy with mildew and open the door into the porch, and you enter a world of snapping monsters and twisted foliage as a collection of carved gravestones and fragmented crosses queue up to enter the church out of the Anglo-Saxon twilight. But inside, the church is cold and comfortless, bare whitewashed walls and glum brown pews, plain glass in the stark east window. Long-life bulbs hang from pendant lamps. This is religion pared down to its barest piety, cold, colourless, commanding respect only because of its great age and miraculous survival. Many of the stones are from the Roman fort at Binchester. There's an inscription to the VIth Legion in the north wall, set upside down to ward off evil spirits, a notice tells us. Another tells us that whiskered bats hang from the roof boards - a fact that it was now too gloomy for me to confirm.

147

Despite its cheerless interior, I liked Escomb church. I liked it because of the way it hides behind its trees and tall walls, sheltering from the insipid tidiness of the twenty first century estates, locked within its stern Anglo-Saxon integrity and surviving down the years with the tenacity of the Christian faith itself.

Today it is almost impossible to capture the sense of God our early ancestors must have felt as they stumbled out of the shadows of Dark Age heathenism into the light of Christian revelation. Today our national religion is too worn out, too stale, dare I say, for us to comprehend the shock of the new they must have felt. Time may invest old stones with magic but the down side is that they also become worn and lose their incisiveness as objects of marvel. Journey to Hexham and the cross of Bishop Acca in the Abbey church which may have once dazzled with its painted colours now lurks somewhat disconsolately in a corner of the south transept, the dull surface of the stonework never to be revived by the play of sunlight or its swirling patterns of leaves and fruits never etched by shadows or importunate lichen like the cross in the churchyard at Bewcastle. In fact, the heathen monument across the aisle opposite fares better. Lit by a spotlight in the roof, the Roman standard bearer Flavinus rides his horse over a cringing Briton, his feathered panache fluttering proudly above his head. But in the setting of this Anglo-Saxon church, the glory that was Rome begins to ring rather hollow. Ubi sunt? Where are they now? Just another empire that has passed away. Just a heap of stones to be scavenged.

Carved Roman stones are to be found everywhere in the Saxon crypt at Hexham. Some of the olive-leafed patterns seem as sharp as the day they were cut, not surprising when you consider the crypt lay buried under the church until 1725. But it's not the Romans you think of as you negotiate the steep steps beneath the nave. Here's where the Saxons placed their sacred relics of saints, a central chamber fitted with a stone altar between two ancient piscinae lit by lamps. It's an affecting place - or would be if you could have it to yourself for a few moments. People come clumping down the steps, especially children, rush into the two side chambers as far as the blocked-up staircases at the end and out again. There, done it! There's nothing here! And then they're off, leaving only the smell of acrylic clothes, deodorant, sweat, to mingle with the resident mildew. After all, what does a Saxon crypt have to offer the twenty-first century? I stay to try to answer this question, waiting for a lull in the visitor traffic. It is the end of the tourist season and my moment comes. Conversation from the nave at the top of the steps drifts away. The hollow tolling from the church clock trembles into nothing. And silence steps softly down to sit with me in the half-light.

Do stones remember? Stones which have witnessed bacchanalia, the solemn processing of monks, stones where prayer has picked at their surface and left them mottled with pale, dissolving mortar? Stones that today exhale damply until after a time you feel your breathing shortening as they squeeze the goodness out of the air? Is it the sheer weight of their longevity which suffocates us as they turn their cold gaze upon yet another age, one which surely, certainly, like all the others will one day disappear? Are they here only to discomfit with their message of mortality? Small wonder people rush out of here so quickly.

But it is in the crypt of the church at Lastingham on the edge of the North Yorkshire Moors where a real sense of the spiritual still resides. Bede tells us how the monastery was founded in the seventh century by Cedd 'among some high and remote hills, which seemed more suitable for the dens of robbers and haunts of wild beasts than for human habitation'. Today's visitor to Lastingham may well wonder what Bede was on about when they arrive at the idyllic village in its secluded wooded hollow, so I would advise a stroll to Ana Cross on Spaunton Moor north of the village before a visit to the church. Here is that familiar Palaeolithic landscape of the moors where the vegetation has been cleared off to reveal grey bones of stone and roots of burnt heather reaching up like supplicating fingers. Scattered around are the tumuli of ancient heathens. Upon one of them rises Ana Cross, an assertion of the Christian triumph over the pagan. As Bede writes of Cedd, quoting from Isaiah, he chose

Lastingham because, 'in the haunts where dragons once dwelt shall be pasture with reeds and rushes, and he wished the fruits of good works to spring up where formally lived only wild beasts, or men who lived like beasts'.

If God is to be found anywhere today, it is in the Saxon crypt of Lastingham. As you make your way down the stone steps from the nave above, you are met by a misty glow, an emanation. It is a distillation of candlelight and pale stonework, of sanctity and history. Dozens of night lights prick through the gloom, revealing the tiny aisles, the vaulted roof set upon dwarf Romanesque columns adorned with curling ram's horns, the ammonite whorl, the infinite spiral of creation. And as the candlelight creeps into the shadows of the aisles, the vault reveals the secrets of its past. Saxon cross shafts laced with coiled serpents. A huge cross head with a maze of knotwork. A Viking hogback tombstone with eyes which stare up at you out of the darkness like some monstrous tribal mask. It is as if the whole atavistic world had come to kneel and pray at the shrine of the new religion, to submit to a new order, like the dumb beasts at Bethlehem. Amazement leads you on towards the single lancet window where the nervous daylight blinks, and to the stone altar set on a cobbled floor which conceals the yellow bones of saints.

There's a small rail where you can kneel which contains some lines from T.S. Eliot's 'Four Quartets':

> *'You are not here to verity*
> *Instruct yourself or inform curiosity*
> *Or carry report. You are here to kneel*
> *Where prayer has been valid...*
> *Here, the intersection of the timeless moment...'*

It is such a timeless moment which you may be lucky to experience if you arrive at Lastingham on a late Autumn afternoon and find you have the place to yourself like I did. Without any self-conscious striving - unlike Cuthbert on his rock - but because of some chance coincidence of place and time and yourself being inexplicably receptive to the spirit of the place, you experience a moment when all the nonsense, anxiety and inconsequence of the world disappears and you feel a sense of oneness with Creation. Here you may come face to face with God.

The belfry clock strikes the hour and the spell is broken. I step outside into the afternoon sunlight of the churchyard. A plume of dark smoke is rising from the moors. They're burning the heather and I can see orange flames licking the sky from a great horseshoe of fire. The peace and sanctity of the North's golden age of monasticism is drawing to an end. The Vikings are coming.

6. THE VIKING LEGACY

The entry for the year 793 in the Anglo-Saxon Chronicle announces the arrival of the Vikings in apocalyptic terms:

'Here terrible portents came about over the land of Northumbria, and miserably frightened the people: these were immense flashes of lightning, and fiery dragons were seen flying in the air. A great famine immediately followed these signs; and a little after that in the same year on 8 January the raiding of heathen men miserably devastated God's church in Lindisfarne Island by looting and slaughter.'

The image of the Vikings as godless, murdering monsters whose evil deeds were orchestrated by cosmic turmoil is the judgement of the scribes of the English king, Alfred, the writers of the Chronicle. It is the same view as that of the Church, principal victims of the North Sea plunderers. Bishop Alcuin, at one time master of the monastic school at York, writing from the security of Charlemagne's court, records:

'Never before has there appeared in Britain such terror as we have now suffered from a pagan race. Behold the church of the holy Cuthbert bespattered with the blood of the priests of God, despoiled of all its ornaments, the most venerable place in the whole of Britain prey to the pagans.'

Despite the latterday success of the Scandinavians to redeem their ancestors' image, and nineteenth century artists' and musicians' efforts to romanticise Viking horn-helmeted heroism, it has, until recently, suited our patriotic purpose to side with the Anglo-Saxon

153

King Alfred and continue to view the Vikings as murderous monsters. But today all that has changed. Now, geneticists are keen to prove how much Viking blood runs in modern English veins and archaeologists stress the civilised aspects of Viking life. In his book from the television series, 'Blood of the Vikings', Julian Richards points out that the Vikings were essentially farmers, so fond of their animals, he adds, that they 'invited' them into their farmhouses in the winter to keep themselves warm. And, as if to anticipate the modern Ikea, the Scandinavians were homemakers whose houses boasted the luxury of insulated cavity walls - stones outside, wooden planks inside, and in between lined with moss and grass - snug retreats where they could sit around the fire enjoying stories of their ancestral heroes, stories which inculcated the heroic values of brave adventurism bound by warrior codes of honour and loyalty (The Anglo-Saxon Beowulf, too, let's remember, was a Scandinavian warrior) and must have helped to legitimise their more violent antics. Their skill and undoubtedly highly developed aesthetic sense as builders of beautiful boats like those discovered at the ship-burials at Gokstad and Oseberg can also be cited as instances of their refinement. And, of course, to appeal to the modern fixation for entrepreneurship there is their reputation as renowned traders with a commercial empire the envy of any modern multinational, extending from Greenland to Spain and Byzantium, and from beyond the Caspian Sea to Newfoundland. But there again, to set beside their legitimate trading activities we must place the discovery of sacred reliquaries, gold and silver jewelled book clasps and ornaments, all uncovered at sites in the Viking homelands and damning proof of the Vikings' taste for Christian valuables looted from ransacked and blood-stained British monasteries. So you can take your choice. You can emphasise the Vikings' civilised practices like their craftsmanship, intrepid commercialism and even law-making or else you can remember that they were often nothing more than berserkers - the name given to a Norse warrior who whipped himself into a frenzy of aggression before going into battle - ruthless and murderous plunderers who even by the standards of violence of the

154

Dark Ages were beyond redemption.

But redeemed they are today. A visit to York's Jorvik Centre will take you back over a thousand years to York in the tenth century where they have converted the site of the Coppergate Viking excavation into a warren of Viking domestic and commercial harmony. Friendly young actors dressed in cloaks and tunics shepherd you into your time capsule which takes you along a street of straw-roofed huts where a collection of dirty-faced, jerkily animated, life-size models chatter away in Old Norse. They argue and gesticulate, play, gut fish, smell and, in one Rabelaisian touch, strain away noisily at the toilet. It's great fun, cheerful, sociable and disease-free. And there's not a hint of a trembling monk about to be eviscerated. There have been millions of visitors to the Jorvik Centre since it was opened in 1984. This, it would seem, is how we like to think of our Vikings today. You peer into the passing huts, into the warm, marmalade light where figures crouch over cooking pots or busy away scratching combs out of antlers amongst their cats and stuffed dogs (I reckon when they set this up no domestic pet was safe on the streets of York) and you almost wish you were there. It's the sepia-tinted school of romanticised history which presents life as as cosy and uncomplicated as a weekend camp in the woods with the wolf cubs.

But then the journey ends and you're dumped in the real world of the exhibition centre where some of the harsher realities of Viking life are laid out. In the middle is the skeleton of a six foot two inch warrior, his bones fastidiously marked to reveal each vicious blow that killed him. First there's the chip in his pelvis where his shield failed to deflect a sword blow, then another in his leg. Then on to his skull and the splintered bash to the bones of his face made by the pommel of an iron sword, (where we get the word pommelling or pummelling). And finally there's the slash to the throat that finished him off for good, captured forever in the jaws which are dislocated in a final howl of anguish. Each stage in his lethal and bloody dispatching is carefully, almost lovingly, listed by our guide, a young man who gleefully withdraws first a sword then a dagger from his green baize cloak to illustrate his theme. And if this isn't enough to erase any lingering feelings of nostalgia for ye olden days, there's a display case full of yet more grisly injuries. There's a skull, top scooped off like a boiled egg, a decapitation, smashed pelvises, tibiae and fibulae, and looming menacingly black over all this, the powerful Viking battleaxe responsible for inflicting all this mutilation. And finally, if your appetite for such morbidity is not yet fully sated, there are bones showing the effects of illness and disease: puss holes in legs caused by osteomylitis and deformities of the spine due to spina bifida. Any sentimentality you may have entertained during your journey through the streets of Coppergate is finally expunged. As our guide observed of the life of the warrior skeleton: he could have been married at twelve and may well have been a grandfather at the time he was hacked down at the age of twenty-five, a life to which the epithets nasty, brutish and short hardly begin to do justice.

One of the most startling ideas which the exhibition at the Jorvik Centre introduces us to is the notion that many of us Northerners will have Viking blood running in our veins. Whether that makes us any more prone to violent larceny, prolonged maritime travel or a propensity to attack gentlemen of the cloth, is open to debate, but the facts, according to genetic studies, seem to be that many of us share Scandinavian DNA and that, for example, in the Wirral, in West Lancashire, which the Norwegian Vikings populated via Ireland, it amounts to as much as 50% of the male population. What I find most discouraging about this is not so much that it may confirm a notion that I've long held that the drunken young men who rampage through the streets of our Northern towns and cities on a Saturday night have more in common with berserking Vikings than civilised human beings, but that discoveries like this seem to indicate that history in the future may no longer be left to the passionate archaeologist sifting through the soil in remote and exhilarating places for artefacts that have been touched and used by our ancient ancestors, but become the preserve of laboratory-bound boffins in white coats waving test tubes. I mentioned my fears to one of the inexhaustibly cheerful female assistants at the Jorvik Centre used to firing the imaginations of parties of small schoolchildren. She was not going to allow a few analyses of blood samples to dampen her enthusiasm for real history. She pointed out that any particular genetic signature would, after only ten generations, be mixed with over a thousand others. And after forty generations, from the time of the Vikings, this number would increase to millions. Which, I suppose, is a way of saying to the geneticists, 'We have some Viking genes, so what? By the same token, we've all got some of Adam's genes. It proves nothing except that human DNA is about the most complicated chemical thing on the planet, much of which we share with monkeys and jellyfish or any living creature or race you care to mention.'

It is as well at this stage to distinguish between the Danish Vikings who came across the North Sea to invade eastern England and the Norwegian Vikings who, from their bases in the Northern Isles, were soon striking the Celtic monasteries of Ireland, overwintering and laying the foundations for settlement in Dublin and ultimately the northwest of England. According to the entry for 855 in the Anglo-Saxon Chronicle, the Danes were overwintering on the Isle of Sheppey in Kent. The Anglo-Saxon phrase for the invading army was 'se here' or 'se micla here', the great army. The words come creeping out of the arcane shadows of the past into the half-light of modern intelligibility with their own special kind of dread, a dread that must have been felt in every native English heart at the news of their arrival:

'...on sumera on thysum gere tofor se here, sum on Eastengle, sum on Northumbria.'

With the threat of plunder and bloodshed from their army, the Vikings extorted vast amounts of money from the English leaders in exchange for promises of peace which the Vikings invariably broke as soon as they sniffed the prospect of more silver. So we must now add duplicity to the list of their less endearing traits.

157

As far as the North of England was concerned, the Vikings, under one Ivar the Boneless, captured York in 866. Ivor was reputed to have been nine feet tall and, if this is to be believed, must have stood out like a flagpole at the head of his marauding army. When Ivar defeated the Northumbrians to capture York, one of the English, Aella, was said to have been put to death by means of the 'blood eagle'. This gruesome ritual involved cutting a cross upon the victim's back while he was still alive in order to cut away all the ribs from the spine before removing the heart and lungs. This is butchery in as literal use of the term as you can get. As the amount of plunder to be gained by excursions from their great Danish camps began to run out, the business of permanent settlement began with the annexation of areas of England away from the West Saxon kingdom of Alfred the Great. In 886 the land north and east of a line from Chester to London became what is known as the Danelaw. Yorkshire place names give a clue to the extent of the Danish settlements in the North. Scores of villages where Danes and Angles integrated are indicated often by suffixes ending in -by or -thorpe. Hence Flasby, Thirlby, Thorpe (near Grassington where I terrified myself with echoes from the Celtic Otherworld arising from Elbolton Cave), Fylingthorpe, near Whitby, and many others. Kirkby, as in Kirkby Malham and Kirkbymoorside, is the Danish name for a village with a church. Now these were most likely Anglian churches, often of wood, established before the Viking invasion. But the fact that they were incorporated into Viking settlements could support the contention that I met with in the Yorkshire Museum in York that the Vikings accepted Christianity 'within a decade or so'. Now I find it astonishing that a pagan race that had been the scourge of early English Christianity should so readily have converted to the new religion. Was it a case of guilty consciences? Belated anguish for all those poor monks wriggling away on the ends of their battle swords? It seems to me unlikely that their conversion could have been so sudden. In fact, in the Yorkshire Museum you'll find an Anglo-Saxon cross which has been recut so that the typical Celtic knotwork is replaced by the figure of a Viking warrior holding a sword as big as himself whilst thrusting back a female figure with his other hand. On such an image rests the Viking reputation for rape and pillage, presumably. Elsewhere the iconographic message is not so clear. The museum has three stone carvings said to be the work of a tenth century Anglo-Scandinavian known as the 'York Master'. They are admired for their sharpness of detail because instead of sandstone they are carved in the native magnesian limestone - the stuff of York Minster - which gives the chisel marks a fine, white etching. One shows a 'beast chain', a contorted dragon-like creature whose head is upside down and has huge, staring eyes. It reminded me at once of the beasts that comprise the infilling of the illuminated letters of the Lindisfarne Gospels. A cross fragment contains a 'fettered bird'. There is the unmistakable figure of Christ bearing a dish-like halo but the decorative scrolls are the pure ammonite whorls of pre-Christian carvings. You begin to see how the Celts, Angles and Vikings had so much in common when it came to self-expression through visual symbols, an uninterrupted tradition. Where the Vikings differ significantly is their fondness for including their own pre-Christian Norse mythology upon their crosses and tombstones.

A grave slab recovered from beneath York Minster and now in the Yorkshire Museum shows the Norse hero Sigurd killing the dragon Fafnir. With none of the clarity of the limestone carvings you can nevertheless just make out the figure of Sigurd if you kneel on the floor to inspect the sandstone slab. Wreathed in the knot of the dragon, he is a rather chunky figure raising his sword. The scene above then shows Sigurd roasting the dragon's heart prior to eating it - heroes must have relied heavily upon a high-protein diet. Actually, eating the flesh of dragons was thought to enable people to understand the language of birds and beasts. This ability serves Sigurd well when the birds warn him of the treachery of Fafnir's brother (Fafnir is really a man who has turned himself into a dragon) who is called Regin and is sneaking up on Sigurd in order to kill him. The whole story is told on the Viking cross in the churchyard at Halton, a couple of miles into the Lune Valley northeast of Lancaster.

The church at Halton is overlooked by the gorse-strewn mound of a

Norman motte and bailey castle topped by a rather incongruous gleaming white modern flagpole. Entry to the churchyard is through a lych gate set amongst gloomy yew trees where the chill of last night's frost still lingers. Snowdrops pierce the brash between the trees and are dotted amongst the cheerless gravestones. High above in the sunlight is the church tower, jackdaws perched upon the worn crocketed pinnacles enjoying the warmth. Away from the dismal yews the sunlight is starting to dapple the rest of the churchyard and it's here where you'll find the Viking cross.

Translating the scenes carved upon the two panels in the bottom section of the cross shaft can be fun once you are made familiar with the Sigurd story. First, in the lower panel, there's Regin the blacksmith forging the sword with which Sigurd will kill the dragon Fafnir who had stolen Regin's treasure. The symbols of the blacksmith's trade - much venerated by the Vikings - are all about him. As he wields his hammer you can make out his pincers and the two bellows which fire the forge. Above him is the dragon Fafnir represented by interlocking knotwork. In the panel above, the story moves on. Sigurd has slain the dragon and is roasting its heart. He is in the process of sucking his thumb which he has burnt on the hot meat, though you might be forgiven for thinking he was making a rather rude gesture and raising his thumb to his nose. The immediate effect of tasting the dragon's flesh is visible above, where the birds in a stylised representation of a tree are warning Sigurd of Regin's treachery. For the final outcome you have to return to the lower panel where Regin is shown with his head removed. The story is literally all over the place and you need a good eye, some imagination and a lot of patience to piece together the episodes. A millennium's weathering and the patina of green lichen don't help. And, rather ominously, a nasty flake in the stone of the top panel augers rather badly for the carving surviving much further into its second millennium.

But why should the survival of the cross matter, you might ask, disappointed by the almost childishly primitive depiction of the story? Well, I suppose the answer is, here is one of only a precious few graphic records of a civilisation which, admire them or not, have contributed to the shaping of the North and our Northernness, even if that is mostly in an imaginative rather than material way. It enlarges our perceptions of ourselves, should we choose to consider ourselves as the products of a slow, organic historical continuum rather than creatures who just arrive upon the stage of the present, strut and fret our bit, and then disappear without trace. And the very nature of the pictures, however crude (An early collator of Norse crosses refers to the cross's 'coarse decadence'), begs another important question. What was this fanciful and bloodthirsty narrative doing on a Christian cross? Does it call into question the seriousness of their conversion to Christianity, their piety, that they could include such stuff? Should we judge it as a measure of their spiritual depth, or lack of it? Or would that be as absurd as calling into question the faith of someone today who happens to have his favourite Elvis record played at his funeral? The commissioner of the Halton cross was clearly much moved by the Sigurd story to want it featured on his gravestone. Why? Was it a sentimental hankering for the old ways, the favourite sagas of his childhood, his Norse ancestry, the sort of personal roots to which we all want to return at the imminence of our death? It is the very fact that the carvings excite these sort of questions which touch on the Vikings' humanity, their similarity to us today, which I think makes them important. They may be images which are worn and muddled and clumsily executed but they begin to offer an insight into the minds of our Northern ancestors absent from notions of them as sword-waving monsters. And if their workmanship is regarded as crude, it is because there was no native tradition of cross-carving amongst the Norse settlers. They were copying from Anglian examples of the craft like that at Bewcastle. The Vikings seem to have shown an adaptability uncommon in an immigrant race, not least in their conversion to Christianity. But the retention of outright pagan images in the Christian sculpture is something to look at next. It is at its most puzzling in a section of cross to be found sheltering from the elements in the parish church at Kirkby Stephen where upon entering you are immediately confronted by a pagan Norse devil. Or is it?

A somewhat austere orderliness afflicts the church at Kirkby Stephen. It begins in the roomy churchyard where all the gravestones have been removed to leave bare lawns and the trees which line the path have been savagely polled to a subtopian nightmare of grotesque, arthritic trunks. I don't know when this massacre took place but the consequences, no doubt desired by the tidy-minded authorities, are that not a single fallen leaf litters the approach to the church door. Once inside, the same cold severity extends. The joyless spirit of the Victorian restorers still hangs about the place. Yes, I know it's Lent, but we should be allowed some sense of spiritual uplift in a church whatever the season. Instead, the dark wooden roof presses heavily down, the Norman arches remain stubbornly anchored to the earth and black and terracotta floor tiles convey a dingy austerity. The pews have been arranged in ranks with the formidable precision of a well-drilled army. The clerestory windows admit the winter sunlight only grudgingly while the stained glass east windows are so narrow you'd think colour was being rationed. A quite horrid organ dominates the chancel, its pipes made of some grim, grey metal which is positively industrial. But then, a sudden and unexpected burst of opulence - a pulpit of green and red Italian marble. Nevertheless I can't help feeling that I've stepped into my late grandparents' front room and I must hold my breath in case it fogs the shine on the best china.

But then, at the back of the font, under the church tower, at last a muddle. Behind glass doors where the choir's cassocks droop from their hangers, waiting patiently for Sunday, and the ladders are stored along with a big, yellow cone to warn when the cleaners are busy (Pretty often, I should think), here's what I'm looking for. It's a motley collection of ancient masonry. I can make out a large piece of a Viking wheel cross head, bits of a cross shaft and what looks like a hogback tombstone. But I can't get at them because the glass door is locked and I must content myself with pressing my nose to the glass like a pauper child at a sweet shop. But no matter. I've deliberately saved describing the most tantalising feature of the church until the last. And it's right by the south entrance door. It's a piece of Viking sculpture known as the 'Bound Devil' and the presence and sheer iconographic mystery of the stone has the power to light up the stern formality of its surroundings.

The church authorities will be reaching for bell, book and candle when they read this. The very notion that the Devil could light up their church is probably a sacrilege. Yet it is a tacit acknowledgement of the impact of this piece of Viking sculpture that they have given it the prominent position it enjoys. That it is a depiction of the Devil is open to debate. The stone is about two and a half feet high and is clearly a section of a cross shaft. It shows a human figure with powerful shoulders and large hands hanging limply down, bound hand and foot by a ring of rope. But the most striking and controversial feature is the head. It has round, arresting eyes, a flat nose and a long, pointed beard. He wears a wry, crooked smile. To describe it as mischievous would be accurate and it's this which leads him to be identified by many as Loki, the Norse god of mischief and destruction. And to clinch the diabolical interpretation, he has horns, horns which turn downwards to his shoulders. But those able to pronounce upon these matters, and I'm not one, having only Dennis Wheatley to go by, say that if it is the Devil, his horns should curve upwards. As it is, they're more like ram's horns, which leads them to speculate that they're not horns at all but an attempt by the sculptor to fill the space between the head and the edge of the stone with an ornamental scroll. This being the case, some suggest it is not Loki at all but the figure of Christ, symbolically bound in a struggle with evil. But one thing is for sure, the expression on the face of the Kirkby Stephen stone would suggest to me that he is enjoying all this confusion immensely. The challenging eyes, the wry, impish smile, seem to be saying, 'Well, go on, sort it out. Who the Devil am I?'

It has been calculated that some 115 Viking age carvings are scattered around Cumbria. The most celebrated of the crosses and thought to be the largest piece of pre-Conquest sculpture surviving in

Britain, is the one in the churchyard at Gosforth, two and a half miles inland from the coastal town of Seascale. A slender and elegant structure, carved, astonishingly, from a single stone, it rises to almost 15 feet. The pink west coast sandstone is covered in complicated details of Norse mythology. Figures, sometimes upside down, sometimes at right angles to the cross shaft, wrestle for interpretation, something I can't pretend to provide. Many are on horseback and are belligerently armed. Everywhere curl dog-faced dragons. But, as always with these carvings, the east face of the shaft is reserved for the Christian symbolism, in this case, a Christ-like figure with outstretched arms. The only explanation I can find for this amazing juxtaposition of the Christian with the pagan pantheon is to conclude that here was a period in the development of our Viking ancestors when both old and new religions vied with one another for a place in their spiritual sensibilities. Bede, who hated non-Christian iconography, would have been horrified that 200 years after his death Christianity in the North hadn't progressed further than this.

The church outside, with its strange triple bell-cote which looks as if it has been bolted on Leggo-like to the west gable, is an unhappy late eighteenth and late nineteenth century restoration. But it is full of surprises inside. There are no Lenten or Victorian austerities here. It is one of the cosiest churches I've been in, especially for a cold winter's afternoon. Even though it is a Saturday, the central heating has been thoughtfully switched on and the whole place is carpeted. They are proud to show off their Norse connections at Gosforth. Viking crosses are set into the wall of the north aisle where there's also the famous Fishing Stone. It shows two Vikings in a typical high-prowed Viking boat. Below them in the ocean huge fish teem about the bait, an ox's head. A helpful leaflet from the back of the nave points out that far from being a simple scene of Viking everyday life, the fishing expedition depicts the god Thor with the giant, Hymir, fishing for the wicked world serpent which has grown so large it is overcoming the earth. Above is a hart, trampling a serpent which is said to be a symbol of Christian good overcoming evil. The interpretation offered by the leaflet is typical of what is to be found in churches containing pagan relics. They put a Christian spin on the Norse myths, suggesting that the wily Church fathers allowed the pagan images within a Christian context as a means of weaning their new converts off their old religion while apparently converting to the new as a kind of double indemnity against not missing out on salvation, not an interpretation likely to be much favoured by today's faithful. I recall when visiting the hogback tombstone in the church at Heysham Head being told of the disquiet felt by some parishioners at an essentially pagan monument being allowed inside their place of worship. I have no idea whether there are any amongst the congregation at Gosforth who share such reservations, but two powerfully impressive hogbacks, one measuring five feet in length, occupy pride of place on a specially built plinth at the west end of the north aisle. (One guide rather alarmingly described the plinth as an 'altar pedestal'.) Based upon the shape of a rather thin Viking long house with a sloping roof decorated with a pattern of roof tiles, these houses for the afterlife were uncovered from the foundations when the church was restored during the nineteenth century. The least tall of the two is known as the Warrior' Tomb because it depicts a procession of men with raised spears and shields facing another armed group. They are badly worn. The other stone, known as the Saint's Tomb, shows a figure on either gable with outstretched arms, said to be the crucified Christ but without a cross.

It is difficult to convey the profound impact of these stones. Wedge-shaped and lumpish, they possess a crude, blunt belligerence so in keeping with their Viking origin. Despite their worn, shallow carvings, they have still not been successfully transformed by art, by the human imagination. They retain some of their lithic monstrousness, some of the primal power of standing stones. They arch with a charged, almost threatening natural potency. Compare them with the slender arcade of the nave, stone that has been tamed into an ordered symmetry by the mason's chisel to rise and soar, to express human hopes and aspirations of salvation. But these hogbacks remain firmly rooted in the physical, material world. Even their carvings express the violent, martial aspirations of their age. Whatever you may make of the figures with outstretched arms, there's precious little of the spiritual about them. This is art and spiritual expression in its infancy from a culture still unable to cast off its brutal past. (Look again at the violent images on the cross outside.) The hogbacks are the work of a people who still belong to a darker world. Whatever the gloss the Church might like to put on them, they are still shockingly primitive and pagan.

I have suggested elsewhere how some of the ancient, historical aspects of the Northern landscape seem to accord with the uses to which it has been put today, especially where these uses involve some of the more disturbing aspects of modern scientific technology. So, in the desolate fastness of Spadeadam Forest, redolent of the 'Beowulf' monsters which so haunted the Anglo-Saxon mind, was hatched the modern nightmare of Armageddon in the Blue Streak missile programme. And in the Palaeolithic moorland of Fylingdales with its mysterious Neolithic carvings was constructed that grotesquely sculptured truncated pyramid which is a part of the early warning radar defence system. And here in West Cumbria, I can't help but think that the industry which has dominated and endangered the area for the last half century or more is not out of place on the shores where the first Norse longships landed.

Here at Sellafield, three miles from the Gosforth hogbacks, people routinely handle the most dangerous materials known to mankind. They have drained the appalling energy from the heart of matter and they have created enough fissile material to blow apart our solar system. An awareness of the enormity of what has gone on at Sellafield and the substances which it houses has stayed with me since I was a schoolboy when my parents used to bring me here on holiday to Ravenglass. The first sight of that familiar profile of buildings - today, the round, silver reactor has disappeared - has always felt to me like entering a room wired with explosives. Call me febrile, paranoid or over-imaginative, but that's how it is. Today, as I walk northwards along the wide expanse of empty beach from Seascale, I still feel twitchy, one eye on that tall, infamous chimney like the one (or is it the same?) that spread its lethal plume in the 1957 accident. (We were in Ravenglass around that time, but I can't be sure whether it was the exact day of the leak, just as I can't be sure that my current bad chest is merely the fall-out from a stubborn cold or traces of radioactive caesium.) But in addition to my long-term, over-charged reaction to the nuclear plant, I must now include a heightened sense of a Viking presence. Like the raw potency of the crouching stone hogbacks and the strange but powerful myths of warring men and gods, the whole violent spirit of the Vikings seems to accord with a place dedicated to the splitting of atoms and the release of cosmic forces of destruction.

Today the coastline lies still under a cold blue sky. The low winter sun shadows the ripples in the sand left by the retreating tide. Seagulls have pierced and picked clean every stranded seashell. From the many sea-polished pebbles I pick up a piece of granite, smooth and round as a ball. From its grey and mottled surface flashes of mica dart in the sunlight and I am suddenly thinking of broken atoms again, of scintillating, deadly particles with names which inspire fear: strontium, polonium, plutonium. Somewhere, far out, in a dazzling splash of sunlight, distant breakers burst with a dull roar. Whether the Norse longboats arrived here in the early tenth century on a wave of dread and fear or by then the Vikings were war-weary and were on the lookout for somewhere to settle and lay down their swords for roots, we shall never know. But soon they were fanning out into the Eden Valley and eastwards into the hills and valley heads of old Westmorland and North Yorkshire, places they liked because they resembled their Nordic homeland, somewhere to find peace and acceptance amongst the native Anglian community.

If I were asked to select one place which epitomises that complex mix of factors that add up to the essence, the spirit, of the North which it is the underlying aim of this book to explore, Ribblehead would come close to being my first choice. Foremost, the natural landscape affords an impression of almost boundless expansiveness. Stand anywhere in that sea of shivering reeds and hidden gullies where the water sings, in the shadow of the great railway viaduct, and in whatever direction you look, one or another of the encircling peaks will draw your eye outwards and onwards. To the south, Pen-y-ghent, rising out of the flatlands of the river valley, the combination of mist and light snowfall today giving its solid bulk a strangely transparent, wraith-like quality which makes me think of those dissolving 'cloud-capped towers' from the end of Shakespeare's 'Tempest'. And visible through the great framing arches of the viaduct, Ingleborough, spinning coils of fine cloud around its great gritstone buttresses. Whilst at my back is Whernside, a massive presence felt rather than seen by the cold breath exhaled from its bare, gully-wrinkled flanks. Or it may be one of the other heights which draws you away, of Plover Hill or Dodd Fell to the east or Cam Fell where the Roman road sets bravely off over the fells to Bainbridge fort.

For it seems to me that a way of looking at this idea of North which helps to explain its physical and emotional impact, is to strip it to its cardinal element of a compass needle, forever pointing and drawing you onwards to its own mysterious magnetic core. For the Northerner like me, other places don't seem to have this quality. They seem content to be embedded in where they are. Go to the flat east and you can seem almost shrunken to the spot by the vast pressure of so much open sky. And south? Well, south, certainly the southeast, is the complacent centre of the known universe from where its dwellers wouldn't dream of removing. But to feel the pull of the North is to feel an expansion of the spirit, a sudden liberating sense of freedom, like a prisoner casting off his shackles. When I lived for a while in London, I recall the journey back home from Euston station. There's a tunnel at Borehamwood from which when the hurtling train emerged I always felt a surge of release, like a bullet from the muzzle of a gun. This was the point where the terrible claustrophobic weight of the city, the conflated mass of humanity, seemed to fall off and I was propelled at last upon my exhilarating trajectory north. I wonder if this is like what astronauts feel when they finally break the bonds of the earth's gravity, when they suddenly become a part of stellar space? I imagine that once you have sampled it you never want to return to earth. Just as, once you have been amongst them, you never want to leave these hills and they forever tug away at you all your life, ever in your waking dreams.

The railway at Ribblehead is to me a symbol of that restless reach of the spirit which the Northern landscape inspires. Conceived by the Victorians it was constructed with an almost hubristic disregard for the difficulties presented by the mountain terrain through which it passes. Impelled by the impulse to follow the magnetic needle, the irresistible lodestone, the line was driven through rock, bog and cloying clay left undisturbed from the great ice ages. Taking six years it lost over a hundred lives and hundreds more must have died prematurely through the sheer physical punishment of the work and hostile climate. The viaduct at Ribblehead, with its 24 massive arches, is like a leap of faith, an emblem of Victorian self-belief and confidence to defy and defeat nature. It epitomises the North of England's massive investment in human muscle which made it the powerhouse of the industrial age. Today, despite the small but steady traffic of diesel trains, it stands as much a monument to a lost age as Hadrian's wall or the standing stones and henges of Neolithic Yorkshire.

People have always been drawn to Ribblehead. From the first hunter-gatherers who trekked west from Malham Moor or sheltered in the caves of Attermire, to the Brigantes who built their forts on Ingleborough, all the better to sledge the passing Roman armies, and right down to the navvies who came in their thousands to live in the shanty towns of Batty Moss and pioneer the railway. Today, people are still coming. Rarely a day passes, whatever the weather, when there aren't cars parked along the verges where the Horton and Hawes roads meet. And at the weekend it's often chock-a-block. The permanently stationed snack cabin is a tribute to its popularity. What do they all come for? Many just seem to stand there, warming their

169

hands on their cups of tea and gazing out into the landscape. Others set off and are rapidly absorbed into the wilderness. They are all Northerners, at least in spirit, stirred like so many iron filings by the ineffable magnetism of their surroundings, reaching out in his or her private way to the quietus which the place affords. And, if they are like me, they are also responding to that other quality which defines the spirit of the North: a sense of history, of human continuity which pervades the landscape and peoples it with the ghosts of our ancestors. For, like all the others, it wasn't long before the Vikings found Ribblehead and liked it enough to settle here.

In all my emphasis on the brutality of the Vikings, it is easy to forget that they were principally farmers before they took to the easier option of sacking monasteries and extracting ransoms with menaces. I'd heard of a Viking farmhouse found at Ribblehead at Gauber High Pasture from the exhibition in the Yorkshire Museum, so, armed with a map reference, I set out to find it.

My instructions were to follow the English Nature waymarked trail round the old limestone quarry just to the west of Ribblehead station. It was my first venture out of a new year following a seemingly interminable period of heavy rain and I blinked at the sun as I would a forgotten acquaintance. As I approached the quarry a kestrel swept low over my head on an arc as pure and clean as any ice-skater's. His plumage was the soft chestnut colour of the sunlit reeds on the surrounding fells. I took it as an omen that the day was going to be full of quiet surprises. The quarry, as I've mentioned before, is a sort of experiment by environmentalists to recreate the colonisation of bare, ice-scoured limestone landscape after the last ice age. Saplings have been planted but seem to have made scant progress in over a decade. Despite a notice promising various new colonists, on this January day there was nothing to suggest that nature was in any hurry to readopt the quarry. Bleak pools milky with lime dust swallowed any colour from the sky. The rest was grey mud and broken stones, reminiscent of those settings from old Dr Who programmes when disused gravel pits doubled for alien planets. But what more can you expect from Ribblehead in January? The waymarkers, bleached wooden posts with small squares of green paint that was already fading, take you on an eccentric tour of the quarry bottom before crossing an area of shattered rock and rising to a gate at the quarry's southern limits. Then the misery of Malham Moor returns. We're onto an extensive area of limestone pavement which makes the discovery of the remains of human habitation almost impossibly difficult. I wander around for close upon an hour, harbouring a conviction that the powers that be - the archaeological world that discovers these places or the public bodies that are supposed to be dedicated to encouraging our interest in our history and environment - don't really want us around, we, the great unwashed, troublesome people disturbing the wildlife, trampling over historical remains. Unless they can install a gift shop and make some money, they'd rather have us somewhere where they can keep an eye on us on a Saturday afternoon, out of harm's way spending money at the Trafford Centre or else shouting our socks off at a football match, not wandering at will with our big feet over their precious countryside. Cynical? Well, I was getting cold. At first, in my joy at being outside again, I'd not noticed what a cold wind it was creeping down the valley and into my bones. Wandering around disconsolate limestone pavements, peeping into grykes and thinking dark thoughts, I needed shelter. Maybe lunch at the Station Inn half a mile away? And then I thought again. Shelter. That's it! If I was a Norseman looking to build a farmhouse, I'd want it in the most sheltered spot I could find, out of this nasty wind. And the only place that fitted such a description was over there, up-wind towards Ingleborough, just at the edge of the pavement where a low ridge not more than 15 or so feet high lay. At last, I was thinking like a Viking now, not like a stupid, cosseted modern with his hand on the central heating switch. I walked over there, felt the cold wind lessen, and was immediately rewarded with the sight of the remains of a long, narrow building, walls about two and a half feet high of stones welded together by moss. I felt triumphant, sat inside one of the walls, and offered thanks to Odin, god of ancient wisdom.

There are three buildings: the farmhouse, more than 20 yards long, and two smaller outbuildings on the Ribblehead side of the farm building. According to Alan King, whom I understand to have been the farm's discoverer and I know to be a man undaunted by acres of limestone pavement when it comes to recognising historic settlements here in the Dales, coins, a spearhead, iron knives, spindle whorls and grindstones or querns were all uncovered here. Today, the thick grass and moss have covered the site and it's well on the way to being absorbed into the anonymity of the limestone landscape. It's poignant to see how precious little is left of the lives of these settlers who made their homes here, grazed their cattle and sheep, grew their grain and spun their woollen cloth, and enjoyed the peace of these empty hills; just these ruined walls wrapped in their shroud of moss and broken bents, the rest, their passions, hopes, fears, all that imbued the spirit of these restless adventurers, brutal plunderers and ultimately peace-seeking farmers, lost, absorbed into the massive indifference of this unchanging landscape.

But a more permanent legacy of the Vikings is to be found if you leave the Ribblehead farmhouse alone and cross the Roman road and take the track under the viaduct to Gunnerfleet. Armed with an OS map, you will discover the Vikings are still alive in the names of the places and features of the landscape around you.

At Gunnerfleet there's a modern farm enjoying the same protection from the elements in the valley bottom as the Vikings sought over a thousand years ago. Gunnar is a Norse name. Whether 'fleet' makes reference to the fast-flowing stream that passes close by, I'm not able to say. To judge from the sound of cattle and sheep coming from the large wooden sheds that surround the farmhouse, stock is herded in here to afford protection from the worst of the winter weather. Just to the north of Gunnerfleet farm is Winterscales, -scale being a Scandinavian suffix denoting an outlying farm, indicating the practice of choosing these sheltered locations for wintering stock back in Viking times, too. Beyond Winterscales, high on the flanks of Whernside, is Greensett Moss, named from the Old Norse word saetr, the name given to the spring grazing grounds or shielings. And the linguistic legacy of the Vikings here is even more fundamental.

The words beck, rigg, scar, force, fell and moss, all features of the Northern hills which we are familiar with today, come from Old Norse words. The Viking settlers really made these hills their own. Where would the descriptive language of our Northern landscape be without them? Alan King has calculated that in the district between Settle and Sedburgh, between 60 and 70% of the place names are of Norse origin.

I make the round trip from Gunnerfleet to Winterscales and up to Blea Moor signal box then back down the stepped path before returning to Ribblehead. The fields are full of rooks whose shining black feathers have caught the winter sun. The sun is turning hard and cold like platinum as it sinks into the valley, notched briefly in the western buttress of Ingleborough. Ash and sycamore trees hang by the river, their trunks pale and bleached. One ash tree has clung on to its keys and holds them out to the sky like brown, tattered rags. On the lane to Winterscales the moss is choking-thick upon the dry stone walls, vivid green against the limestone blotched with powdered white lichen. Somewhere on the heights of Whernside the distant wind roars restlessly but down here everything is calm. Winterscales is as near today as you'll get to a Viking farmhouse. There may be a tradesman's van outside and some ladders where a man is fiddling with a satellite dish, but forget the facile frills of modernity. The basic things haven't altered. It's the same essential location, with sheep sheltered in the winter shielings by the river under the snow-clad flanks of Whernside. There are the barns for winter fodder (I saw none of those blights of modern agriculture, the hideous silage bags like giant shiny, black maggots). And the same basic rule applies: keep your stock alive and they'll keep you alive. The farmer may be up and down the lane in his Land Rover but I suspect he may be nursing the same genes as old Gunnar.

Beyond Winterscales the outlying farms are all tumbled, exposed roof-beams bowed and thin with worm and weather. Next to the river there are sudden astonishing outbursts of rock, ragged like giant drawn teeth. After weeks of rain the ground sops. Moles drown. Stoical sheep make a meal of nothing. Trying to negotiate these becks and mires (another Norse word) I feel I'm walking in the footprints of Gunnar. A figure moves in the bleak signal box at Blea Moor but no trains pass. Nothing disturbs this hiatus in time, this silence between the slow heartbeats of the hills. The sky sinks back after the day's sun into a sulky greyness. Briefly my kestrel returns in switching flight across the valley before threading an arch of the Ribblehead viaduct and disappearing northwards. It has been a good day, an afternoon indeed of quiet surprises. And the sort of peace the Vikings themselves must have at last enjoyed.

7. The Middle Ages. Power and Piety.

There couldn't be a greater contrast than that between the mountain landscape of Ribblehead and the flatlands south of York. But they are linked. First, by the River Wharfe which begins its journey eastwards high on the slopes of Oughtershaw Side close to the Roman road which climbs the fells from Ribblehead to Bainbridge fort, and ends by spilling into the Ouse near Riccall between York and Selby. And there's an historical connection too, so far as our Viking narrative goes. For it is at Riccall that events that were to put a stop to any further Viking settlement of the North began to unfold. In September 1066, King Harold Hardrada of Norway sailed up the Humber with a fleet of 300 ships and anchored at Riccall, ready to play his part in a conflict which was to end a month later with England in the hands of the Normans and devastating consequences for the North.

I went to look for where this giant fleet which could have carried as many as 10,000 fighting men would have been moored on the Ouse at Riccall. The first villager we met pointed across a huge field to where the river was hiding in the flat landscape. We set out uncertainly. No peaks here to draw the eye or lift the spirits; nothing to relieve the pressure of the huge sky which challenges any presumption that we dare reach out to relate to any of the landscape, but merely leaves you feeling shrunken, insignificant and directionless. The only reference points are transient human features: a water tower, a sail-less windmill, the skeleton of a disused greenhouse, and on the horizon, the squat spools of the power stations, Drax and Eggborough, reeling out ribbons of steam that merge into the overwhelming grey sky. And the villages seem to shrink under this pressure too, contained as they are by the territorial aggression of an agriculture which has allowed the fields to grow so large and featureless they seem to rival the sky itself in depressing anonymity. For an early afternoon it is oddly silent too, as if land and sky lie so tightly together they endeavour to squeeze out all sound. Until a police siren starts up, sharp, fretting pulses of sound growing closer before suddenly stopping. And then a skylark rises close by and, fluttering like a moth, spills bright slivers of song that pierce our hearts.

Still no sight of the river. But then we come across a girl taking her dog for a walk, a tiny baby strapped to her breast, cocooned in a fluffy, white babygrow. Yes, the Viking fleet was moored over there beyond that stile, she tells us, as if it had all happened yesterday.

And here's the river, the Ouse, 60 or 70 yards across, the current flowing thick and fast. A heavy task to row upstream today, so maybe a good place to quit, moor up and march. The surface of the water is smooth and unbroken but swirls and eddies give a sense of power, like skin tensing with the stirring of underlying muscle. Where the river has flooded it has left small lakes and meres full of drowning willows and sharp explosions of reeds. The trees lean in their flooded swamps like a primordial forest. The catkins are swelling into silvery life in their own fluffy babygrows. Early daisies are out before the celandines at the water's edge. Mating mallards flap around anxiously and power overhead in panicky flight.

We can only guess why Hardrada's army moored their fleet here and set out for York on foot. All we know is that the Viking army engaged the English - or should that be Anglo-Danes? - under the Northumbrian earl, Morcar, at Fulford, two miles south of York and defeated them on the 20th of September, 1066. It is said that as many as a thousand of the best English troops were killed as well as a 100 of the clergy from York. The notion of the clergy taking up arms is one that can only be received with astonishment by the modern reader. However, it must be remembered that the English raised their armies, or fyrds, by enlisting the support of local citizens and there seems no reason to believe that this would not include the clergy. Besides, as history has shown, the Church had most to lose at the hands of the plundering Vikings. So not much room for turning the other cheek in eleventh century England.

Hearing about the English defeat at Fulford and the subsequent capitulation of York, the second protagonist in the events of the autumn of 1066, King Harold of England, set out northwards, postponing his plans to confront the weather-stranded fleet of William of Normandy as soon as it crossed the Channel. In a strike that made lightning seem slow, he and his army marched north in only four days, taking on the might of Hardrada at Stamford Bridge, eight miles east of York, on the 25th of September.

Stamford Bridge is a most sorely neglected site when you consider the part it played in the events which culminated at Hastings in the loss of the English kingdom to the French. The first thing that you notice when you leave the village and walk to the site, known as Battle Flats, is how a rash of modern housing development has been allowed to encroach. Moreover, the rest of the site has been commandeered by agribusiness. Spring wheat and rapeseed fields stretch before your eyes in all their mundane glory. I don't know what the plough has turned up over the years but it's known that unlike the English who buried their dead, the Vikings left their soldiers where they had fallen. Pylons march across the battlefield and there's the embankment of a disused railway. Everywhere, the imperatives of the moment have been allowed to smother our history. The pathos of neglect hangs heavily over Battle Flats. Not agricultural neglect, I hasten to add, for the hedges are neatly trimmed, the Keep Out signs freshly painted, the shoots of wheat and rapeseed laid out with military precision. Like flags of truce, white bags have been pegged out across the land, the purpose of which defeated me unless they were there to scare off scavengers, the bane of battlefields. Cars hurry past on the B-road. There is nothing I could find to indicate that here is a stage where once one of the great acts of history was played out. No curious archway here like that which announces the Northumbrian township of Ad Gefrin at Yeavering. Nothing to stop us, however briefly, in our tracks and jump-start the imagination, help us to ponder some of the grim realities of our history. For example, those injuries to the skulls and bones in the Jorvik Centre's collection of gruesome relics were inflicted in just such a battle as this, delivered by the blunt iron pommel or the grim blade of the black battleaxe - mortal injuries which must have led to the agonising loss of blood, the defenceless, abject dysfunction of those broken bones, so that all the victim could do was lie there appealing to a mercy which it seemed had fled the earth, before dying horribly. (Is it our reluctance to face up to the horrors of war that leads to our failure ever to put a stop to it?) And on another, some would say more fanciful level, does such collective horror as these battles entailed leave an imprint upon the landscape? Do the residents of Battleflats Way wake up in the night screaming? Is there a great welt, a bruise of psychic energy, left behind to haunt succeeding ages should they stop to think too precisely on such events? Perhaps this is why we prefer to hurry past and leave no monuments, let time heal. But time doesn't heal, not if you're an inveterate picker of historical scabs like me.

Back in the village no traces remain of the bridge where, according to the Anglo-Saxon Chronicle, an unnamed Viking hero held the bridge 'so that the English people could not cross…nor gain victory' until an Englishman came underneath and 'stabbed him through under the mail-coat'. Today, the river hides behind substantial properties, an old mill converted into exclusive apartments, gardens where willows weep like widows, trailing their flaxen hair over the river. The water is grey-green and the afternoon light dances on the rippling surface. Downstream a weir thunders like a distant battle roar and spindrift of broken water rises from it like a ghost, soon to evaporate like all the ghosts of Stamford Bridge.

Outside the public toilets on the main road, local schoolchildren have decorated the walls with a rogues' gallery of the English and Viking leaders of the battle - as good a use for a toilet wall as I've seen. Harald Hardrada was killed in the battle and so was King Harold's renegade brother Tostig who had sided with the Vikings. Of the 300 boats that had arrived at Riccall only 20 could be manned in retreat. As every schoolchild knows, Harold was unable to repeat his Viking success against the Normans when he returned south and fought at Hastings on the 14th of October. It could be argued that

Harold's army and the English forces he might have mustered against William were sadly depleted by the fighting at Stamford Bridge. Yes, the defeated king would have raised a fresh fyrd on his march back south, but his crack troops, the housecarls, must have suffered debilitating losses against the Vikings. In this, perhaps, lies the significance of Stamford Bridge.

But the Vikings hadn't done with us yet. A year after the Conquest, in 1067, the Anglo-Saxon Chronicle tells us that King Swein of Denmark arrived in the Humber with a huge fleet. It was this persistent determination of the Vikings to plunder and colonise which was to have the most devastating consequences for the North. For the new king, William, put into effect a scorched earth policy in a deliberate effort to make the North unattractive to any would-be settlers. Allied to this was the need to quash the rebellion of the North's Anglo-Danes against their new masters. As the Anglo-Saxon Chronicle records for the year 1068:

'Here in this year King William gave Earl Robert the earldom of Northumberland. Then (1069) the local men came against him and killed him and 900 men with him. And the Aetheling Edgar (the exiled descendent of the West Saxon kings, who had his own claim to the throne) then came to York with all the Northumbrians, and the men of the market town made peace with him. And the king William came from the south with all his army and ravaged the town and killed many hundreds of men; and the aetheling went back to Scotland.'

The period between 1069 and 1071 is referred to as 'the Harrying of the North'. William's success in reducing the North to ruin is recorded elsewhere throughout Yorkshire in the Domesday Book. Villages and land which before 1066 had flourished are described by 1086 as being laid waste. Take Wensleydale for example:

'In Middleham are 5 carucates to the geld (The carucate is a measure of ploughland for the purpose of geld or tax), and there

179

could be 3 ploughs. Gillepatric had a manor there (before 1066). *Now Ribald has it, and it is waste.'*

And:

'In Leyburn are 7½ carucates to the geld, and here could be 5 ploughs. Eskil and Othulf had 2 manors there. Now Wilhomarc has them, and they are waste.'

And so it goes on. Even William himself on his deathbed was said to have been remorseful for the miseries his armies had inflicted upon the North. The appearance of Halley's comet prior to William's arrival did indeed turn out to be a bad omen.

But if the peasant smallholders found their ploughlands ravaged to ruin, what of their landlords, the English aristocracy? It has been estimated that only 8% of the English thegns were left holding land by the time of Domesday. The rest was lost to the Norman barons. Many of the English fled to Scotland or abroad or had simply lost their lives on the battlefield.

William's inventory of his conquered kingdom, the Domesday Book, does not even bother recording the vast tracts of Northern England outside the rich flatlands of Yorkshire and a few parts of Lancashire. There's no way of knowing how the momentous events of 1066 may have affected the likes of Gunnar, quietly minding his sheep on the windswept slopes of Whernside. I should imagine the great sweep and tide of history, of politics and the machinations of princes, made little mark on the remote highlands of Northern England. Just as the Brigantes before them had thrived in their high isolation, so the Viking settlers got on with their business under their one master, the seasons. It's the beauty of the North, even today, that there are places where you can get by, if you choose, tucked away from all the madness of the world, and still find yourself alive, heart and soul, to the joys of your surroundings.

A measure of the Norman military dominance of their newly-won territory was the arrival of their castles. Initially of wood, they soon became the formidable stone keeps set upon mounds and surrounded by defensive enclosures: the motte and bailey. We've seen at places like Brough and Bewcastle how the stones from Roman forts were reused to build such castles. The comparison with the Romans is a handy one as far as the North is concerned. Here, with the Normans, is a new army of occupation, taking over dangerous frontier territory where the threat of insurrection was rife. The castles were initially barracks for fighting men, just like the Roman forts. The appropriation of land and demolition of homes to build these castles and fortify their surroundings must have been a source of bitter resentment to the native population. But the Norman barons who took over England were military adventurists, the lands they received being the spoils dished out by their grateful commander-in-chief, William. Moreover, the kingdom's wealth was now concentrated into much fewer hands so the barons were exceedingly wealthy. They could afford to build dauntingly impressive strongholds. Here they surrounded themselves with their retinues of professional fighting men, many of them cavalry and all needing to be housed, fed, watered and entertained in between sallying forth into the surrounding countryside to strike terror into the hearts of any local who dared so much as to even think of stepping out of line. Amongst these were the knights, but knights before any notions of chivalry and rescuing damsels in distress had appeared, that is, before the concept of knightly courtesy. It's tempting to see them more as a bunch of arrogant arriviste louts who today would be barging about in giant four-by-fours with blacked-out windows and chrome bull bars, swaggering male chauvinists shoving their snouts to the front of every trough. Thatcher's children, some might say.

I hesitated before dwelling on these Norman castles, symbols of military repression and exploitation, when there are more positive aspects of Norman culture to explore, such as their church and monastic buildings. But my aim in this book is to explore many of the exhilarating and inspirational features of our Northern landscape and its history, and it would be hard to ignore the romantic appeal of the mediaeval castle. So I went to examine a couple of them.

Richmond Castle is the ruined Norman fortress begun by Alan Rufus in 1071. Alan was from Brittany, a relative of William the Conqueror, who had led the Breton contingent at the battle of Hastings and was rewarded by becoming one of the foremost landowners of the new regime. He crops up, as you'd expect, in the Domesday Book and his share of the plunder is prodigious compared with your average entry:

'Count Alan has within the jurisdiction of his castle 200 manors…In all there are to the geld 1,153 carucates of land. (There is) land for 853 ploughs.'

After the Conquest as much as a quarter of the country was held by only eleven men. It is no wonder that such consolidation of power within Norman hands required extensive military fortifications to stifle any native resentment.

The keep at Richmond dominates the town, its square walls rising to a height of a 100 feet. It is a brute statement of physical supremacy. So are the massive stone walls that enclose the triangular great court within. And to the south the castle stands impregnably on a bluff, beetling over the fast-flowing Swale hundreds of feet below. This is everything you could ever dream of a mediaeval castle being, but it is underpinned by the harsh realities of the politics of power. Nature has done its best to soften the severity of the stone walls. In places it is so flaked with weathering it is like millefeuille. Elsewhere it has been invaded by stonecrop, mauve ivy-leaved toadflax just coming into flower and wallflowers, living up to their name. But in the walls to the east side of the courtyard are dark cavernous doorways. One leads into a rare surviving eleventh century chapel. No more than 12 feet long and 9 feet wide, it is a church in miniature, with a round window at either side of the altar arch. It is a reminder that Norman strength was allied to religious piety. Here too are the domestic buildings, the Rufus family's living quarters, known as Scolland's Hall, one of the oldest surviving Norman domestic interiors in England, built in 1080. Even today without its roof its grandeur is evident. A two-storey building, the great hall is on the first floor above an undercroft and occupies almost the entire length of the 80 foot block. It is lined with arched windows and is where the family dined at their high table, set upon a dais. Behind them was a door which led into the solar where the count retired to sleep. The opposite or low end of the hall contained the main entrance where the servants brought food and drink from the kitchens in the castle bailey.

When imagining the scene in Scolland's Hall as the count and his family sat down to dine, it is interesting to reflect that the Norman invasion force of 1066 was only between 10 and 20,000 strong. They were serviced by native slaves. These were the people who provided them with their food, grazed sheep (Old English sceap) and cattle (OE cu), reared pigs (OE swin) or shot deer (OE deor). But when these foodstuffs arrived at table they had been transformed into mutton (Old French moton), beef (OF boef), pork (OF porc) and venison (OF venison). This is a linguistic legacy of the invasion and the feudal class system it brought with it. To be fair, the English did have slaves themselves before 1066, but it was the Normans who refined the system of slavery into the divinely ordained social order of lord and vassal which it became, something, it could be argued, that lived on in England for another 900 years and can still be detected curling its privileged lip in some of our hallowed institutions to this very day.

If you leave the hall by the gatehouse to the east you enter the Cockpit, a garden area now laid out with cobbled walkways between yew hedges. There are fine oak seats where you can sit and watch the sunlight dancing on the waters of the Swale down below and reflect, despite its ruined walls, upon the solid permanence of the castle and the Norman contribution to our English heritage. They brought a European culture not just reflected in their culinary vocabulary and a whole new Latinate language to enrich our own but also in a new architecture. They brought their churches and monasteries, a concentration of power into the hands of a few mighty landowners and a sense of hierarchy which, however subordinate it made the vast majority of the population, somehow suited the conservatism of the English temperament, for no popular revolution seen in other European countries has ever arisen to overthrow it. After the Harrying of the North by William we settled down under our new masters and within a 100 years intermarriage between French and English was fashioning a new nationhood.

Legend tells of an underground passage from Richmond Castle to Easby Abbey a mile downstream. This is probably the site of an Anglo-Saxon minster with a community of priests serving the surrounding area. Evidence of this was discovered when fragments of an early Northumbrian, late seventh century, cross were found within the walls of the nearby parish church of St Agatha. When reassembled it showed Christ and 11 apostles with fine carvings of beasts and convoluted vine scrolls. This now stands in the Victoria and Albert Museum in London, having been replaced by a truly vile replica. Standing close to the altar, it looks to be made of some sort of plaster painted in a milk chocolate brown colour. It is an excrescence which demeans its surroundings, especially when you view the chancel wall-paintings, much restored but from the thirteenth century and showing biblical scenes as well as scenes from mediaeval rural life. The agricultural activities follow the seasons of the year. For spring there's a peasant scattering seed and being pursued by a hungry rook and a woman pruning a tree. Winter shows a bearded fellow digging, He's wearing rather fetching boots with tulip-shaped rims. It must have been rather comforting to the peasant congregation to find their humble activities elevated to the same level as the stories from the Bible. But I think I spot a clever reason for this. Nearby is the most dramatic of the didactic Bible stories - they were, after all, to instruct an illiterate peasantry - the expulsion from the Garden of Eden. God and the angels are twice the size of Adam and Eve and are dressed in lavish coloured robes. In contrast, Adam and Eve are small, pale and almost doll-like in their nakedness. A distinctly androgynous Eve offers Adam an apple before they are driven away by an angel bearing a flaming sword. In

184

the final scene, Adam delves and Eve spins while an angel stands over them pointing rebukingly. And so the point is made. It is original sin which consigns the peasants to their lives of seasonal drudgery. Just where the other painted scene of a gentleman prancing along on horseback with a hawk in his hand fits into the divine scheme of things has vexed egalitarians ever since.

Just as castles like that at Richmond dominated the political horizons in the wake of the Conquest, so the arrival of Norman churches and monasteries began to dominate the spiritual landscape. Saxon churches were pulled down and replaced by many of the structures we still see today. At Easby Abbey the Saxon foundation was taken over by Premonstratensian canons from the abbey of Premontre near Laon in France. What they built in its place was impressive, particularly the refectory building whose walls still stand with their high arched windows, their edges ragged with the remains of shattered tracery. It's a two-storey building with a row of central pillars only the bases of which remain and a 20 foot high east window whose tracery still survives, rising dramatically above the high table where the abbot dined. It is the ecclesiastical brother of Scolland's Hall in the castle further upstream and is so grand you would be forgiven for thinking it was the abbey church and not just the dining room. It's not thought that this belongs to the original foundation of 1152 because extensive rebuilding occurred during the following century. Nevertheless, to the casual modern visitor it looks suspiciously luxurious, one is tempted to say, sybaritical, for men who reputedly renounced the temptations of the flesh for a life of piety and prayer. To dine in such splendid surroundings before taking a pleasant stroll in the cloisters next door, a blackbird shouting his heart out in the churchyard like he is today, might even lead me to renounce the world and live here, in spite of having to rise at 2am every morning to celebrate nocturns in the abbey church. But the truth to be gleaned from an inspection of the architectural extravagance of ruins like these at Easby Abbey is that the Norman religious foundations were immensely rich and quite determined that the Anglo-Saxon world that they had taken over should not forget it.

185

Yet Easby is modest compared to other better known Northern monasteries.

Just as Richmond Castle had its ecclesiastical counterpart in Easby, Helmsley Castle, 11 miles east of Thirsk, became the secular patron of Rievaulx Abbey, two miles away in the valley of the river Rye. The castle at Helmsley was built in the early twelfth century on land granted to Walter l'Espec. Apart from its handsome ruined east tower, the castle's most prominent features are the ditches and ramparts which surround it, primitive but effective fortifications which present a 30 feet deep obstacle to any assailant. The banks are immaculately maintained and on the day of our visit, despite the wet weather, they were being mowed and scraped as bare as a Plantagenet's neck shave.

The east tower was built in the twelfth century by Robert de Roos, according to the guidebook, 'as a statement of his power as Lord Helmsley'. It certainly dominates the rather prim town today, which is a model of genteel restraint with its biscuit-coloured stone and terracotta pantiles. Perhaps the potent, thrusting stonework still exercises its control over the townsfolk? The yellow sandstone of the keep is weather-frayed, only two of its four turrets remaining to claw at the sky along with a single section of battlement. Five narrow Norman windows gaze vacantly down upon the empty courtyard. Opposite, the later west tower has fared rather better and you can stand inside and gaze up at what is left of its four storeys. Doorways step giddily out into the empty interior and seven yawning fireplaces pay tribute to the intemperate nature of the climate. Today, vivid green lichen lights the roofless stonework. Stumps of wood are all that remain of the roof beams, their ancient medullae radiating from the walls like secret, rotten flowers. Walter l'Espec led the English against the Scots at the Battle of the Standard at Northallerton in 1138. The continual threat of hostility from the Scots is reflected in the castle's defensive features: its narrow windows, thick walls and outer earthworks. Nevertheless, these were no match for gunpowder and Helmsley was severely damaged during the Civil War when it was a Royalist garrison. Today, 'in this weak piping time of peace', the mountainous defensive banks are full of wild primroses and starred with sun-lacquered celandines.

It was the Lord of Helmsley, Walter l'Espec, who gave land to monks from Clairvaux in Burgundy to establish the first Cistercian abbey in the North at nearby Rievaulx in 1132. Here, hot on the heels of the Conquest, was another invasion, somewhat more peaceable but bringing with it its own massive and wonderful symbol of intent, the monasteries. Ironically perhaps to us today, many of the Norman knights became monks. But so far as the twelfth century was concerned, society was neatly divided into a divinely ordained trinity of those who prayed, those who fought and those who toiled. Not many of the toiling classes ended up as monks. Qualification for acceptance into the monastic life entailed, along with piety, an ability to bring with you a gift, usually of land. This is why so many of the nobility were to be found joining holy orders and why the monasteries became so inordinately wealthy. And why, today, we are left with such magnificent ruins as those at Rievaulx.

When I first visited Rievaulx more than 30 years ago I was not as impressed as I should have been and today I can see why. It had to do with the setting more than anything else. The narrow, wooded Rye Valley fails to provide any kind of a grand open aspect. It is somewhat claustrophobic, especially in the early part of the year before any leaf burst when the unlit browns of the wooded slopes under a grey sky press down and tend towards monotony. But the mediaeval monks were practical as well as spiritual people. They wanted shelter and, of course, their vision was of a spiritual horizon. They deliberately sought out the claustrophobic. After all, doesn't the term come from the same word as cloisters, the place where they spent their hours when they weren't in the church at prayer, where their focus was on the inner life? It was to be another 600 years before the sight of vast, open prospects of nature was to engage man's spiritual being and Romanticism was to become the new religion.

Today the best preserved of Rievaulx's ruins are the remains of the abbey church. In the rain, the stones, especially the blackened masonry of the original building, the nave, are sombre looking. Nevertheless, some of the stonework carries a pale skin of lime-washed plaster and a notice reminds the visitor that the stonework would have been painted white both inside and out. So it would shine out against its surroundings, however drab the season or the weather, a symbolic beacon of spiritual enlightenment here in a region so recently blighted by the ravages of conquest and, for many in these remoter parts, still in the shadow of the Dark Ages. The arrival of the Norman monasteries signalled a new age of monasticism not seen in the North since the time of Bede.

Avoiding the rain I shelter in the only building in the monastery left with a roof, a small chapel set in the north transept of the church. The pigeons have found it and it's splattered with droppings. The culprits coo contentedly above the clerestory arcades like old men burbling away into their pipes. The nearby crossing is a good place to observe the contrast between the nave and the chancel. The nave is where the lay brothers worshipped. These were the toilers, the farmers who worked the monastic granges that fed and clothed the monastery. The Cistercians were self-sufficient, as the rule of St Benedict required, but it was largely the lay brethren who saw to that. So their nave is bare, the stonework dark with plain stone piers. But the chancel is where the monks prayed, ordained priests often of aristocratic background who performed only little manual labour. Their surroundings reflected their more exalted status with its spiritual priorities. The stonework is light and honey-coloured, finely and elaborately carved. The piers with their clustered columns support arches which soar ever heavenwards to yet more finely carved arcades and a clerestory of lancet windows and columns from whose capitals spring the stone fans which supported the vaulted ceiling. Here are two different worlds which may have served the same end but reflected a distinct social hierarchy. Tensions were inevitable between monks and lay brothers, so that over the next centuries the number of lay brothers gradually decreased until eventually the monasteries became landlords, renting out their estates to local farmers, an ecclesiastical barony little different from the secular

188

feudal pattern. But, of course, the monasteries didn't offer the physical protection of a lord of the manor and his knights. So what was their purpose?

Rievaulx's most famous abbot, between 1147 and his death in 1187, Aelred, wrote that the monastery offered peace and serenity and 'a marvellous freedom from the tumult of the world'. I can go with that. In fact, while not wanting to underestimate the brutality of the Middle Ages, I think a good case can be made for a return to monasticism today, somewhere where those of us bruised by the imbecilities of modern life, or simply temperamentally unsuited to life today, could retire. But in the unlikely event of our political masters offering such free sanctuary to their overwrought citizens, we'll just have to settle for an English Heritage membership card and a day trip visiting the ruins of those monasteries the Normans were good enough to leave us.

The other great Cistercian house of the North is Fountains Abbey near Ripon. And here is a setting which will never disappoint. At the neck of a wood-lined valley, Fountains is surely the archetypal Romantic ruin. A stroll through the vaulted west range, which runs from the church southwards across the river for a full hundred yards, is to experience, in its shadowy stillness, the essence of a forgotten age of monkish withdrawal. Shafts of dappled sunlight spill in through the arched windows through which the afternoon sun catches the ivy-clad stonework until it glows with green flames. The river runs beneath, murmuring softly like the lost voices of the men who passed this way in quiet communion. The earthen floor muffles the tread of the visitors to a respectful silence. Here is the antithesis of everything that is the twenty-first century, that is noisy, crass, vapid and prosaic. Here, locked in the silent stonework survives some of the universal mystery which inspired men to build their astonishing monuments to their faith.

And outside, if you move to the crossing in the abbey church, the tower rises before you, 172 feet of pale lemony limestone where the jackdaws soar and chivvy and where worn outlines of saints and martyrs gaze out from their weathered niches. And on the side of the tower, a faint inscription reaches out of the worn masonry like ghost writing, a palimpsest from the distant past warmed into life by the sun and etched by the shadow from the raised surface of the letters before melting back into obscurity as a cloud covers the sun.

Here at the crossing the church reaches out west and east in vistas of ruined holiness. Down the nave the great round Norman piers ride, the stones a subtle mix of colours, yellows and pinks and some almost purple, but all weather-worn like sandstone rock at the foot of a sea-cliff. I stride out from west to east measuring the length of the church which must be 120 yards. Today a green lawn covers what was once a brightly tiled floor. Only the arching sky overhead fills the vacancy that was once the vaulted roof. On either side of the chancel stretch the stone stalls, once ornamented with columns of Nidderdale marble. Today, only one column survives and if you inspect it closely you will find it full of crumbling fossils, petrified annelid worms, segmented and smooth to the touch. The columns' sandstone capitals are weathered to an amorphous nothingness, like faceless gargoyles. And what can you say about the vast east window, a huge arch of stone 50 feet high framing nothing now but the empty canvas of the sky? It is as poignant a symbol as any of the transient nature of human works, even those devoted to the glory of God. And here's something on the north side of the heavily buttressed east wall, above the last of the lancet windows, a rare piece of figurative ornament: an angel, inserted to disguise a crack in the top of the window arch, a result of the over-ambitious dimensions of the east window. But go outside and inspect the same window from the other side and the angel has transmogrified into a green man, his grimacing mouth stuffed with coils of leafwork, worn until they look like snakes twisting down his face and down his chin. Even from 40 feet below you can still make out the anxious furrows on his brow. He is in a state of misery. An exile, outside the church, forever excluded from God's grace and redemption.

More modest statements of our conquerors' religious supremacy are to be found outside the monastic foundations in the Norman parish churches which replaced the native Saxon structures. A near-perfect survival of a Norman church, retaining most of its original features, is to be found in the tiny village of Birkin between Ferrybridge and Selby in North Yorkshire. There's a rare semi-circular apse and a small but wonderful southern doorway with a round arch lavishly decorated with carvings displaying a fascinating mix of both pious and primitively superstitious symbolism. Protected by a wooden porch - but sadly shadowed by it, making the time-stained carvings difficult to observe - the arch of the doorway is a typical Norman layering of different decorations set upon triple columns on either side of the door. First there's a layer of beakheads, fabulous birds with hungry-looking beaks and round, staring eyes. They are interspersed with bearded human heads, warrior-like. Next is a row of chevrons and finally there are roundels, medallion shapes containing figures both human and monstrous. The Lamb of God keeps company with a grotesque lined face with a great lolling tongue in an extraordinary juxtaposition of the Christian and the pagan. There are interlocking knot-like patterns and whorls which had me thinking of the Anglo-Norse crosses I'd seen. Nothing new then about the iconography. But then, should we expect it? The Normans were of Norse origin, having settled in France in the tenth century. Or perhaps they weren't even French masons who did this work but local Anglo-Norse craftsmen doing the bidding of their Norman masters. What is new, however, is the overall impact of the finished result. The intricate patterns which radiate above the door are all varied and diverse but are drawn together within the unifying harmony of the hemispherical arch, miscellaneous images captured within the symmetry of the new order. There is none of the tumult, the chaotic jumbling of the images, say, in the Gosforth Cross, with warriors and beasts upside down and scattered all over the place. Here is a new order and discipline which the Norman mind with its particular mediaeval world-view has brought to our shores. It is as if they are saying to the local population: from now on this is the way to do things. But outside the porch, running round the edges of the roof, the corbel table of chancel and apse, is an array of the damned, those excluded from the salvation of the Church and, by implication, the new social order of Norman England. These carvings might be described as devils and demons, but many are still undeniably human-looking. Yet what terrible dismay in those hooded eyes, those horrified gasping mouths. Time has not eased their predicament but weathered their expressions into a new semi-amorphous horror, like the indistinct, inchoate terrors of, say, MR James, no less but more terrifying for being incompletely realised because they then reach deeper down into the sub-conscious mind and invoke the primal fear which lies hidden there They have some of the same raw, moon-shaped, imbecile horror of those Celtic stone heads from a darker age. Surely they offer the direst warning to those who would step outside the boundaries of the new order?

Inside the church, beyond the round chancel arch, the apse retreats via its simple vaulting into a grey, stone-cast shadowiness. You might almost expect to see a knight kneeling, keeping a vigil before the altar in the pale, faded, wintry light that filters through the narrow windows. And here he is in stony sleep, lying in the north wall of the chancel, his legs crossed, his dog at his feet and his heart held in his hands clutched in prayer. The dust of ages is deeply etched into the folds of his cloak and a distant, almost beatific smile rests upon his face.

Like the knight, Birkin church sleeps too, out of its time and place here in the flatlands north of the M62, with their modern power plants and their pylons striding across the fields of garish yellow rapeseed; in the shadow of the great Yorkshire conurbations from where, when I returned the key of the church to its custodian in the old village post office, I was told that thieves had come and stolen from the offertory and made off with brasses and lead from the ancient church roof. And we think the Dark Ages are a thing of the past.

Six miles northeast of Birkin is the market town of Selby. A charter granting Benedictine monks permission to build an abbey there was given by William the Conqueror around 1070, said to be a thanksgiving for his victory over the Northumbrians during the Harrying of the North. At today's abbey you can enjoy the early Norman craftsmanship and observe how it changes to Gothic or Early English as alterations and additions were made. This process culminates in the exhilarating east window with its extraordinarily elaborate tracery.

As you walk from the market place towards the west door you are met by a typical Norman circular archway. No fanciful carvings here like Birkin, just semi-circles of meticulously patterned stonework: lattices and zigzags soaring from five pillars at either side of the door - pure Norman order and symmetry. (The workmanship is identical in the lovely north doorway.) Superseding the Norman work and above the west doorway is a blind arcade, not of round arches this time but of trefoils, and above that, the pointed arches of the window with its blind side arches. In these simple alterations to the arches we have the transition from the Norman to the Gothic. This change is further seen inside the church. Stand at the crossing under the great tower and look back towards the west door where you entered. The piers nearest the tower are solid and round. Two are scored with a latticework of zigzag patterns, perhaps copied from Durham's Norman cathedral. But then they change to clustered columns, a sure sign of Gothic workmanship. And turn to face the chancel, and through the screen you see how the piers support arches which are pointed.

The pointed arch was the great innovation of the Gothic period. It meant that arches of different span were able to reach the same height and rib vaults on the roof could distribute the load to different points on the walls. With the help of buttresses this meant thinner walls and more slender columns and room in the walls for greater spaces and windows of stained glass. The result meant a much more refined style of architecture with a greater sense of light and air and upward movement to take the eye and the spirits skywards. Who has not experienced this almost giddy, soaring sense of uplift as they looked upwards towards the vault of a great cathedral roof?

At Selby there are sumptuous gold bosses at the apex of the roof ribs. Some are new, others old, rescued from the great fire of 1906 when the bells in the tower melted and molten metal poured down on the church. Here's one showing two warriors fighting with swords and shields. There's a crowned monarch, a mermaid, an antlered deer, a green man, a woodwo or wild man of the woods, bearing a great wooden club. You can stare up until your neck aches at this gilded gallery of the mediaeval mind. But as you step further into the choir it is not the gold bosses but the stonework which electrifies the imagination. All around you it bursts into bloom in a flowering of the most elaborate carving. The capitals of the piers are so encrusted with foliage they seem to ignite the arcading into skyrockets of soaring stonework. Under lavishly crocketed canopies saints stand serenely amongst all these sculptural pyrotechnics. They stand on the backs of cheeky-looking crouching scullions which I later learnt were supposed to be half-man half-beast with faces based upon the masons who carved all this. They deserved better. The saints are Victorian, carved to replace those smashed up during the Reformation. And just when you think carving can't get more elaborate, you spot the four stone seats or sedilia to the right of the altar. Soaring above them is a forest of minute spires bursting with bud-like crockets in a haze of masonry. You can barely believe that they are carved from stone the workmanship is so fine. Then, behind the altar screen is blind stone arcading piled high with extraordinary tracery in which the tops of the arches are alive, pullulating with the most extraordinary leafwork. And hidden amongst the stone foliage you are suddenly startled to see, peering out at you, tiny carved heads no bigger than walnuts. But this is only a prelude to the renowned east window. Supported upon slender mullions the tracery curls and dances like celestial flames. And the window itself, a mediaeval Tree of Jesse, is of such density and richness of stained glass, whoever is allowed to walk along the gallery in front of it must think themselves taking a stroll in heaven.

Selby's chancel is from the thirteenth and early fourteenth century, that later period of Gothic architecture when it flowered into its most flamboyant expression known as Decorated. John Ruskin, that great art and architecture critic and latterday Northerner - he retired to Coniston where he died in 1900 - had a lot to say about Gothic architecture. Earlier critics had dubbed it Gothic because, being besotted with the Classical, they thought it rude and barbaric. Writing in 'The Stones of Venice', Ruskin lists the characteristics of Gothic, principally the condition of 'savageness'. There could be nothing further from the savage than the exquisite intricacy of the chancel at Selby, but Ruskin explains himself in a remarkable passage which is music to the ears of anyone in love with the North by arguing that the Gothic took its inspiration from the physical characteristics of the Northern landscape and climate. Long before air travel he imagines himself a swallow flying northwards and viewing the landscape from on high. As the Mediterranean lands are left behind and France and Germany begin to disappear, he sees:

'...the earth heave into mighty masses of leaden rock and heathy moor, bordering with a broad waste of gloomy purple that belt of fields and wood, and splintering into irregular and grisly islands amidst the northern seas, beaten by storm, and chilled by ice-drift, and tormented by furious pulses of contending tide, until the roots of the last forest fail from among the hill ravines, and the hunger of the north wind bites their peaks into barrenness; and at last, the wall of ice, durable like iron, sets deathlike, its white teeth against us out of the polar twilight.'

Phew! This is prose to set the hairs rising on your neck. But then, Ruskin soars further ahead to suggest that the Northern craftsman, a creature of his environment, reflects this savage landscape in his creations, and:

'...with rough strength and hurried stroke, he smites an uncouth animation out of the rocks which he has torn from amongst the moss of the moorland, and heaves into the darkened air the pile of iron buttress and rugged wall, instinct with a work of an imagination as wild and wayward as the northern seas; creations of ungainly shape

195

and rigid limb, but full of wolfish life; fierce as the winds that beat, and changeful as the clouds that shade them.'

I offer this wonderful flight of fancy of Ruskin's because I believe that no book which attempts to deal with the inspirational appeal of the North should be without such a heady and poetical tribute to the region. But is it only a flight of fancy? Or does it throw any light upon the extraordinary outpouring of church architecture which we can still enjoy today here in the North, especially in North and East Yorkshire? Perhaps we need to turn our backs for a while on the flamboyance of the late Gothic period and return to the ruins of the two great Cistercian abbeys of Yorkshire, Rievaulx and Fountains, to capture some of the savageness Ruskin found in Gothic architecture. With the roofs lost to time and no arching vaults or dazzling gold bosses to seduce the eye, it is the shifting backdrop of the sky which truly sets off the wild spring of the stonework - the 'wolfish life' - or the huge empty east windows of Fountains or Bolton Abbey which capture the scale and drama of the builders' self-belief, something on the scale that for its time only nature could achieve in the balance and thrust of rocky buttress or 'the heaving of the earth into walls of rock'. Here, in these ruins, is the Gothic, spare of decoration and pared down to its bold, yes, savage, essentials. It shouts, 'Look. This is what we can do with stone', like a noble savage showing off his physique.

The trouble with these abbeys and churches is that you want to keep going back, looking again and testing your ideas as new thoughts come along, as you develop a feel for them, an understanding. In a day trip you scratch only the surface. You need the equivalent of those benches you see in front of old masters in famous galleries, somewhere to sit and gaze, until you've bitten through to the core of the experience.

The west doorway of the priory church at Bolton Abbey in Wharfedale is somewhere I never tire of returning to. Cut short by the Reformation, the west tower of the abbey church was never completed. Roofed in modern times it now provides a protective lobby for the west front of the thirteenth century church and its quite perfect Gothic doorway. Here you begin to appreciate the elegant transformation achieved by the pointed Gothic arch. No need for an assortment of sacred and pagan symbols to underscore the sweep of the curve, for the arch itself is perfection and knowing this, the early English craftsmen have repeated it again and again in layer upon layer of chamfered stonework rising from clusters of shafts supporting plain capitals. The masons have allowed themselves just four chains of dogtooth bands to draw out the power and elegance of the new geometry, and apart from a single floral stone boss to punctuate the apex above the door and thus to emphasise the perfection of the pointed arch as an innovation, there is nothing to deflect the attention from the glory of the shape and the loveliness of the honey-coloured stone. Here is somewhere to sit and gaze - if there were seats, which there aren't, so you may have to sit on the cold floor - until they close the doors and send you away for the night. And because it's the original west doorway of the Augustinian priory church, blind arcading runs along the whole of the west front - interrupted in the porch by the pillars of the sixteenth century tower but continuing again outside - and flanking the doorway like maids of honour attending a bride. Above the west doorway is more arcading but this time so curiously shaped it looks halter-like. (Another feature of the Gothic singled out by Ruskin is its 'changefulness'.) Here the stonework alters colour from pale honey to pink mixed with yellow, and the spaces between the arches, the spandrels, are filled with trefoil patterns. One is so distorted it looks like the work of an apprentice who hasn't quite got the hang of things yet. Inside the church is more early Gothic work. Six twinned lancet windows set with Victorian coloured glass by Pugin fill the south aisle: ruby reds, deep cobalt blues and emerald greens set amongst the pale white faces of a congregation of figures telling the story of the gospels in stained glass, great panels of colour and light to complement the restless reach of the stonework. And in the west wall of the north aisle, a tiny window making up in brilliance for what it lacks in size, showing St Cuthbert, Bishop of Lindisfarne,

197

cradling the head of Oswald, a reminder of that other great monastic age here in the North of England. Subdued music of plainsong chants adds to the atmosphere of heightened spiritual intensity, so that we hardly need reminding that prayers have been offered here for over 850 years. The soaring arches lead us backwards as well as upwards.

But who were these masons whose stonework can still steal our breath away? Their names are lost and were probably never set down, such was their lowly status in the mediaeval hierarchy. It's this contrast between the uncouth lowliness of their lives and the loftiness of their unsung achievements which is the subject of a poem by John Ormond called 'Cathedral Builders':

> *'They climbed on sketchy ladders towards God,*
> *With winch and pulley hoisted hewn rock into heaven,*
> *Inhabited sky with hammers, defied gravity,*
> *Deified stone, took up God's house to meet him,*
>
> *And came down to their suppers and small beer;*
> *Every night slept, lay with their smelly wives,*
> *Quarrelled and cuffed the children, lied*
> *Spat, sang, were happy or unhappy,*
>
> *And every day took to the ladders again...'*

Yes, you think after reading it. I'll bet it was just like that.

Bolton Abbey is a small and manageable ruin for the visitor because so little of the monastery buildings survive. You are not overwhelmed by its complexity. And its setting is unequalled. No sense of claustrophobia here. It looks out across open sheep-grazed pasture to a sweeping bend of the River Wharfe and beyond to the open moors of Barden Fell. Today it is still early spring and no green life has yet lit the winter trees which crowd the banks of the river. The moors are bare and burnt-looking. A cold wind is slicing out of the east sending the daffodils in the graveyard into yellow disarray and the wallflowers shivering in their shallow niches in the ancient abbey masonry. The whole eastern end of the abbey church is a ruin. The great east window soars above the ruined chancel where the interlaced round arches of the choir stalls, their pillars lost, rise from their surviving capitals like fountains of stone. It's moody and silent inside the chancel shell, roofless yet insulated somehow from the world outside, enclosed in its aura of ancient sanctity. The east window, like Rievaulx, is hugely ambitious, an act of such architectural self-confidence, the very height of Gothic structural audacity. Two buttresses survive to support its vaulting ambition. One is crocketed but worn to a jagged grotesqueness, a grizzled, lichenous sentinel still defying the assault of time. As ruins, these places are indeed full of an 'uncouth animation'.

Just when you think you've had enough of mediaeval churches you find there's another one you simply must see. Beverley Minster, like Selby Abbey with which it is so often compared, is the apotheosis of the Gothic, even more ornate and exotic than Selby in the sumptuousness of its carvings. Remember the four sedilia next to the altar at Selby? Well, at Beverley this sort of thing, dare I say, becomes almost a commonplace. First viewed from the outside from the south, at Beverley there is another lesson to be learnt in the gestation of the Gothic. But a proper inspection of the outside of the church is difficult because there's no access to the graveyard. Iron railings and trees prevent a close-up view of the stonework. Only by peering through the railings from the pavement next to the main road can you begin to appreciate the luscious detail of the craftsmanship. Doing this you run the risk of stepping back in involuntary awe and being run over by the traffic. An alternative is to choose to stand further back still across the road in Hallgarth meadow, which was moated and dates back to the thirteenth century. But when I attempted to do this a group of rather frisky-looking bulls began to take an interest in me, making my stay a very short one. Such are the unexpected perils of church appreciation. Having settled upon somewhere to view the south side of the Minster, to the east you'll see the twin transepts. The triple lancet windows of the largest are

Early English and as you proceed westwards you move along the Decorated nave to the west tower which is Perpendicular. This is a delightful journey for the eye. It takes you along ten nave bays with reticulated window tracery standing erect upon their stem-like mullions like stately flowers. Between the bays are pinnacled buttresses which suddenly fly outwards to support the main thrust of the nave wall where the clerestory windows flow in an elegant wave of rippling tracery. Each buttress sprouts a crocketed pinnacle separated by a frieze along which groups of carved figures appear to be wandering. Further round and you arrive at the stunning west doorway. You've moved on 200 years from the Early English transepts. This is considered by many to be the finest west front in England, if not in Europe. Carved figures, restored by the ever-confident Victorians, crowd either side of the doorway. They stand head to toe upon the four great narrowing buttresses, accentuating the vertical lift of the tower. The pointed arch has reached its apogee and, as if to honour its pre-eminence, both the arch of the door and the west window above are crowned with an ogee, a sinuous decorated moulding which rises to a point like the dome of an Arab mosque.

For all its magnificence Beverley is run in a pleasantly homely way as befits the minster of a small market town of less than 30,000 souls. There's none of the cold hauteur of York, with its insistence upon an entrance fee. Any charge at Beverley is voluntary and the assistants that greet you are friendliness itself, so you're glad to chip in to help maintain their wonderful building. (We found the same warmth at Selby where, despite the fact that the Abbey was closing, the verger went out of his way to take us back and show us a feature we'd failed to spot on our tour: a tiny hole in the wall where lepers outside were permitted to peep in at the high altar.)

Inside the Minster, after the warm sunlit yellow of the exterior limestone stonework, all is cool shadow. There is a misty stillness reminiscent (Ruskin again) of misty Northern forests that seems to be exhaled by the rising columns of stonework. And the densely detailed Victorian glasswork in the nave windows filters the light into an ethereal glow. But in the north aisle above the arcading supported by black Purbeck marble columns, all is mediaeval musical jollity. Each capital is topped with a fourteenth century carving of a musician, enough for the craziest orchestra. There are pipers and whistlers, drummers and fiddlers and lyre players, over 70 for you to discover throughout the Minster. But as you progress eastwards towards the crossing the motley band is transformed into more grotesque figures. A half-man, half-beast is wrestling with the Devil. A cloven-footed jester stands on his head while another cloven-footed figure is clutching his backside and straining costively, a bad case of mediaeval constipation. This is the mediaeval imagination at work, happy to encompass both the jolly and the scary, the sacred and the profane, within the same tumultuous universe.

The roof of the nave is a triumph of elegant simplicity. Nothing brash or over-elaborate at this stage, it has just two kinds of rib, pointed arches for the cross ribs and rounded ones for the diagonals. Its simplicity allows the light from the clerestory to do its work, flooding into the roof space and drawing the eye and soul heavenwards. The same roof style runs the whole 365 feet of the church and would be a glorious soaring progression were the view from the ground not interrupted by the eighteenth century organ, its lavish gold pipes thrusting high above the choir screen. In the chancel everything is more shadowy, as if the oak canopies of the choir stalls gave off their own dark light, so that the attention is instinctively drawn to the light of the east window and its mediaeval glass, serene panels of saints and martyrs set against a background of daylight pearl glowing through the wishbone of tracery.

But the jewel of Beverley is the canopy over the tomb of Lady Eleanor Percy, from around 1340, situated to the left of the altar. You can inspect it from both sides and you will be mesmerised by the sculptural detail. Angels seem suspended in mid-air as they hang from the phalanges of the ogee arch. Knights bearing lion-crested shields fill the spaces between, and all is surrounded by cascading riches of nature in fruit and foliage. While above them all sits Christ in glory. The Gothic has come a long way from Ruskin's savageness. Here is sculptural voluptuousness, yet without decadence or empty superfluity. The tomb as a whole has an integrity of vision: the symbolic expression of a unified Creation, with civil, natural and spiritual fullness united under God. It is the mediaeval world-view captured in brute stone.

The Percies were one of the great Northern families of the Middle Ages, king-makers and protagonists in the Wars of the Roses. One of them, Henry, was the 'Hotspur of the North' of Shakespeare's 'Henry IV':

> '...he that kills me some six or seven dozen of the Scots at a breakfast, washes his hands, and says to his wife, 'Fie upon this quiet life! I want work'.'

Earls of Northumberland, the Percies had extensive estates north of the Humber. Their name survives in the mediaeval village of Wharram Percy, which is more than can be said for the village itself. It is the most thoroughly studied lost or deserted village in the whole of England of which there are over 3,000, all falling into disuse during the fifteenth century. It was long thought that this was a consequence of the Black Death, the plague which swept the country in 1348 and in just two years cut the population by two million to less than three million people. It was a time of misery and panic when people fled their homes and left their fields and crops to rot. (They had some assistance in this, 1348 being one of the wettest harvests on record.) Seen not for what it was, a bacillus spread by fleas and rats, but a divine judgment upon the wickedness of mankind and a precursor to the biblical Apocalypse or end of the world, people either performed extravagant acts of repentance such as public self-flagellation or else indulged in further wickedness while they still had the chance. People are said to have joined hands and danced in the streets, a macabre dance of death which may have done something to ease the pain of the swellings or buboes that had

202

developed in their armpits and groins. The most intensely memorable image of the plague, albeit fictional, comes from the closing scene of Ingmar Bergman's film 'The Seventh Seal' when the silhouettes of the villagers are captured as they dance across the horizon led by Death himself.

Worst hit of the mediaeval classes by the plague were the clergy, who had lived their lives in the cloistered confines of the monasteries. It is thought that the subsequent shortage of properly trained priests played a part in the general decline of the Church which was to lead to the Reformation. Certainly the shortage of peasants to till the land had a significant effect on the rural economy. But research at Wharram Percy indicates that the village was beginning to decline before the plague, as early as 1320, when several of the 40 houses began to fall into disrepair. The village had been a place of settlement from prehistoric times - it's only two miles away from the Neolithic burial mound at Duggleby Howe - and by the time of Domesday the king is recorded as being the owner of nine carucates of land, until there were probably about 200 people living there at its height. Even after the plague 30 of the households were still occupied, so researchers have had to look for other reasons for the village's decline. The protracted war with the Scots could have been one reason - the nearby village of Thixendale was raided and ransacked - but no evidence of burnt-out cottages has been found at Wharram. The main period of decay came after 1400 and it's now generally believed that the problem arose not from rats but those least demonstrative and docile creatures, sheep. The landlords, seeing their rents decline from falling tenant numbers, decided they could make more money turning their land over to grazing sheep. And so, a record for Wharram Percy for 1500 tells of the eviction of the last four tenants. It is a poignant postscript to what must once have been a lively and vibrant community - I'd say as lively as a mediaeval peasant's vest, had it not such fateful undertones - that archaeologists tell of unearthing the last of the inhabited dwellings and finding the remains of a tramp who had been sheltering there when the roof fell in on him.

I've got an iron nail about four inches long with a square shaft and a flat head nearly three quarters of an inch wide and obviously hand-made. It's rather bent and pitted with rust, yet I hold it precious because it is a tangible link with the mediaeval village which today is nothing more than a series of bumpy rectangular outlines on the side of a Yorkshire Wolds valley six miles southeast of Malton. Our diligent prospector of all things lost, our archaeologist in a black fur coat, the mole, presented it to me on my last visit to Wharram Percy.

There is something particularly atmospheric about Wharram Percy for a place which is no longer there. Perhaps it's the lack of anything much to see set against all we know about the village which accounts for the overriding sense of the forlorn which the valley exhales. How could a village, you ask yourself, which has survived over so many centuries, witnessed the arrival and departure of different races and people, suffered the traumas of war, famine and plague, been steeped in the day to day dramas of human life with all its joy and misery, hopes and fears, have disappeared so comprehensively? The empty fields of Wharram Percy loosen our very hold on mortality and leave us with a sense of the transient, fragile, almost futile nature of human existence. And there's also a sense of strangeness, of other-worldliness, which, I find, comes from the larger setting of the Yorkshire Wolds themselves. What do I mean?

A good way to approach Wharram Percy is from the south, leaving the Bridlington road from Stamford Bridge and turning north at Fimber village from where the road follows the course of a dismantled railway before reaching an empty crossroads lost amongst shallow sloping hills. At once I am reminded of a line by Louis MacNeice where the poet urges us to escape from the shackles of the town into 'some blind tunnel where the world recedes'. And here it is, the gateway into one of the narrow, silent valleys of the Yorkshire Wolds. Within a mile of the busy coast road, a sudden oasis of silence and emptiness. It is like the closing of a door on the clamouring, fractious world. It is quite magical. Is this why it's called Fairy Dale?

The road to Wharram Percy takes you up along the side of Fairy

204

Dale. Half way up we stop, switch off the car engine, open the windows and let the silence wash over us, wash us clean. And then, true to its name, Fairy Dale offers us yet more enchantment. A huge hare comes lolloping down the road towards us. Tawny red, erect black-tipped ears, he seems so awkward on his long, thin legs, like some tottering newborn deer or calf. But he's made for speed and anything less is ungainly. He seems so relaxed, so disarmed, so at ease with his surroundings, even the metalled road. Perhaps cars are a rarity here and he's just not used to them. Or perhaps the place really is magical and he knows that if danger threatens he can transform himself into something else, as hares are fabled to do. We stiffen in expectation that he is going to amble right past. But then he smells us and pauses, and then, without any hint of alarm, saunters back into the hedgerow and into the field. A couple of minutes later we see him back on the road behind us continuing his journey, having made a detour around this evil-smelling machine with its gawping human passengers.

The day is grey, still and calm, a humid late May. All around us is hidden birdsong, birds nesting amongst the may blossom which spills in milky tresses. Fairy Dale twists eastwards ahead of us, a smooth, green, sinuous canyon in the wold. A line of trees on its crest stands out, starkly accentuating the hazy horizon. At the opposite side of the valley a disused quarry exposes the rock that underlies these smooth, undulating folds in the land. It is a half-moon of yellowing chalk bitten out of the hillside and full of the sound of jackdaws, their harsh calls fretting at the tranquillity. This chalk begins in the Wessex downs, moves northwards skirting East Anglia and then into Lincolnshire before sweeping round us in an escarpment and hurling itself into the North Sea at Flamborough Head. It is the deposits of marine animals from the Cretaceous period when the dinosaurs died out. It leaves us with a 300 square mile plateau swept with sudden folds of mystifyingly dry valleys like dunes in a green desert. But it's good arable land and you can see how the plough has followed the contours sometimes deep into the dip slopes. The soil is red, peppered with stones but full of chalk particles which retain moisture and make it fertile. It's a richly satisfying landscape, too, both visually and ecologically. I met a local man coming down the road with two greyhounds straining at the leash after the smell of the hare. He tells me that he sees peregrines and red kites here. The jackdaws in the quarry have suddenly fallen silent and I wonder if the peregrine is about somewhere. At the same time a wind has sprung up out of nowhere. It shakes the cow parsley in the roadside verge and sends the hawthorn blossom cascading like white rain. The hare makes a final appearance, this time back in the field where he disappears towards the horizon, merging into the red earth.

Less than a mile further on and there's the path down to Wharram Percy. It's a heavily, heavenly-scented path between fields of corn which churn in the breeze. The path is fringed with spring flowers. There's red campion, colonnades of misty yellow crosswort, purple vetch, wild veronica or speedwell, exquisitely veined, and the creamy-white flowers of the deadnettle like strange, beaked mouths rising from a green explosion of spikes, natural forms and beauty to inspire the masons of Beverley Minster 20 miles away. At the bottom of the path you begin to see why Wharram Percy was such a popular place of settlement. A rare stream meanders through the thick vegetation whispering to itself. It will lead us to the lost village where swallows skim the grassy slopes of the plateau on which many of the mediaeval farmsteads once stood. The site was excavated between 1950 and 1990 and they have edged the foundations of the house walls and the central hearth with curb stones so that you can appreciate the size of their living space. It looked rather more generous than the pokey holes the Vikings lived in in Coppergate in York. But they did share their homes with their animals here at Wharram Percy. Only two long houses have been marked out in this way, the rest are just bumps and ridges in the meadow, rectangular enclosures full of nettles and buttercups. The two long houses were built on the site of an earlier manor house which was demolished in the thirteenth century, leaving only the Percy's manor house at the other end of the village. Today, the cows lounge uninterested.

'What's all this history to us? Give us more grass, we say.' Their lowing echoes eerily in the deserted valley.

Walking up what once was one of the two village streets is a salutary experience for the modern moralist. It's not enough to know that there were houses at each side, like many traditional village streets today, that the houses were surrounded by tofts or yards and had crofts for growing food at the rear, and that they were built of wattle and daub and were held up by cruck beams. You want to know the secrets of the people's lives, what they felt and thought. Were they like us or little better than savages? Or did the very confined nature of their lives, rarely straying beyond the boundaries of their birthplace, make them subtle, intensely aware of detail in the world around them, a microcosm which they were able to explore and understand with an intimacy which we today, with the whole wide world at our beck and call, can barely comprehend? Were they instinctual rather than the rational creatures we pride ourselves on being today, and as a result were they sensitive in the way they monitored and responded to the world around them: their grasp, for example, of natural lore and the use of herbal remedies to cure illnesses? It is interesting that modern researchers at Wharram Percy have analysed bones from nearly 700 skeletons found in the churchyard which reveal a very low incidence of infant mortality which is directly attributed to the discovery that mothers breast-fed their children for up to two years. Life expectancy was between 40 and over 50 years, much higher than in the mediaeval towns, and in some cases people lived into their 70s and 80s. TB, however, was a scourge. Further analysis of the skeletons also revealed evidence of arthritis and much disappearance of cartilage and consequent wearing out of bone due to excessive hard labour, harder than in the towns. And one eleventh century skeleton revealed how surgery had been undertaken by cutting away the bone of the skull to relieve pressure on the brain after a heavy blow to the head. Ouch!

A uniquely detailed picture of mediaeval life here in Yorkshire emerges from all the work done at Wharram Percy. Although roofless, the church still stands. It was completely rebuilt by the

Normans, probably on the site of a timber-built Saxon church. Arcades were added to the north and south aisles in the village's heyday, the thirteenth century, before being demolished in the fifteenth century as the population dwindled. You can see how the double-arched windows have been fitted in to the infilled arcades. And the tower half stands, mediaeval tombstones with ornate cross carvings incorporated into the buttresses. Worn and blackened faces look down from the corbels, impassive witnesses to the destructive passage of time.

Beyond the church is the village fishpond, a clay-lined dam which captured water from the stream which powered the watermill. Today, the placid blue-slate surface of the pond is troubled only by the occasional rising fish nudging circles in the water which rapidly expand then disappear under their own lost impetus. A water hen emerges from the yellow flag irises in the far bank, moving as if propelled by some mechanism inside his jerking black head. It is, of course, his feet which, as every observer of the singular and ridiculous motion of hens must know, are mysteriously attached to his head and incapable of moving independently. Then, suddenly a squadron of swallows arrives from the meadow, dipping into the surface of the water for insects and sending it into a flurry of agitation. The water hen croaks disapprovingly at these aerial hoodlums. It is the only hiatus in the tranquillity of the afternoon. It is hard to imagine the terror of the Black Death stalking this peaceful valley. Perhaps it didn't and Wharram Percy was protected by its own isolation. Bones, however many you dig up and study, will not reveal the ravages of plague. Nor, today, are there any signs of the sheep whose wool was deemed more profitable than the peasant's labour and left this village and its valley to desolation. Now the surrounding wolds have been returned to the plough and seas of quivering corn and yellow-flashing rapeseed fill the horizon. As we climb out of the valley, how quickly Wharram Percy disappears into the sudden, secret folds of the landscape.

The overwhelming power of the Church to shape men's thinking about life lived under the unremitting shadow of death produced a work of the imagination which perfectly expresses the anxiety of the Middle Ages. It's to be found in a stained glass window of the church of All Saints next to the River Ouse in North Street in York. Known as the Pricke of Conscience window, the glass, installed around the year 1410 depicts the end of the world. It is based upon a hugely popular poem written 60 years earlier around the time of the outbreak of the Black Death. But for those of the population unable to read, which must have been the vast majority, the impact of the events depicted in the fifteen panels of the window in the north choir aisle must have been nothing short of nightmarish. They illustrate the last fifteen days of the Apocalypse, an event that people believed would happen in 1500. In blood red, cobalt blue and yellow, the glass mirrors the end of the world in a terrifying sequence of illustrations.

First, in the lower panels, the sea rises, falls, then rises again. The vicar, who just happened to be on hand as we puzzled over this state of affairs, pointed out that this is precisely the sequence of events witnesses have subsequently recorded of tsunamis: a tidal wave followed by a scouring of the sea bottom before further inundation. But how could a fourteenth century poet, probably writing here in the North, have known about such an exotic natural catastrophe? Travellers' tales or even race memories are a possible explanation, said the vicar. But the name tsunami conjures up a very recent nightmare, relating to our own anxieties over climate change and global warming. This glasswork from 600 years ago suddenly takes on an alarming modern perspective. On the fourth day fishes begin to rise from the sea. Each panel has some words from the poem written beneath it, but you need to flit from the glass to the words of the poem to fully grasp what is going on. The fishes become 'wondreful fisshes' or perhaps sea-monsters, for in the poem they 'mak swilk rorying That it sal be hydus til mans herying' - they make such roaring that it shall be hideous to man's hearing. That they are no ordinary fish is clear from the window which shows three fishes which look more like snarling dogs baring vicious teeth. In the next series of panels the sea burns and trees drip with fire. In the seventh panel earthquakes destroy buildings. There's a toppled spire. Now the church's 120 foot octagonal tower was erected only fifteen years earlier. It is the tallest in York and it is as if the glass-makers were saying: You may be proud of your fine tower now but remember, it too will be destroyed. There's something powerfully effective in the simplistic depiction of things which heightens the weird and cataclysmic nature of the events. The trees resemble exotic mushrooms. As the stones of the earth burn, jagged bones rise up between them like pale tubers. It is this spareness and simplicity of the art which emphasises the horror, as do the stark limitations of the colours, the blood-red flames contrasting with the deep blue of the threatening sky and the ghastly colourless faces of the human beings. The people are shown hiding in holes in the ground or else emerging to huddle together on their knees in prayer. Another panel shows their corpses crammed into lidless coffins, heads rising above piles of bones, dramatically conveying the sheer scale of the death toll, something still fresh in the memory after the devastation of the plague. The corpses are not skeletal but have round, baby-like faces. Not only does this child-like representation of the humans intensify the horror but it also adds a compassionate dimension to the scenes. The impression is not of wicked people caught in the enormity of their sins but of vulnerable, bewildered victims. It is deeply fatalistic, suggesting that we are all doomed because of our flawed humanity. In the lowermost panels are depicted the donors of the glasswork, thought to be members of two well-known York families. The shock and dismay etched upon their faces as they kneel and pray is something to behold.

The final chapter in the destruction of the world is in the topmost of the three panels below the window's tracery. The stars and heavens fall in great bolts of yellow light. On the fourteenth day Death creeps into the panel with his spear to gloat over the laid out corpses of a lord and his lady. Death's pale face is almost split in two with the most ghastly grin. His eagerness is palpable. This is the end of all human life and it leaves the final panel, Day 15, to the flames, jagged red teeth in a maw of blue which gives a shocking new meaning to the word 'consumed' by fire. It is a deeply pessimistic creation. Only high above the window in the two quatrefoils of tracery is there any hope. Not to the right, where devils carry off the damned, but to the left, where St Peter is seen holding open the door of heaven to the righteous. But this is almost an afterthought and in no way mitigates the horrors we have witnessed below. Hope is marginalized in the overwhelming fatalism of the mediaeval mind-set. The window is a fitting postscript to an age of violence, death and unparalleled spiritual intensity.

8. The Bloody Borders

For almost the whole of the 500 years from the Conquest to the union of the crowns with Scotland in 1603, the North was a war zone. In fact, if you add on the 350 years of Roman occupation and the struggles in between with Germanic and Scandinavian invaders, there seems to have been few years in our history when the native Northerner was able to fall asleep without his sword or cudgel under his bed. It would not be over melodramatic to say that large areas of our region were stained with blood, particularly to the east and northeast where the great ancient highways to Scotland ran. Even the most utilitarian of today's road maps will pick out the battlefields: Northallerton (1138), Myton-on-Swale (1319), Boroughbridge (1322), Neville's Cross (1346), Otterburn (1388), before we stop at the Border and further killing fields beyond. But these were battles where great armies clashed and casualties ran into thousands. What about the local slaughter where death crept over the Border at night and sliced the throats of families and their children as they slept? The Northern Marches must have been a nightmare place to be while war between England and Scotland raged during the later Middle Ages.

But it's an ill wind, as they say, and historians argue that the North of England prospered during the wars with Scotland. Because of its strategic importance it brought successive kings to the region with their armies. In 1312, Edward II set up his government in York, and in 1307, Parliament met in Carlisle. Great Northern families like the Nevilles and the Percies rose to power and could soon afford their lavish tombstones. Even the peasants prospered. Instead of the feudal obligation to follow the lord of the manor to war, knights began to pay for their levies and bonuses came down to the foot soldiers from the plunder and heavy ransoms paid out for important prisoners. The Scottish wars spawned a culture of mercenaries akin to the great

213

Viking raids of the ninth and tenth centuries. (At the time of writing this, the government has announced a multi-billion pound project for building aircraft carriers which will provide work and wages for shipbuilders and aerospace workers here in the North, and it set me wondering whether there has always been a tradition of the North being an inadvertent beneficiary of warfare.) Nowhere were the profits of war a more important part of the Northern economy than in the Border regions of the late Middle Ages when cross-border theft of goods, cattle and sheep sustained families and whole communities. So much so, that raiding and its rewards became known as the 'winter harvest'. A measure of the violence and larceny which afflicted this region during the fourteenth, fifteenth and sixteenth centuries is to be found in the astonishing number of castles, towers and fortified farmhouses in various states of repair still to be discovered in Northumberland and Cumbria. I didn't think it would be long before I was returning to the realm of that hoary old Celtic war god, Cocidius.

A journey up Liddesdale from Longtown just north of Carlisle towards Kielder Forest provides plenty of evidence of the insecurity which constant warfare brought to the Border region. Crossing the Esk near Gretna you enter what was known as the Debateable Land, an area of constant dispute between England and Scotland where laws no longer operated and notorious felons took refuge. Here was the stronghold of the Grahams and further north were the Armstrongs of Liddesdale, families made famous by folk legend and ballads and glamorised today by the tourist industry under the title of Border reivers. United under a common surname, they were clans or extended families and their followers, sometimes numbering into the hundreds and occupying fortified towers and houses from which, armed and riding sturdy ponies, they would issue forth to supplement their farming income by plundering the possessions and livestock of their neighbours. They owed little allegiance to any but their own and often put self-interest before nationality. Enlisted into the armies of England or Scotland for their fighting prowess, they could not be relied upon to remain loyal to either where the spoils of war were at stake. They were, in a word, freebooters.

If you drive towards Gretna from the bridge over the Esk at Longtown you are still in England. The Border today follows the line of the River Sark further to the west and in the triangle of land between the Sark and the Esk lies Solway Moss, scene of a battle between the English and the Scots when a force of only seven or eight hundred English Borderers on their ponies beat back between fifteen and eighteen thousand Scottish troops. The vast Scots army had been caught between the banks of the river and the marshes of the Moss, which was their downfall. Today, outside the Solway Moss Works, a sign boasts that here is the 'oldest peat extraction plant in the world and the site of the Battle of Solway Moss on the 24th November, 1542' One can scarcely help wondering how many Scottish bones get dug up by their earth-moving equipment or appear in the mountains of dark brown peat piled up inside their yard. This is a grey and sullen spot, as befits a place of national humiliation. Dark clouds gather over Galloway and you can watch the rain creeping southwards down the valley like smoke. Pylons stride brazenly across the Border while the rail traffic between the two countries is restless, echoing noisily across the flatlands round the upper reaches of the Solway Firth. Swallows skim the fields, enjoying the glut of insects which the wet weather has brought. They'd surely grow fat if they didn't expend so much energy on catching their dinners, sewing a maze of invisible threads through the sky.

Alongside the Moss is a feature that as an inveterate browser of OS maps I had long puzzled over. The map shows a rectangular area measuring a mile and a half long by three-quarters of a mile wide and filled with seventy or so buildings all set equidistant from one another. A further smaller complex is across the road to the north. Both have rail links to the main line. But there are no names or indications of what the installation is for. Now, I'm probably running the risk of incarceration in the Tower for even writing about this, but a visit soon reveals that this is Ministry of Defence land. By a remarkable coincidence, on the morning of the day of my trip, I'd listened to an item on the radio about the Carlisle State Brewery. Pricking up my ears, as I always do when beer is mentioned, I learnt that the state took over the breweries in Carlisle during the First World War to inhibit drunkenness by munitions workers in the area. So this was it. A munitions factory. This accounted for the security fence and the kind of intimidatory notices I'd witnessed at Fylingdales. 'This is a prohibited area and persons may be arrested', says one. 'Seen anything suspicious?' demands another. The notices look somewhat faded and you may be entitled to think that the whole place has now been shut down. But that would be a mistake. Further along the road, MOD Longtown is bristling with activity. Only afterwards - in the middle of the night, to be precise - did I wake up in a sweat when it dawned upon me that there I'd been, with my nose stuck through the fence, notebook and pencil in hand. Thank goodness I didn't try to take a picture. There's a fine line - some would say invisible - between curiosity and mischief in this era of universal surveillance from CCTV cameras. I still await with a shudder the knock on the door from the military police. I doubt that my excuse that I was researching the Border reivers would pass much muster.

Rationalists would argue that there were good practical reasons for locating this facility in the Debateable Land. But as at Spadeadam, with its secret missile plant, I myself hear the dark chuckle of old Cocidius. 'Blood will have blood', as Macbeth bemoaned. The events of history have left such an indelible bloodstain on this land that it can call down to the deepest subconscious reaches of our nature and cry, 'This is the damned spot. This is the place to hide your ghastly weapons of war. This is where they belong, here among the ditches and marshes where the dead cry out, where cruelty ruled men's hearts!' Fanciful? Our ancestors, before their instincts became smothered by the artificialities of modern life, could recognise the spirit of a place. They sensed holy places to erect their sacred shrines and churches. So why not murderous places too?

Two miles further north up Eskdale is the pele tower of Kirkandrews, a stronghold of the Grahams. Even though today it has been converted and is lived in, it stands solid, a square tower with gargoyled parapet rising 30 feet to its battlements and a pitched roof, truculently dominating its surroundings. The valley may be peaceful now, quiet parkland dotted with trees and gently grazing cattle and sheep, but there can be no doubting the tower's original belligerent purpose to guard a ford across the Esk facing the Scotch Dyke to the west. The entrance is via a flight of stone steps to a door in the first floor - in the past these peles had access by means of ladders which they raised in times of danger - and I climbed them rather tentatively to knock on the door and ask for the owner's permission to inspect the outside of his home. There was no answer and I was glad, half expecting a burly Graham to emerge brandishing his dagger and shouting oaths. But we were to find that there was rarely anybody about in this wide, open Border country. Even though it was approaching high summer, the roads were empty, the noisy modern world elsewhere. The books say that Kirkandrews Tower was built in the fifteenth century by the Grahams of nearby Netherby but destroyed by their enemies the Armstrongs in 1527 when it was later rebuilt as a farmhouse. Latterly it was modernised as a fishing lodge, which may explain why no one was at home, its occupants busy flicking their flies into the racing waters of the Esk to lure the passing salmon.

The tower has an incongruous companion in the field nearby, a small neo-classical church with an uncomfortably crowded graveyard. The headstones, fashioned from the same terracotta sandstone as the tower, are mottled with lesions of pale lichen, like the ravages of some dreadful disease. They stand like ranks of mute spectators who have just emerged from the trees beyond to silently witness some overwhelming event. Judgment Day? Their apparent watchfulness was unsettling, but I was looking for reiver names. At a glance I found a Bell and a Little, West March surnames, and here were the Grahams. A Jessie Graham, and Harold, son of John and Ann Graham, a child who died in infancy in Victorian times. And two modern Grahams, one who died as recently as 2002. Sir James Graham, I was told, still lived at Netherby Hall.

Another Graham stronghold is at Brackenhill. A journey of four miles, travelling due east from Longtown along quiet lanes past verges of creamy meadowsweet and tall foxgloves and hedgerows full of honeysuckle, brings you to this pele tower - in modern parlance, a 'towerhouse' - rising above a clutter of farm buildings. It's a massive square tower which reaches to double gables inside a battlemented parapet from which protrude round gargoyles like giant ovipositors. To one side a Victorian wing has been added, with a bay window, which gives a somewhat discordant suburban dimension to this most doughty of structures. Inside, off the cobbled courtyard, a date stone above a doorway reads 1548, although it's so badly worn I wouldn't swear to it. The doorway itself is eerily impressive with two projecting heads, one at either side, worn and grizzled guardians rendered featureless by time but with enough latent aggression in the thrusting stonework to stop you in your tracks. In the wall above are notches where the roof timbers once slotted. One is full of nesting material and the broken remains of a dead jackdaw. The red-stained stonework has been invaded by mauve toadflax. But human intruders would have been less successful. The windows are only inches wide and you can measure the thickness of the walls through an aperture into the basement. They are between four and five feet thick. This is a fortress. The remains of an eighteenth century farmhouse cling to the tower. Daylight gapes through the wormy roof timbers and cracks track dangerously across the crumbling brickwork. We learn from Mrs Carlyle who lives in one of the surrounding buildings (Carlyle is another Western Marches surname) that there was a gathering of the Graham clan in 1999 to save old Richie Graham's tower. Since then, we were told, English Heritage have been excessively pernickety over the authenticity of the restoration work and the cost has risen to £4 million. This is a pity and a bit of realism is required. It seems to me that each generation adds its bit to our historical heritage, witness for example the Victorian wing. Whatever we might make of this, it's an organic process which reveals how each age left its mark and guarantees the continuous use of the building. Now while I'm not suggesting that we leave our mark today by adding on a breeze block bungalow - there are enough of those around the area - surely some leeway must be allowed if the alternative is that the building will disappear because no one can afford to keep it to English Heritage's exacting standards. I know of too many buildings that have gone this way and would hate to see it happen to Brackenhill. Meanwhile, the Herculean task of restoration goes on, with heaps of rubble, salvaged stone and timbers, all in a sea of mud surrounding the tower, while the cloying smell of slurry from the farmyard hangs over everything like despair. One day it might all take shape again. It depends on the resolution of the Grahams, a quality they never seemed to lack in the past. In the short interregnum after the death of Elizabeth I, an unholy alliance of Grahams, Armstrongs and Elliots rode into Cumbria, stealing almost 5,000 cattle and sheep in one raid. It was to be one of the last audacious acts of the notorious reivers because, with the accession of James VI of Scotland to the English throne in 1603, the raiders were outlawed and many of their scores of fortresses demolished. When the chairman of today's Clan Graham Society, Bruce Graham, was recently challenged with the view that the Grahams were bloodthirsty murderers, he replied that they didn't murder people 'because there was no profit in murder'. Humph. So what happened to the people who got in their way?

A Border clan which shared the Graham's notoriety was the Armstrongs of Liddesdale. One of their towers, Gilnockie, is off the Canonbie to Langholm road just over the Scottish border. Luck would have it that we arrived at a time when the tower was open to the public, and none other than the chairman of the Armstrong Clan Association, Ted Armstrong, an Englishman, was there to show us round. Ted is a proud ancestor of Kinmont Willie Armstrong, subject of the eponymous ballad in which Willie is audaciously sprung from incarceration in Carlisle Castle. Sir Walter Scott collected many of these ballads. His roots were in the Border country and he was clearly blinded by regional chauvinism and therefore quite happy to romanticise the blatant criminality of these Border 'heroes'. The same sentimentality exists today, whether it be by the promotion of reiver trails and the like by the tourism authorities or the revival of

219

the reiver clans. Gilnockie Tower has been bought and restored by members of the Armstrong Clan Association and is now their headquarters. American Armstrongs, if so minded, can return home boasting that they have spent the night under the laird's roof and produce a certificate to prove it. To make their stay more comfortable, if somewhat less authentic, a modern tiled bathroom has been installed next to the original stone latrine set into the tower wall. There is also a shrine to the most famous modern Armstrong of all, complete with close-up pictures of his footprints on the surface of the moon.

But what impels people to want to be associated with bygone thieves and murderers who must have made life hell for the honest and decent citizens of the North during the sixteenth century? (Their raids were not just confined to the Border regions but penetrated deep into England as far as South Yorkshire.) One obsessed soul has spent four and a half years of his life making a model of Willie Red Cloak Bell, the man apparently responsible for the rescue of Kinmont Willie. It is on display in the tower and is a life-size replica with typical reiver armour - a steel bonnet, a sword-proof jack or jerkin, a pike and a fully operational pistol ('They didn't murder people …'). When I asked Ted Armstrong the awkward question as to why he was so proud to be associated with a band of homicidal blackguards, so infamous that even their own king undertook a campaign to exterminate them, he looked as if the question had never occurred to him. Finally, he blamed the times. 'They had to do it. They had to do it to live,' he replied. Undoubtedly the romantic glow of history can blind us to many of its realities and even confer a glamour to some of its greatest villains. The portrayal of the American wild west in the cinema of the 1950s, whose outlaws most readily compare with our reivers, is a case in point. As kids we all wanted to be Jessie James or Billy the Kid. But however many bodies may have strewn the screen at the end of the film, villainy always got its due deserts and heroes emerged on the side of law and justice. With the reivers the moral compass seems to have been readily tossed aside by their latter-day admirers. But for how long?

With time, sensibilities shift and it may not be long before the Border reivers suffer the same fate as the wild west outlaws and become nothing more than a squalid footnote to history.

Still, I was indebted to Ted Armstrong for the opportunity to inspect the interior of a towerhouse. A stone spiral staircase links the four storeys at Gilnockie. On the ground floor a stone slab over the threshold is marked by a carved whorl akin to the prehistoric markings on the stones of Fylingdales Moor. Was this the Dead Stane I'd read about, marking the place where the remains of the chieftain's family were buried? I'm afraid I forgot to ask. I was too eager to escape the tiresome memorabilia of the modern clan - photos of Armstrong Haulage's trucks, lino courtesy of Armstrong Flooring Inc of America - and get up to the battlements. The stone staircase has 107 steps, winding past windows only four inches wide. Stepping over the corpses of dead bats we were allowed onto the parapet, but only so far (Health and Safety, you might know) to witness the vantage these towers gave over the surrounding countryside. At the apex of the stepped stone gable is a stone slot into which an iron basket was placed for a beacon fire to warn of an enemy invasion. What magnificent and effective defensive structures these towers were. Towerhouses like this would originally have been surrounded by a defensive stone wall or barmkin. To the north side of the tower at Gilnockie is a deep hollow from where the stone for the tower was quarried, providing the house with a further defensive obstacle. This hole gave the tower its other name of Hole House or Hollows. It was the custom at times of threat from rival cattle thieves to bring stock into the barrel-vaulted basement. It was a vicious cycle of dog eat dog. Darwin's survivalism at its most savage and remorseless. As a public record of Border affairs for 1595 to 1603 reveals:

'Although contynuall intercourse of winning and loosinge of goods do ebb and flowe like the sea, yett the game hath ever of late rested in the strongest takers handes, and forceth the loosers, eyther to take again, or to wast by little and little to nothinge; so as, which of eyther side are theevishe and strong, must of necessitie make the

221

opposite side eyther theives or beggers.'

As always with history, the losers are forgotten or ignored. Scott's ballads ring with the stirring derring-do of Armstrongs, Elliots, Bells and 'Gallant' Grahams. The modern day clansmen hang their coats of arms and tartans over their fireplaces and bore their visitors with stories of their illustrious pedigrees. But their victims lie forgotten under the ground of this Border Country. Today its very peacefulness is their requiem. Looking out over the parapet at Gilnockie Tower northwards up Liddesdale one is struck by the tranquillity. None of the encroaching harshness of Bewcastle Waste to the east or the furtive reminders of war at Solway Moss. Just the sheep and cattle grazing unmolested in the fertile valley, the swallows dipping amongst the meadowsweet near the water's edge, and the ancient Esk, the silver sky on its back, bearing everything away - triumph and sorrow, good and ill - like time itself.

Nowhere has nature more mollified this region's shadow of war and violence than at Liddel Strength, an earthwork the aggressiveness of which is preserved only in its name. A motte and bailey castle, it towers above the junction of the Esk and Liddel Water, a mile south of Canonbie. But not a stone lies standing, just a massive ditch nearly a 100 feet deep rising to a plateau upon which stands the mound which held the fortified castle. In fact, it was probably a wooden, pallisaded structure relying more upon its impregnable natural position for its strength. To the west there is no need of a ditch because there is a vertical drop of 200 feet into Liddel Water. It's thought to have been part of the Border defences from the twelfth century, and the presence of a Roman road running northwards up the Esk, with the remains of a Roman fort at Broomholm, has led some to speculate that Liddel Strength was used as a Roman station too. Layer upon layer of troubled history underlie this Border region.

Today, Liddel Strength is approached by a path from High Moat farm. The farmer was as gentle and courteous a figure as you could ever wish to meet, and you do seem to meet them in this part of the world, which leads me to think that if there was once violent Border blood running in their veins it has long evaporated. His farmyard seemed to be full of tame animals, ducks that waddled up to greet you, rare breed hens that pirouetted in the dust in a feathery ecstasy of welcome. Only the farm dog on his chain was hostile, some dark suspicion still lurking in his doggy brain that we were rustlers come to carry off his sheep. Ever-simple, the long-eared sheep rushed to meet us as we tramped through the field to where we'd been directed. Soon the path had petered out into a bog and then we were met by the fosse, full of briars and brambles. To breach these natural defences you need a lot of determination, a strong pair of knees to tackle the steep sides and a resistance to thorns and nettle stings. And I imagine the fort relied upon exactly the same defences in the past. Having assailed the summit we were rewarded by a view on only two sides. To the south, beyond Carlisle, the north Lakeland peaks serrated the skyline. To the east lay Bewcastle Waste and the dark smear of Kershope and Spadeadam Forests. Tall trees mask the other vantage over the confluence of Esk and Liddel Water into Scotland. Nevertheless, you can still appreciate the strategic importance of this place and why it deserves its name. Someone should take responsibility for clearing this impressive earthwork and making it less of a wilderness. Or should they? On a rare patch of open ground on the summit we found a slowworm sunning itself. Disturbed, it slipped its way through the grass into cover. As well as nettles and brambles the ditches are full of scented meadowsweet, tall and intensely purple thistles, herb Robert and gleaming yellow stars of tormentil. Fight your way off the top to the brink of the bluff to the west and through the tangle of beeches and birches you can glimpse the river far down below flashing in the sunlight. Liddel Strength is a secret place which stays with you long after you have left, a place where the violence of the past has been sublimated into the introspective harmonies of nature.

The same cannot be said of Hermitage Castle, the memory of which will return like a bad dream to sour my waking hours. It is located in an empty valley off Liddesdale on the banks of Hermitage

Water. As you turn west up the valley it leaps out at you like a mailed fist, a brutal assertion of martial might. It has been described as awesome, but is more than that. It is terrifying. It is a vast, square, oppressive monolith, threatening and disturbing in the way that the truncated tower of Fylingdales radar station can affect you. Some of its menace derives from the setting. It was said to have served as the 'guardhouse of the bloodiest valley in Britain'. The bare moors and mountains which ring it in a wild complicity know that it belongs to them. It is of the same elemental, Palaeolithic ancestry. Its bare, blackened walls rise to a hundred feet and are punctured to west and east by huge, gaunt archways serving no purpose, it seems, but to impress, to intimidate by casting dark internal shadows which augment the menacing potency of the fighting force it once concealed. When it was first built in 1240, fighting platforms were ranged around the parapet, thrusting defiantly out from the battlements. It was fought over like some ultimate machine of war. First it fell into the hands of the Douglases before being taken over in the fourteenth century by Lord Dacre who held it for the English before it was again back in Scottish hands with the Earls of Bothwell. Prisoners starved to death in its dark dungeons. Walk round it inside the ancient bank and ditch and as you look up at the battlements you feel that sense of vertigo when the stonework begins to gather strength as if it was about to topple and crush you. It is a lithic monstrosity. There are mean windows ranged below the corbelled parapet, and others, lower down, which are flattened and oval-shaped with chamfered edges, presumably to facilitate the firing of missiles from within, which taper inwards to a central hole which gapes like a cruel Cyclopean eye. One, near the south door, is only head height and you can run your hand around its edges and feel the rough cruelty of the stone before peering into the fortress's interior, its black, empty heart, fearful that someone or something will thrust something nasty into your eye. This is the Dark Tower of the imagination, the one to which Childe Rowland came to meet his sickening Nemesis. This, if anywhere, is the hideout of the dark war god, Cocidius, and you know that if you were to knock on the bleached door in the wall nearby, all will be lost, the game will be up. You will be confronted by your worst nightmare, the ultimate horror.

I am glad the castle is closed for the day and we have arrived too late to go inside. Nor do I ever want to go inside. I want to run away and return to some sort of civilisation and leave this, pitiless, desperate, brute of a place to its dumb, belligerent isolation. It has muscled out all those other images of the Borders as a tranquil retreat of flowers and fertile river valleys and gentle people, and underlined it as a place of violent inhumanity, usurped the romanticism of idyllic nature, the harmless sentimentality of wanting to be associated with daring figures of ballad and legend because they shared your surname, and stamped the grim reality of man's bloody past upon the whole region so that all that remains is to repeat the cynical and sickening assertion that all history is the history of cruelty.

What is left of the Borders after Hermitage can only be an emotional anticlimax. Next day we journey further up Liddesdale towards Northumberland. Our horizon is etched by ragged ranks of dark conifers which are steadily closing in until we are hemmed in by narrow corridors of trees. We see a large raptor clinging to the top of a tree. His beak is short and hooked like a lethal barb. He sweeps off into the heart of the wood before we have chance to identify him. It is our last close encounter with real wildness because we are now in Kielder Forest and the forest is the invention of man. It is nature marketed, a place where your credit card is as vital a piece of equipment as your walking boots and anorak. First created in 1926, it is 250 square miles of forest, bog and giant reservoir where you and the family can live in a log cabin in the wood for a week or spend a day 'blazing a trail' in your 4x4. There's pottery and poetry workshops, basket-weaving and mini-golf, sailing, water-skiing, mountain biking, trips round the haunted castle, a Christmas deer safari 'to spot Rudolph's distant cousins', fungal forays and dining in restaurants. You name it and, if they can charge a fee for it, it will be there. There's even a toll to drive through the forest into Redesdale.

The reivers of old are alive and well and they've found a way to plunder the pockets of today's tourists without spilling a drop of blood. And on top of the tourist revenue there's the money from the tree-felling. They plant one million new trees a year, they tell us, and you're more likely to meet a giant trailer stacked with pine logs haring round a corner as encounter Rudolph's cousin in the road.

Kielder Forest says so much about what we can expect from our countryside today. Or what the vested interests think we want. They think we want it organised, with weeded walkways and WCs, with car parks and craft shops, rustic playgrounds with an officer from the Health and Safety Executive behind every other tree to make sure we do ourselves no harm. Today the sun is shining and people are arriving in their hundreds to enjoy the 'Woodland Experiential Trail' or any of the other carefully contrived pseudo-experiences on offer. It is as if today we have somehow lost the power to rely upon our own natural curiosity and sense of adventure to discover things for ourselves. It is all so deeply patronising. And it is as artificial as the architecturally designed light structures which have been set up around the forest, stainless steel surfaces to reflect the natural world around them. In fact, this is what the Kielder experience of nature offers: a reflection, an illusion of wildness, nature at one remove, carefully mirrored through works of human artifice, through strictly imposed human boundaries. It is our Claude glass again, where the observer turned his back upon nature's shocking uncouthness to view it tamed, captured in the comfortable confines of the mirror, in the secure framework of the civilised. The forest's creators seem to have no idea that tiring of the artificiality and commercialism of modern life we might just want to escape into the truly wild, into a bit of genuine wilderness; that lurking hidden deep within us may survive some of that same awe and terror, that primal fear, inspired by the Great Forest of old and which haunted the mediaeval imagination, finding expression in their church carvings of wodwos or wild men of the woods, or green men with foliage grotesquely spilling from faces contorted with the anguish of eternal damnation; or that we may need to confront those vestiges of terror of waste places, of fen

226

and bog, haunts of devils and demons and exiled monsters, of hell's reivers. These may, of course, only be metaphors for the chaos and fear that an honest look at nature in her supreme indifference to the fate of mankind inspires. But to deny room for these ancient instincts, to nanny them away with centrally-heated cabins in the woods and jolly rangers dressed in Lincoln green to hold our hands as we wander through the trees, is to turn our backs upon the dangerous otherness of nature. So that in our cosy, protected view of nature we ignore the signs that it may have already turned against us, that today's floods and storms and weather extremes are the prelude to a world when nature shrugs us off and returns to a planet without us, to the chaos of a new Hadean Aeon. Only by experiencing the true wildness of nature can we come to terms with our precarious position in the scheme of things and act with a due sense of our own expendability should we fail to respect the potent and alien forces which surround us. Is this what that inveterate backwoodsman and philosopher, David Thoreau, meant when he wrote: 'In wildness lies our salvation'?

In my own effort to shrug off the commerce and cosseting of this bogus 'return to nature' I have fled the paths and picnic parties and set off into the heart of the wood. It soon swallows you up within its unnatural stillness. The pine brash underfoot deadens any footfall apart from the occasional explosive crack of a dead branch, the wet suck of the moss. I am enclosed by a sterile calm where the senses begin to be denied any interest. The eye follows the line of countless bare tree trunks to the green flush of the distant canopy where the sound of the wind arrives like the sudden rush of water before sinking again into a sullen silence. The trees have been thinned and there's no undergrowth. It is free of any entanglement, a forest reduced to a single commercial imperative of economic exploitation, the rectilinear monotony of pine and spruce, of spruce and pine. It is a forest robbed of its diversity, its complex patterns and natural dependencies, its chaotic but carefully balanced network of different species, its terrifying, maddening muddle, its exhilarating enchantment. It is no longer nature at all. It is a woodyard.

The reduction of vast tracts of Northern England, particularly here in Northumbria, into arboreal wastelands is a desecration of our natural heritage. Evergreen forests cast a monotonous blanket over the landscape both visually and historically. Moorland may not be to everyone's taste but it offers expansive and often exhilarating vistas of our landscape. It also surprises and mystifies with its wealth of tumuli and earthworks and ancient crosses. Working forests are boring monocultures, no-go areas for all but the introverted and suicidal disposed. They are not the great forests of old but ersatz recreations of them, devoid of all magic and mystery. They are MDF as against seasoned carved oak. Like most modern commercially inspired activities they sacrifice interest and variety to size and uniformity. They may help to cleanse the atmosphere of carbon pollution but I suspect only to a fraction of the degree to which well-spread broad-leaved plantations would do. And despite what the promotional material of the tourist boards would have us believe, few of us eager to transplant from our homes in the conurbations for a weekend or a holiday would choose the lifeless monotony of a pine forest. In fact, all the activities they are eager to sell us could happily take place without a pine tree in sight. The Romantics of the eighteenth and nineteenth centuries would turn in their graves at the sight of the Northern landscape being put to some of the uses it is being put to today and it is to them who we must now turn to explore the most liberating of all the aspects of the North.

9. THE AWESOME SUBLIME

For me, the essence of the North is locked in its mountains and high places. It is an elusive sense of exhilaration which lifts us and sustains us beyond the frustrations and vacuities of everyday life. Yet it never lasts but always leaves us hankering for more. To describe the experience, you find yourself, as others have done before, reaching into the mystical or religious.

Wordsworth was the high priest of that most revered of mountain regions, the Lake District. It was he who interceded between we lesser mortals and the sublimity which lay there. From lump rock and stone he mined rich veins of poetry and spiritual elation. Of course, the Lakes had always been there - for 450 million years since Silurian volcanoes thrust the central mountains skywards for ice and water to chisel the valleys and screes - Wordsworth and his coterie simply taught us to look at such things in a different way, taught us to feel differently about them. They wrote nature with a capital N, imbuing it with divinity. When the mysterious person dies in the Lucy poem, 'A slumber did my spirit seal', she doesn't go to heaven but is:

'Rolled round in earth's diurnal course,
With rocks, and stones, and trees'.

Such natural objects are sacred with Wordsworth. God and Nature have become the same thing. It's pantheism and has more in common with the beliefs of the henge builders of Neolithic times and the Celtic river worshippers than the mediaeval cathedral builders and pious Victorians. And when we set off in search of this god experience into the Lake District today, it's not Wordsworth but another W, Wainwright, who is there with his maps and thumbnail sketches to show us the way.

Wainwright was a milltown Northerner and the spot which first inspired his life-long obsession with the Lake District was the view from Orrest Head above Windermere. As good a place as any to begin. But it's high summer and first you must slip the leash of Windermere's tourism. The shops are a gentrified bazaar of the traditional and the twee. Beatrix Potter pots vie with 'Daffodils' tea towels, ram's head walking sticks with slate house-signs. You can choose between Lakeland rock and heather honey. People sit at pavement cafes eating hummus sandwiches with grated carrot or stuff a Gregg's Cornish pasty on a street corner. You can dine at the Giotto Restaurant or grab a pizza 'to go'. And milling amongst it all or dodging the motorbikes weaving through the log-jammed traffic, dads in straw hats with bare knees herding squads of kids or Lakeland matrons stocking up with breakfast milk for the B&B. I can hear Wainwright growl and Wordsworth rant. 'Getting and spending we lay waste our powers', the bard boomed. Better save your energy for the twenty minute walk up to Orrest Head across the main road to Ambleside and up a well-signed lane.

The lane winds between cool, moss-thick walls and verges lined with nettles, enchanter's nightshade and the straggling remains of bluebell blades. As it climbs there are gullies thick with ferns and woods of birch and slender oak falling away to one side. Suddenly through a gap in the trees you catch a glimpse of Windermere lake and Belle Isle with sail boats weaving through the sky-trapped water. Despite the fact that it's August, an autumn chill hangs over the woods. Rhododendrons offer up pale palms to the scarce light. The track begins to roughen, riddled with roots scarred white with passing feet, knobbled with grey-green Lakeland slate worn slippery. It begins to run with water from the summer's seemingly endless rain. You pass memorial seats, their varnish flaking as memory fades. A loved one's favourite view, high up. Closer to God? And at last you step out into the daylight to harebells and flowering heather, scabious and yellow tormentil. And strewn across the sandstone boulders round the viewing point, a crowd of twenty or more people chattering or shouting into mobile phones.

I wonder if Wainwright on first coming here would have been quite so enthusiastic if he'd been met by such a scene. One American, unable to shake off the national stereotype, is holding forth loudly to a small audience. A woman in large pink trousers gives one of the scrap-seeking jackdaws a wide berth and I hear her say, 'I don't really like birds'. Another group is discussing supermarket shopping and parking charges. Meanwhile to the northwest the Langdale Pikes ripple in a ragged sea of rock, the remains of half a billion year old volcanoes. They rest in a grey matrix of light, the sporadic sunlight doing its best to draw out their might, to etch their wrinkled mass with shade, animate them with light and emphasise their staggering musculature. But it is midday and the light falls flat, bathing everything in a milky opacity. And so the mountains sleep.

To invite us into this view, to assist us in briefly relinquishing our petty human concerns, there's a stone lectern for a map, a map perhaps with ancient mountain names to mutter like a spell - Helvellyn, Glaramara, Blencathra - to draw us into the circle of their powerful enchantment, so that we can put aside the merely picturesque, the comfortable, accessible, view-from-the-car sort of view that this is from Orrest Head and make us feel compelled to strike out into the real, primal, savage-or-divine heart of things. But the view point has been vandalised, the map a few flapping shreds of paper. Undifferentiated, unnamed, the view remains just that, a view. The mind reaches out but bounces off. It cannot take in such an incoherent mass of landscape, it needs some contact, some personalising, before we feel it, before it can release our human passions which is the true source of its power over us. Without this, these mountains are simply vast, obdurate lumps of matter. Or pretty backcloths. Before the Romantic poets and painters, nature was just a stage cloth against which the real business, the play of human activity, took place. That most civilised, drawing room of poets of the eighteenth century, Alexander Pope, declared, 'The proper study of mankind is man'. Wordsworth turned all that on its head. He quit the world of men to immerse himself in this landscape, so much

231

wilder then than now. He poured all his passion into it and a whole new philosophy of human nature emerged. We are a glorious product of Nature ourselves, he proclaimed. The hand that shaped these mountains made us too. We share their same grandeur and nobility however humble our origins. Left to work upon us, this whole majestic panorama would imbue us with moral elevation. Forget the monks in their cells at prayer or their noses in the great mediaeval manuscripts of the patriarchs, real moral enlightenment would come from exposure to Nature. It was an extraordinary idea and we still subscribe to it today. We still believe that time spent 'communing with nature' is valuable spiritual refreshment.

But it doesn't seem to be working on Orrest Head today. I see no silent, rapt faces, awed by the view across the Grasmere valley to the hills. Instead, people continue to chatter happily. The American is drawling on as his listeners' gazes glaze over. The woman in pink pants, thinking no one is looking at her, aims a sly kick at a jackdaw, her bete noire. Perhaps they just feel relaxed, back at home in the landscape we all came from before our hankering after material prosperity imprisoned us in our towns. But that's another notion.

Another priest of high art enthralled by the Lake District was Ruskin. For him the view from Friar's Crag on the northwestern shores of Derwentwater was the most memorable. Strolling along the lake side from the Boat Landings half a mile from Keswick town centre you pass along an avenue of beeches which breaks into sturdy pine trees as you progress. Amongst the trees on a small hill, hardly a crag, is a ten foot high memorial to the great Victorian art critic. Set into the rough slate monolith is a bronze profile of the man, the truculent thrust of his jaw indicative of the determination of someone whose literary output was prodigious - his published works run to 39 volumes. And on the other side of the stone are the words: 'The spirit of God is around you'. Unfortunately you'll not see much of that from where the memorial stone stands today because of the trees. To get any idea of the impression made by the setting you need to move away from the trees to the open lake side.

The lake stretches to the foot of the Borrowdale fells to the south.

Opposite rises the ridge of Cat Bells, thick lakeside woods giving way to screes before the fell tops are scribbled across the western skyline. The lake water is still, creeping gently around the headland of Friar's Crag in a soothing stream of light. The islands rest like corals of trees. The lake is wonderfully clear and you can count every pebble in its lucent shallows. Despite the fact that it is holiday time and the voices from the pleasure cruisers carry across the water and children and dogs paddle and splash ecstatically at the lake's edge, the surrounding hills clasp the lake in a protective embrace of peace. The 'spirit of God'? Doubt creeps into my mind like a gathering storm cloud. This is where on the 12 August 1898, five young Sunday school teachers from milltown Nelson, girls as transparently innocent as the lake is clear today, set out in a rowing boat only to be overwhelmed by a sudden violent storm and drowned. I tell the whole tragic saga in my book 'Real Lancashire' and the memory of it sours my feelings for this spot today. What was at work that day over a hundred years ago when those innocent lives were lost? The inscrutable 'spirit of God' or the chilling moral indifference of nature? Ruskin was alive to these conflicting views. He had rejected his stern religious upbringing to turn towards denouncing the social evils of industrialisation. He provoked the wrath of the Victorian commercial world by attacking the way the factory system had been allowed to dehumanise people. And he lived through the shocking discovery of Darwin that creation was not the anthropocentric master plan of God but the slow evolution of the species through random adaptations propelled by merciless self-interest, that we were not only descended from the same ancestry as apes but a product of the primal swamp. There could be nothing more calculated to deflate the high seriousness of Wordsworth than a dose of Darwinian realism. What are mountains but the raw cosmic material, the atoms which would one day combine to create the protoplasmic slime from which began the long journey to mankind? And if God ignited the fuse which started all this just to create us, he sure took the long way round.

Yet whichever way you look at mountains, either with the

reverential awe of a Romantic poet or the wary scepticism of a modern day scientific rationalist, one thing is clear. You need to get up close to them, look them in the eye and slug it out with them step by step. You need to climb them.

I've long been fascinated by Stickle Pike in the Langdales. It was the discovery that Neolithic man climbed it over 5,000 years ago that first took me up there. Close to the summit of 2,300 feet, climbers had discovered the remains of a very hard volcanic rock which had been worked into axe heads. Here was an axe factory, artefacts from which found their way all across Neolithic Britain. From here came many of the tools responsible for the early deforestation of our landscape. What first struck and amazed me was not just that they had discovered this vein of hard volcanic tuff in such a remote spot but that they had then toiled up here on a regular daily basis to work and remove it. There is a cave in the side of the scree-filled gully near the summit which some seem to think might have afforded shelter for a longer stay. But this hardly alters the hostility and sheer inaccessibility of this as a place to work. Here in Stickle Pike we not only have a mountain redolent with all the exhilaration and mystery of wild Northern places, we also have the hand of our early ancestors at work to resonate down the centuries and intensify the heady emotional appeal. Irresistible.

From the well-trodden path along Mickleden from the Old Dungeon Ghyll Hotel, the Langdale Pikes jab at the sky, bruising it, which then the grey clouds try to bandage. Today, everything is grey. The incurious local sheep share the same dirty grey look as the sky, and the only other sign of life, the grey wagtails, flit and palpitate amongst the grey glacial rocks that strew the valley floor. Worst for cloud today is Bow Fell, a surly brute of a mountain which blocks the northwest progress of the valley. In fact, Mickleden is a cul-de-sac, a blind appendix terminating in the great wall of Rossett Crag up ahead. This is why we have left the path which takes the rest of the hikers trudging up Black Crags and Stake Pass to get to Stickle Pike. There's an easier route, according to the ubiquitous Wainwright, that has not appeared on a map since 1901 but is an old sheep drovers' road which zigzags up the left flank of Stickle. But it's hard to find and you have to wander through the bracken just a few yards to the left of Troughton Beck (again, unhelpfully not mentioned on modern OS maps). You know you're on the track only when you start to see stones laid diagonally across it at intervals to divert the water. You begin to see why Wainwright preferred this hidden track to the well-worn Cumbrian Way up the valley head. You are on your own. The old curmudgeon didn't like meeting other people. Rather cruelly he called them the 'red and orange blobs', from the colour of their anoraks and perspiring faces, no doubt. His misanthropy has always struck me as being ironic, coming from the man whose guides have done more to encourage walkers into the Lakes than any number of Wordsworth's verses.

To the east of Stickle Pike (It's more commonly referred to as Pike o'Stickle which I don't care for because I think it sounds uncharacteristically quaint for such a remote and hostile land mass) is Gimmer Crag. Between the two crags the bracken rises to meet the scree. Vegetation and volcanic rock confront one another, establish an uneasy truce, eventually conceding their territorial limits. As a younger man I once scrambled up the scree searching for stone axes, but today I wouldn't dare tread such perilously steep and shifting terrain. We keep to the meandering drovers' track, turning back to marvel at how quickly and giddily the valley below shrinks. Where we tread, the bracken has given way to heather, struggling into bloom. Rare moss campion reveals shy pink flowers. Yellow hawksbit trembles in the breeze. A cold dampness is exhaled by the stone above us and the nearing cloud. Fat, juicy drops of rain begin to descend. The dark mass of cloud that cloaks the summit of Bow Fell takes a step closer across the valley, menacingly. The wind licks like some beast that greets its dinner. And something new creeps into this mountain venture turning the sweat on my body cold. It is fear.

It was foolish to foresake the popular path for this recluse's route. If the mist descends there are no cairns and who would be around to help us down? We haven't met a single person since we took to this track. And what about a compass? I haven't brought one, and even if

I had, would I know how to use it? And there's no signal on my wife's mobile phone should we suffer the ignominy of getting lost. And worse, people of my age who worry a lot have heart attacks on hills. Suddenly, this mania for reaching the top of mountains which has begun to seize me, looks to be just that, a mental disorder brought on by an irrational obsession. The shaggy dome of rock which is the top of Stickle Pike rears above our heads. A primal entity forged from the magma of a nightmare planet when rocks seethed and mountains ran red like rivers of blood. If it could speak it would say, 'Stay away if you've any sense. Sit in the garden of the pub at Dungeon Ghyll and drink your beer. Admire me from afar. But don't dare attempt to take me on or spar with me. Or I'll swat you away like the impudent, importunate fly you are.'

But then the sky begins to clear and we stop our ears to the mountain's taunts and find new resolve, and climbing out of the shadow of the mountain we reach the plateau of Martcrag Moor and enter another world, a skyworld where far peaks unfurl and distant lakes sparkle. The Borrowdale fells roll northwards and beyond Derwentwater Skiddaw rises. Here we meet the path which has taken the long route round to Stickle Pike, stepping stones that cross the black peat hags and rock and chunk together disturbingly. Invisible water chuckles everywhere. The path leads to the summit by the back door, an easy climb now for those who would play feral and stand up there and beat their chests and risk the wrath of mountains. But I decline the chance to pretend such a cheap victory and keeping to the left, approach the mouth of the gully where the axe factory hides.

The scree heads off into the void between two walls of rock. As I warily approach the edge the wind funnels upwards through the gap, boiling in a surge of twisting, angry air. I peer downwards, 2,000 feet into Mickleden where the valley floor has become microscopic. I'd love to explore the cave in the cliff to the right or clamber onto the scree of broken slate to look for half-finished axes, but only a fool would risk climbing onto such a steep slope of shifting polished slate that might send you surfing a thousand feet or more to a broken leg or worse. And besides, my fear has returned. At first I didn't know why. I'm safely at the summit of the afternoon's climb and the weather has taken up. Then I remember. This dark gully of stone between blackened walls of rock reminds me of Lord's Rake on Scafell. Fifty years ago as a teenager I had a fall, rolling and bouncing down a slope such as this, mercifully coming to rest on a ledge which would have taken me another thousand feet if I'd gone over it. I ended up in hospital at Seascale. Apart from dozens of tiny scratches which made my bare arms and legs run with blood like raw liver, I was unhurt save for a broken thumb. But it left me so scared I gave up my holiday and crept home to my mum and fell out of love with the Lake District for more years than I can remember. Shuddering, I turn away, thoughts of early Northern man's daring presence in these mountains driven out by memories of my brush with death.

On the way down from behind Raven Crag we collect groups of walkers and chatter amiably. You feel an intimacy with others who have taken on these mountains like you. Perhaps it's a camaraderie which, I guess, soldiers must feel in battle. I wonder Wainwright never felt it. Or perhaps he did but wasn't letting on, with true Northern cussedness. But, thinking about that other W, Wordsworth, I couldn't help but acknowledge some intenser feeling, a sense of having been touched by something, a presence which inhabits these high and rarefied regions and, once touched, leaves you feeling both exhilarated and humbled.

Another mountain stamped with the footprints of our early ancestors and their invaders is High Street. It gets its name from the Roman road which, astonishingly, traverses the range of mountains of the eastern Lake District to a height of over 2,700 feet as it journeys from the fort at Ambleside to Brougham near Penrith. So again you can savour that rich experience of a remote and empty mountain landscape which still echoes with the whispers of a long lost human presence. Not only might you hear the tramp of Roman legions hurrying north to put down a Pictish uprising but maybe the call of a Norse farmer rounding up his sheep from the high summer shielings before the onset of winter. Or the hoof beats of Scottish raiders riding south to plunder deep into English territory. Or you may hear sounds of song and laughter, echoes of more recent times when the villagers of Mardale Green climbed High Street to celebrate their annual folk festivals high on the windy plateau. Ghosts from the past lurk everywhere on this lonely mountain. It is one of the less climbed Lakeland peaks, which is not to be expected from the number of cars which fill the car park and line the roadside at Mardale Head at the southern end of Haweswater. From the scarcity of fellow climbers setting out for the mountain, I must assume that people come here to stroll round the lake, an eerie experience when you think that lurking under its grainy waters lie a church, a pub and the cottages that were once home to the folk of Mardale Green. Fifty years ago the hamlet was flooded to enlarge the lake into a reservoir to water and wash the people of grimy Manchester. By all accounts it was an idyllic village too, nestling in the embrace of the hills, a green and flowered refuge with a long history. How Wordsworth would have ranted had it happened in his day! The very proposal for a railway from Kendal to Windermere sent him into a poetic apoplexy. 'Is then no nook of English ground secure from rash assault?' he railed.

Setting out upon my own rash assault of High Street, the way ahead presents a steady climb up a series of small outcrops which lead to Rough Crag followed by a staircase ridge known as Long Stile beyond which the walls of High Street fill the skyline. On either side of the climb the land falls away dramatically, to the south into Blea Water tarn and north into Riggindale. Neither of these places offers a crumb of comfort to those who look for salvation here in the Northern hills. Riggindale is an empty glacial graveyard, littered with the bones of boulders and scoured by bare screes. It is devoid of all other features apart from its ragged crags which are said to be home to golden eagles. I was on the lookout for these mighty birds but had to make do with a pair of crows, one leading the other through the empty skies, craaking hoarsely as it chivvied its mate along upon some meaningless meandering excursion. The only other sound was the roar of the river echoing from the bare walls of this most desolate of valleys.

There's more cheer at the other side of the ridge where a rare shaft of sunlight catches the wind-chopped surface of Small Water, sending it scintillating in a wild, silvery mountain dance. Above is Nan Bield Pass where a huge twenty-one inch Viking spear blade was found. The Norwegians must have felt at home here in these mountains, and over the summit at Bryant's Gill in Kentmere, a Viking farmhouse which bears comparison with the one at Ribblehead has been discovered. Another enthralling warp in the human weave of this mountain fastness.

The monotonous switchback of this rocky spine is starting to take its toll. The summit seems to get no nearer and when Blea Water comes into view below the left flank of the path, my mood begins to alter. I'm on my own today and so far I've met no one on the climb and a kind of mountain melancholy begins to seize me. I'm sorry, Wainwright, walking alone in the mountains is a fool's game. Some conversation, however trifling, with another human being will jolly the time along. Instead of which, on your own you seem to be getting nowhere and time trickles into demoralising stagnant pools fed only, you feel, by the great reservoirs of eternity which are locked in mountains like this. Blea Water is a dark crater of despair, a gloomy circular expanse of black water trapped inside a great basin of scree-lined rock skulking under the sunless flanks of High Street. Its frightening appearance is not helped by Wainwright's reminder that a schoolboy perished here when he fell from the path. To stare down too long into its depths is to risk madness. The surface waters swirl and churn as if some monstrous creature trapped in its depths were trying to scratch its way out. It is said to be the deepest tarn in the Lake District and some have even suggested that it could have been caused by a meteorite. Here is a Gothic savageness to awe Ruskin.

I cheer myself with the thought that once the villagers of Mardale Green came this way, staggering up, maybe, with barrels of beer and home-cooked hams for their mountain-top shindigs, lads and lasses giggling merrily in anticipation of their grassy frolics.

I pass a startlingly white outcrop of rock, crystals of quartz sparkling like snow amongst the summer tormentil, a sudden magical trick of the mountain. And the sunlight has found the mountain recess of Blea Water tarn and set the surface water flashing as if it were full of silver fish. Mountains were holy places to Wordsworth but so they are to Christians. Moses climbed one to meet God and the psalmist lifts up his eyes to the hills. When we were kids we always climbed Pendle Hill on a Good Friday and in Ireland, in Mayo, Catholics of all ages still climb Croagh Patrick. What do they expect to find?

The last leg of Long Stile is loose stones which clatter like dominoes underfoot. And at last, there's the cairn, peeping over the edge of the summit like a stone dwarf, a mountain troll. Then it's a brisk walk along the plateau to the trig point to savour the view. To the southwest lies the sea while the bulk of the Lake District mountains stretch out westwards. North is the Solway and the hills of Galloway. I look for favourites on my travels like the unmistakable crouch of Wild Boar Fell far to the southeast. The sun is playing tricks again and lights up the Dales hills until the limestone takes on the appearance of drifting smoke. Placid Eden is a rich green heartland.

Across a broken wall, and after a couple of hundred yards I arrive at the Roman road that has drawn me here. Southwards it marches towards an horizon where Windermere stretches like a jagged pane of fallen sky. Northwards it snakes along the highest contours of the mountains towards the plains of north Eden. Inches from its perilous path the land plunges a thousand feet into the surly depths of Hayswater. And beyond, the western mountains seem to rear up in massive indignation that this impudent nonentity, man, should have the audacity to make light of their elemental might and drive his roadway through their very heart. It may only look like a stone cart-track today but it was once an artery of the greatest empire of history, that fed the muscle of its military power at Hadrian's Wall. The sheer audacity of its construction reflects the same relentless determination to conquer. It is a sky road not only in location but in its reaching ambition.

I wonder if the Roman foot soldiers loved or hated this track? The weather is everything here. Today is fine and the clouds have anchored well above the mountain tops. But the wind carries a bone-sawing chill, especially after the hot slog up here. And, once more, it's the cold breath of the rock you feel up here in this region of stone. Sunlight can never penetrate rock like this. It can play upon the wrinkled skin of the hills, light up the grass and fern beds, round up the shadows and send them scudding across the hillsides, but it can never warm up the grey, tight-grained stone. It has had its fill of heat when volcanoes made it. Now its fire has long gone out. If this region is the heart of the North, it is a cold heart.

There's a sudden rush of air and whirr of wheels. A mountain biker, muscles straining, head down, helmeted, flies past. You're just as likely to see a fell-runner as a cyclist up in these places. It's bad enough walking up here, but riding, running! What stuff are these people made of? Now I'm sure of it, they are deliberately setting out to demoralise the rest of us, we lesser mortals. When you think you're doing so well, when, teeth gritted, you've pushed yourself to the very limit, there they go, sailing past, barely breaking sweat and making a mockery of all your efforts. How can people be so different? But then, after all, this is the country of Joss Naylor of Wasdale, the Blands of Borrowdale, legendary fell-runners who learnt to run because it was the quickest way to round up sheep before softies came along with their quad bikes. Wordsworth was convinced that this environment had a moral effect on those who lived here, but what about the physical effects? Like the stones, have these native Northerners been forged in the ancient heat of these mountains, tempered by plunging into their glacial ice and sharpened by the whetstone of the winds? Nonsense, I hear old Wainwright grunt. But then he would, wouldn't he? After all, he spent long enough in these mountains to be moulded by them himself. His walks, to me, often make light of the difficulties and distances involved. You can almost hear him saying, 'Come on. Hurry up. Cissy!'

The arguments about the effects of landscape on its people will

241

never be easily settled. But you can look back through the history of this region from the mountain excursions of the villagers of Mardale Green, through the Norse settlers and Brigantean Celts, as far back as the axe men of Stickle Pike, and trace an enduring vein of toughness. To survive here demands nothing less.

And what of God? Is He here in these hills as the Romantic poets would have us believe? I didn't meet Him. But I did meet a sense of smallness as I looked out on the Northern landscape, the world I'd journeyed through for many months. I felt a sense of insignificance when I measured my own puny lifespan against the duration of mountains. I experienced a sense of exhilaration at having pitted myself against their unrelenting harshness and made it through. And I enjoyed a feeling of kinship with all those who trod this way through history and those today with whom I shared the journey - those who had time to stop and exchange a few words and didn't go haring past on bikes or iron limbs. All rewards enough without any life-changing epiphany. In fact, I came down from the mountains with a growing conviction that they weren't so much places of great spiritual elevation as inhuman and alien places which we all need to brush against every so often if we are to put our lives into perspective, place ourselves more firmly in the natural context to which we humans belong and this way cure ourselves of our egocentricity, our arrogance, with the realisation that as a species we are expendable and unless we value the wildness at our disposal we will lose it and in so doing destroy the best part of ourselves.

The final leg of my journey through the North takes me back to where we began, to Malham, this time to Gordale Scar. Early visitors, those usually from the south in the late eighteenth and early nineteenth centuries, were shocked to their foundations by what they saw. The poet Thomas Gray looked at Gordale Scar and shuddered, the impression of the rock's 'dreadful canopy' staying with him all his life. Others went further, describing the 'immensity and horror' of the spot. It was 'savage', 'awful' and 'sublime'. And the artist James Ward set about painting it, not to tame it but, like a big game hunter, to bring it back to civilisation in all its awesome power. He ended up with a canvas 11 feet by 14 feet which has found its way today, in the kind of cultural appropriation we have come to expect here in the North, into the Tate Gallery in London. A smaller, earlier study, measuring a mere 2 ½ feet by 3 ½ feet, can be viewed in Bradford City Art Gallery in Lister Park. Even this shrunken version conveys the impact which the scene had upon those early visitors. As anyone familiar with the Scar will immediately recognise, the painting is not a realistic presentation. Everything is enlarged for dramatic effect. The 200 foot high cliffs which overhang the river bed are twice the size in the painting. They loom over the scene menacingly, as if they were about to collapse and crush us. In the same way, the storm clouds overhead are so dense and oppressive they might also be made of rock themselves, turning the setting into a giant cavern into which, through an angry rent in the sky, a ghastly pale light leers. The rocks, applied in crude slabs of paint, like the sky are an unrelenting monochrome, what I can only best describe as bruised sepia, brushed by a lurid, supernatural light, the sort you get sometimes as a prelude to a violent thunderstorm. It renders the whole scene primordial. Were it not for the cattle and deer in the foreground, there to add scale to the vastness of the overhanging rocks, and the white bull which epitomises the primal energy of the scene, you could believe the artist had captured some violent episode in the geology of creation. What Ward has done is to convey the sense of 'sublime horror' which a landscape like this induced in his contemporaries. It is the overwhelming psychological impact of Gordale Scar upon its visitors which looms out of Ward's study, the emotional response to wildest nature where terror outweighs grandeur, and fear, reverence. There is no Providential hand at work in the landscape, which Wordsworth chose to see, no God, only violent telluric enegies, the physics and chemistry of an unruly cosmos let loose upon our landscape. Which is why I believe Ward rather than Wordsworth accords more with our modern post-scientific response to nature. The picture certainly strikes a chord with my own experiences of the wilder aspects of the Northern

243

landscape.

My appetite whetted for the real Gordale Scar I journeyed back to Malham. As you approach the Scar alongside the river from Gordale Bridge, the gorge twists so that the Scar is not visible for a jutting spur of rock, something Ward's painting ignored in order to get a full-on view of the rocks and waterfall. You pass along a defile of grey scree which slowly narrows as you proceed, pressing in. You begin to notice vegetation, scant trees clinging to the rocks by their fingernails, straining to get at the light. This is organic nature struggling to survive in a hostile kingdom of bare limestone. It is an introduction to what happens behind the spur, the curtain of rock. It is the first act before the unfolding drama ahead. A single harebell, a thing of almost pathetically fragile beauty clings to the rock beside the path, a last glimpse of subtlety before you turn the corner to be confronted by the roofless cave with its threatening rocks browbeating any nation of nature as picturesque or scenic, just slobbering masses of stone rearing up like huge, clenched fists to drive out the light. This is the work of creation as bully, oaf, blind Cyclops, throwing matter together in great, insensate lumps, the first crude experiments with the basic dough of nature, pushed and pummelled into amorphous shapes then tossed aside in petulant frustration. A waste of atoms in a meaningless act of cosmic brutality.

Yes, it is perfectly easy to recreate the sense of shocked horror which these first genteel Georgian visitors felt as they left behind their polite salons and studios in the sheltered south to turn this corner in the rock and be confronted by such a monstrosity. How sick they must have felt. (You can feel some of that revulsion when you reach out to touch the tar-like substance that oozes from the warty surface of the rock when it's wet. This is not the limestone we may know or love.) Gordale Scar must have challenged their religious orthodoxy as well as their aesthetic sensibilities. The maker of this lot is certainly not the creator of 'All things bright and beautiful'. More like some ape-god who himself had not evolved beyond the brute beast.

But today we've all seen too much and been too far to be shocked or overawed by Gordale Scar. Television has taken us into the Himalayas and the frozen heart of the Antarctic. We are unlikely to suffer any moral crisis at the sight of nature's more extravagant creations. That small child who looked up at a rock for the first time and screamed may have retained that childish, atavistic sense of horror with which he was born, but the rest of us know too much. We know that when the ice sheets began to melt from the plateau of Malham Moor, torrents of water cut their way through the soft limestone to fashion the scar we see today. We also know that in another million years the waterfall will have cut even deeper into the rock to create an even more impressive sight. But meanwhile, the campers come today to pitch their tents in the open valley and enjoy their barbecues. Their children scramble fearlessly over the stones and splash in the river or test the echo from the walls of rock The Sunday visitors stroll up here for just long enough to feel the chill from the rocks before they turn away for afternoon tea in the Lister's Arms in Malham. No one is staring up at the rock and having a nervous breakdown. And the whole height of the 'dreadful canopy' has been drilled for screws and pitons so that climbers can pit their skills and finger ends against the rock before ticking it off in their notebooks and moving on to something bigger.

Places like Gordale Scar and the Lakeland mountains are no longer theatres for contemplating the awesome or sublime, for fomenting the supernatural terrors of a bygone age or inspiring poetical theories about the moral nature of our Universe. They are playgrounds, outdoor gymnasiums where we climb, pedal, run or trudge to keep fit and healthy for the business of making a living and to stay one step ahead of mortality. Gordale Scar may look like a vast, natural Gothic cathedral, but there are few nature worshippers to be found here these days. Just fun-seekers. We have tamed nature, domesticated it. Or so we would like to think. Climate change, the gradual resurgence of more extremes of weather and more frequent natural disasters, should give us pause, perhaps, to think again. The beast merely sleeps. Here in the wild places of the North we should need no reminding of this.

Bibliography

'The Anglo-Saxon Chronicle' tr. Michael Swanton. Phoenix Press 2000.

'Bede's Ecclesiastical History of the English People'. Penguin Books.

'Beowulf' tr. Seamus Heaney. Faber & Faber 1999.

Peter Hunter Blair, 'Northumbria in the Days of Bede'. Victor Gollancz 1976.

Aubrey Burl, 'Yorkshire Archaeological Journal' 1991.

'Domesday Book', a complete translation. Penguin Books.

Keith Durham, 'The Border Reivers'. Osprey Publishing 1995.

B.J.N. Edwards, 'Vikings in North West England'. University of Lancaster 1998.

Dr William Greenwell, 'British Barrows, a Record of the Examination of Sepulchral Mounds in Various Parts of England'. Clarendon Books 1877.

Robert Graves, 'The White Goddess'. Faber & Faber 1948.

M. John Harrison, 'Climbers'. Victor Gollancz 1989.

Hartley and Fitts, 'The Brigantes'. Alan Sutton 1988.

Hornsby & Laverick, 'The Roman Signal at Goldsborough near Whitby'. Archaeological Journal vol LXXXIX. 1932.

M.R. James, 'Ghost Stories of an Antiquary'. Penguin 1974.

Alan King, 'Early Pennine Settlement'. Dalesman Publishing 1970.

'London Midland Steam in the Northern Fells'. Bradford Barton 1974.

J.R. Mortimer, 'Forty Years Researches in British and Saxon Burial Mounds of East Yorkshire'. A. Brown and Sons 1905.

'The Oxford Dictionary of British Place-Names'. A.D. Mills. Oxford 1991.

Arthur Raistrick, 'Malham and Malham Moor'. Dalesman Publishing 1947.

Anne Ross, 'Everyday Life of the Pagan Celts'. Carousel Books 1970.

Phil Smith, 'Real Lancashire'. Palatine Books 2008.

John Ruskin, 'The Stones of Venice Vol 2.' Oxford.

Rosemary Sutcliff, 'The Eagle of the Ninth'. Oxford 1954.

Arthur Wainwright, 'Twelve Favourite Mountains'. Frances Lincoln 2007.

James Ward's 'Gordale Scar'. Published by the Tate Gallery 1982.

Roger J.A. Wilson, 'A Guide to Roman Remains in Britain'. Constable 1975.

Michael Wood, 'In Search of the Dark Ages'. BBC Books 1981.

INDEX